CONSCIOUSNESS
IS EVERYTHING

CONSCIOUSNESS IS EVERYTHING

The Yoga of Kashmir Shaivism

Swami Shankarananda

SHAKTIPAT
PRESS

Published by Shaktipat Press

The National Library of Australia
Cataloguing-in-Publication entry:

Shankarananda, Swami.
Consciousness is everything: the yoga of Kashmir Shaivism.

ISBN 0-9750995-0-7
1. Kashmir 'Saivism. Title
294.54

Design: Kali Nolle

Also by Swami Shankarananda
Happy for No Good Reason
Carrot in My Ear
Self-Inquiry

Dedication

> I offer my homage to that wonderful teaching of my Guru serving as a boat and crossing the fathomless ocean of doubts and full of such words as express wonderful uncommon ideas.
>
> *Spanda Karikas,* IV.1

The medieval Christian authors spoke of 'the forest of the world', how confusing and dark life can be. In such a forest a light is needed, and to that light I dedicate my work: my Guru, Swami Muktananda.

I didn't learn Shaivism from books and in some sense I was taught Shaivism before I ever heard of it. I learned it by osmosis from my Guru's being. And when I began to read Shaivism it explained what I already knew.

While dedicating this book to my Guru, I must also salute the Self of all. As well, I offer my salutations to the supreme Devi, in all Her forms, who animates and enlivens me.

Finally, I salute that Shiva that lives in every one of you, my readers, as your own awareness. Please remember, dear ones, Shiva lives in every thought and feeling, in every breath, in every object, in every person. Do not dishonour Him by dishonouring yourself. The highest, most truly worthy expression of our common humanity is the search for the Self within. If something in these pages is useful to you in that search, my work is compensated.

Author's Note

The original texts of Kashmir Shaivism were written in the beautiful and powerful language of Sanskrit. Some of these ancient words, such as chakra, karma and maya, have long found their way into standard English dictionaries. For ease of reading in the main text, I have anglicised the spelling of Sanskrit words such as *prakasha* (light) and *vimarsha* (awareness) and have included a glossary. Likewise I have anglicised book titles which appear in their original Sanskrit form in the bibliography.

The appendices list many key sutras of Kashmir Shaivism in English and in transliterated Sanskrit with diacritical marks for pronunciation. The words are generally pronounced as in English except for a few guidelines:

ā	the long a, as in *balm*
ī	the long i, as in *sleeve*
ū	the long u, as in *school*
c	ch, as in *chimney*
ḥ	slightly aspirated, *ha*
ñ	as in *banyan*
ṛ	with a trill, as in *brrn*
ṣ, ś	sh

Acknowledgments

This book is the result of the work of a team of people, a *shakti chakra* in Shaivite terms, whose many talents and specialised skills made it possible.

I am grateful to my editor, Nancy Jackson, for nursing the book through with clarity, calm and sensitivity.

Next I want to acknowledge Kali Nolle for her graphic design, including diagrams and the beautiful cover.

I want to express my gratitude to Jackie Bos, who came to the rescue at a critical time, and Kaymolly Morrelle. Their impeccable copy editing was indispensable.

I am grateful to Dr Isobel Crombie who did the early work, collecting and transcribing some of the talks that became part of the book, and also to Jo Hughson for her help with the Sanskrit transliterations.

I have to acknowledge Dylan Frusher for his charming sketch of the Headless One on page 83.

Finally, I am very grateful to Teri Giannetti without whose selfless dedication and one-pointedness it would simply not have been possible to complete the book on time or nearly as well.

I owe thanks to Ma Devi and the many members of the Shiva Ashram community, whose names cannot fit here, but fit easily in my heart, for helping to create a heaven on earth and an atmosphere in which Shaivite ideas and practices flow naturally.

Beyond all these, I would be remiss not to mention the international scholars on whose work I have drawn. Among them I should especially acknowledge Jaideva Singh, Mark Dyczkowski, Kamalakar Mishra, B.N. Pandit and Paul Muller-Ortega (especially for the long translation on pp. 233–234). A special mention to my friends Dr Gary Witus for his feedback and suggestions and to Reverend Dr John Dupuche.

I want to acknowledge the great sages of Kashmir Shaivism at whose feet I sit, especially Abhinavagupta, Utpaladeva, Kshemaraja, Swami Lakshmanjoo and my Guru, Swami Muktananda.

Finally to Lord Shiva: all this is Your Grace, Your Shining, Your Gift to a dark age.

ayaṃ śaktidaridraḥ saṃsārī ucyate
svaśaktivikāse tu Śiva eva

He is a bound soul who has poverty of Shakti.
With the unfoldment of his Shakti, however,
he becomes Shiva Himself.

Kshemaraja, *Pratyabhijnahridayam*

Contents

Introduction

Consciousness Itself

> This new and easy path has been shown by me exactly as it was given by my teacher. A person putting his feet here firmly, after realising himself to be the Creator of the Universe, becomes perfect, when he enters into unbroken identity with the state of Shiva.
>
> Utpaladeva, *Ishvara-Pratyabhijna* IV.16

C onsciousness is the great unexplored area of life, the final frontier. It is the invisible but essential ingredient that even science approaches with fear and trembling. Yet one ancient philosophy has explored it completely and that philosophy, and Consciousness Itself, are the subject of this book.

Kashmir Shaivism is the study of Consciousness. Since Consciousness is infinite, so our study is without limits. Notice that I didn't say, 'human consciousness'. Consciousness is One no matter where we find it, though its personalities are many. Look at your pet, your dog or cat. A pet lover feels that there is a conscious being there, somehow overlayed by 'catness' or 'dogness'.

Years ago one devotee of my Guru wept pathetically to me that his dog was not allowed in the ashram in India. He said, 'He's a human being in a dog's body!'

I said, 'Richard, we all are'.

I wasn't exaggerating too much. We are all essentially that pure divine Consciousness referred to in the very first statement of Kashmir Shaivism, *Chaitanyamatma*: The Self is Consciousness (*Shiva Sutras* I.1). Like our pet, we too have an overlay, in our case of ignorance, of foul temper, of jealousy and greed. Just as our dog is kept a dog by its surface personality, so we are kept as we are, by ours. We are limited. We experience only a small percentage of what is possible to us. Kashmir Shaivism says that if we could pare away that superficial layer and know ourselves as we truly are, we would discover ourselves as divine beings, Shiva Himself.

Consciousness is an embarrassment to Western science and philosophy because they have no good explanation for it. In college I turned away from studying psychology because of the form of behaviourism that was taught in those days. We worked with rats, trying to reduce psychology to quantifiable and visible phenomena. The behaviourists had a passion for turning psychology into a 'real' science like physics. They tried to get rid of any notion of interiority within a person. Everything could be measured by an observer.

My study of philosophy came up against the same barrier. Descartes was the villain, with his duality between the Self and matter. The new linguistic philosophers like A.J. Ayer were as uncomfortable with the notion of an interior world as were the behaviourists. Gilbert Ryle called the notion of the Self within, 'the Ghost in the Machine', and discarded it. Yet every five-year-old knows that there is a ghost in every machine: a Self within each person. How do we know? It is by direct introspection, our immediate and obvious experience.

Darwinism, too, is weak when it comes to Consciousness. How did this miracle we know as our own awareness suddenly spring into being from amino acids via natural selection? Darwinians don't want to look too deeply at this question.

When Kashmir Shaivism is studied the way a subject at university is studied, it becomes a set of principles and concepts. These principles and concepts are rich and suggestive and many of them will be discussed here. But Kashmir Shaivism is not only food for the intellect. It also implies direct nurturance of the soul, the direct experience of Consciousness Itself. This open-ended knowing is achieved only experientially, through inner contact. It is a mystical knowing. My goal in this book is to inspire spiritual seekers to make use of the sublime methods and understandings of Shaivism in their own practice. Certainly, I will explain many of the essential concepts, especially the ones that are useful to yogis. It is my profound conviction that Kashmir Shaivism is not only of historical interest, but also a saving knowledge for us now.

For the past 30 years I have given talks from the platform of Kashmir Shaivism. Some of these talks were at Intensives and other programmes where I used the insights and sutras of Shaivism to make a variety of yogic points. I have also done many meditation workshops and seminars based on the techniques of the *Vijnanabhairava* Tantra and other Shaivite sources.

On one memorable occasion, I did a weekend workshop with another swami in which we went through the whole of the *Pratyabhijnahridayam*, an important text. I have spoken on the aesthetics of Abhinavagupta at the National Gallery of Victoria (a talk I have adapted for this book), and held workshops in Shaivism with my friend, the Reverend Dr John Dupuche, who is a Catholic priest and also a Sanskritist and scholar of Kashmir Shaivism. In all these cases I have found that a special Shakti, or powerful spiritual energy, accompanies any consideration of the teachings and practices of Kashmir Shaivism. Shakti loves Shaivism and She never fails to show up.

Many times during these years, I have been asked, 'Where do I go from here to learn more about Shaivism? What should I read?' And these natural questions never fail to vex me. The simple truth is that there is no one good source for a layman or an aspiring Shaivite yogi to pick up the basics. Many of the books are scholarly and technical. The essential texts that we have in English, the *Shiva Sutras*, the *Spanda Karikas* and the *Pratyabhijnahridayam* are well-edited by Jaideva Singh and Mark Dyczkowski, but are difficult going for all but the most dedicated. They are in sutra form, the classical style of spiritual texts of the time.

A sutra is a short aphoristic statement (these are in Sanskrit). *Sutra* comes from the root *siv, to sew,* and is connected to the English *suture.* So it is like a 'stitch' or a 'thread' in the fabric of yogic knowledge. The sutras are sometimes poetic verses and often enigmatic sentences or fragments of sentences. They were a convenient way to transmit a teaching before the advent of printing. They could be committed to memory easily and would form the framework of future talks, and thus keep the teaching consistent. By its very nature, the sutra leaves much unsaid. The unexplained is to be taught by an enlightened Guru of a living tradition.

A significant set of sutras generates many commentaries by later sages and scholars. This hints at a characteristic of the sutra form. They are not limiting pronouncements of dogma, but rather multivalent seeds of wisdom that are more fully revealed according to the understanding of the teacher.

In *Paratrishika Vivarana,* Abhinavagupta interprets a particular verse three different ways and then says:

> All these three explanations should be considered to be appropriate. This verse is a sutra. Therefore, by turning its words this way or that way, many kinds of explanations would become quite fit, as has been said that 'a sutra is that which gives scope for manifold senses'. The respected teachers have averred that *Paratrishika* is an unsurpassable sutra. In this way, there can be many interpretations of the earlier verses also which are indeed like sutras.

Early in 1973, after I had been at the ashram of my Guru, Swami Muktananda (Baba) for two years, he began contributing commentaries on various aphorisms from the *Shiva Sutras*, the *Pratyabhijnahridayam* and other Shaivite texts to the ashram newsletter. These short pieces were full of inspiration, Baba giving his unique flavour to the Shaivite teachings.

As I read Baba's writings on Shaivism, along with the other texts that were available, I became intoxicated with the breadth and nobility of the Shaivite point of view. One of the things that had appealed to me about Hinduism was its conception of a *sanatana dharma,* an eternal religion. This idea, called the Perennial Philosophy by Aldous Huxley, held that behind all the varieties of religious approaches and doctrines, there exists a common core that is the eternal religion of mankind. No individual religion had yet reached this core, and because of that, there is so much misunderstanding and hatred among different faiths.

Reading Kashmir Shaivism, I felt that I was at last face-to-face with the *sanatana dharma,* a spirituality so inclusive, compassionate and human that it transcended all others. Indeed, though it is a spirituality of great sublimity, it rejects none of the lesser ones. Every path has its place within the borders of Kashmir Shaivism.

Sutra 8 of the *Pratyabhijnahridayam* says:

> The positions of the various systems of philosophy are only various roles of that Consciousness or Self.

The commentator explains that the Self takes on the various philosophies as an actor takes on a role. At different stages of the soul's journey, it is appropriate for the soul to adopt a relatively limited philosophy, suitable to its level of understanding. Even the broad highways of yoga and Vedanta, which I had previously embraced, had elements that I found unpalatable.

My soul took to the Shaivite vision without the slightest tremor of doubt. I felt that Kashmir Shaivism had an important message to give to the West.

I told Baba my thoughts about it and proposed to collect and edit his Shaivite writings to create a book that would be useful on his next Western tour, about six months off. He liked the idea and told me he would publish it.

Near the end of my stay in India, I collected all of Baba's commentaries and rewrote the English translations. I decided on the name *Siddha Meditation*, and I worked on an extensive essay that would introduce readers to Baba's approach and explain some of the key ideas of Kashmir Shaivism. When *Siddha Meditation* came out, Baba was pleased. He told me it was very good for me to study Shaivism and asked me to give the first public talk on Shaivism at the month-long retreat in Arcata, California, in 1975. His intimate students began to study the texts available to them and later the swamis formed study groups for intensive examination of the sutras.

In general, Shaivite texts are completely unintelligible for the unawakened. An illumined guide is needed to explicate them. *Siddha Meditation* is, undoubtedly, the most lucid and helpful treatment from a yogic point of view, but it is far from comprehensive.

I always look at the individuals who ask me, 'Where do I go from here?' and wonder, could they read Dyczkowski's *Doctrine of Vibration*? Would they enjoy Mishra's *Kashmir Shaivism*? Could they work their way through Jaideva Singh's *Shiva Sutras*? Most often the answer is, 'no'. I tell them, 'Well, there's really no basic book on Kashmir Shaivism that would suit you. Read Baba's *Siddha Meditation* and *Play of Consciousness* and come here for *satsang* and you'll gradually pick it up'. Privately I would ask myself, 'Why isn't there a good textbook?' And a further question would arise, 'Why don't I write one?'

In 1999 we held a retreat on Kashmir Shaivism. Ma Devi and my students encouraged me to collect my Shaivite talks and writings, with a view to producing a user-friendly introduction to the discipline. So this project has been gestating for a few years.

Since any book on Shaivism would be for more advanced seekers, it had to take a back seat to my more pressing wish to produce a book that was suitable for new meditators and people new to the spiritual path. That turned out to be *Happy for No Good Reason*, and when that was completed, I turned to Kashmir Shaivism.

Oddly, I found myself in a situation similar to that of Kshemaraja in the 11th century. Inspired by Utpaladeva's great work, the *Ishvara-Pratyabhijna*, Kshemaraja's compassionate wish was that everyone could hear that great message. But Utpaladeva's text is a work of profound difficulty and philosophical rigour, and when Kshemaraja considered it, he was moved to create a simplified and more available version. That was his *Pratyabhijnahridayam*. I hope this book, too, serves to cast light on Shaivism for contemporary readers.

TRIKA HRIDAYAM: THE HEART OF THE TEACHING OF KASHMIR SHAIVISM OR SHAIVISM IN THE VERNACULAR

This book is designed for seekers who are well-established in their practice. It is also for those who have a special interest in Kashmir Shaivism and are curious as to how the discipline would be treated from a yogic perspective.

I recognise that I have included a daunting amount of Sanskrit words and technical ideas. Had I not written *Happy*, I would feel guilty about this. On the other hand, I am sure that seekers in the two categories I have mentioned will have no trouble with the text.

Now, what if a beginning meditator wandered in here by mistake? Well, he can't leave without at least reading Chapter Five, You Are Your Awareness. The essence is there. Also, I would refer him to *Happy*, which has sizeable discussions of Kashmir Shaivism. If he is willing to work through this text, however, I am providing here a short, nontechnical overview of Shaivism. It is the *heart* of Shaivism as I see it:

Shaivism is known as 'the three' because it discusses these three subjects:

♦ The nature of the Absolute

♦ The nature of the human being and contraction

♦ The method by which contraction is overcome

Shaivism holds that pure awareness and not matter is the basic stuff of the universe. This can be compared to the situation in a dream, in which the awareness of the dreamer is the fundamental substratum of everything that appears in the dream. The one *Consciousness* that underlies the universe can also be called God. Here we are referring to God as the *Absolute*, beyond any specific form.

For reasons known only to Him, God decides to create a universe and become many. By means of *His Power*, which can be personified as His feminine aspect, He creates the universe in His own being, Himself becoming the *individual soul* by a process of contraction. Though it appears in Consciousness, the created world is real. The universe is actually Consciousness vibrating at different frequencies, becoming more material and gross as it unfolds.

The human individual is nothing but God in a contracted form. When the individual looks at himself, he notices that he has the same qualities as the Absolute, though they are shrunken and vitiated. God has perfect *will*, perfect *knowledge* and perfect *ability to do*, while the human individual has all of these powers in limitation. They show up in him as *three basic knots* within his being.

The first knot is limitation of will. The human individual experiences it in his *heart* as a painful sense of separation, weakness and grief. This is the fundamental birth trauma in which God becomes the individual. The limitation of knowledge is experienced in the *mind*. The human mind experiences darkness and confusion and strains to understand the truth. The third knot is experienced in the *navel* area and is felt as a sense of frustration and lack of fulfilment.

Shaivism asks us to recognise our similarity with God and ultimately our oneness with Him. It minutely examines the human condition as a contraction that moves us from the divine status to that of a human being. It recognises a *power of contraction and delusion* that brings this about. The power is real but is actually an aspect of God. One of the ways it shows up is in language. The language that God uses in His true state expresses His ecstatic song of oneness, while human language tends to perpetuate separation and weakness.

Having looked at the human situation, Shaivism now turns to the solution, a methodology for overcoming the woes and limitations of the human being. Shaivism proposes a comprehensive inner technology designed to restore the human being to his inherent oneness with God. For this, he has to loosen the knots in his heart, mind and navel by means of *three methods*.

To heal the contraction in his navel, he tries to act well in all situations and come into harmony with the higher power. To heal the contraction in his mind, having discovered its cause in the misuse of language, he tries to bring his thinking into alignment with his highest good. To heal the existential angst in his heart, he tries to transcend thinking altogether and merge himself in the oneness of pure Consciousness.

Having profoundly practised these spiritual methods, the Shaivite seeker *recognises* the divinity within his own Self and also outside himself in the world and in other people. His main insight is that the subject, or Consciousness, is not separate from the object, or matter. In fact, he experiences directly that the object is contained within his subjectivity, that is, within Consciousness. He has now reached the culmination and the goal of the practice of Shaivism and he stands as a *liberated being*, fully free within himself, shining with divine wisdom and radiant with love.

ABOUT THIS BOOK

I have made various choices and decisions to create this book. While the greater part of it was written freshly for this volume, some of it was based on talks I had already given. In the tradition of Baba's Shaivism I have not discussed every aspect of academic Kashmir Shaivism. Instead, I selected what I considered important to vivify a seeker's spiritual practice. In editing, some repetition was left in. The material, though informally given, is still dense. Each chapter or talk tends to stand on its own, ending in a meditative mood or an actual meditation. It would be good if the reader uses these meditations to digest the material. That would be in the spirit of my aim.

Among many others, I draw on the ideas of two spiritual teachers I should mention. One is my friend Douglas Harding, whose unique and inimitable approach sheds light on the Self as Consciousness, which is pure Kashmir Shaivism. The other is the enigmatic 20th-century teacher G. I. Gurdjieff. I met his teachings in my earliest days as a spiritual seeker and still find him to have had a matchless ability to express important spiritual ideas. Neither of these two sages is connected to Kashmir Shaivism per se, but I sometimes use them to highlight a Shaivite idea.

Turning to the Shaivite tradition proper, this is not an historical survey. In Kashmir around 1100A.D. a number of schools of Shaivism were operating: the Krama School, the Kula School, the Pratyabhijna School, the Spanda School and undoubtedly others. Each had their own point of view and emphasis, though they agreed broadly on central issues. Here we have to use our historical imagination. What did these schools actually look like? Probably they were the homes or hermitages of a single sage. Copies of the texts would have been very few (many have not survived) and hard to obtain before the printing press. So we are not talking about a mass movement.

It would be fascinating to trace these schools and understand their particular angles of approach, but that is not my focus here. In a real sense, the Krama School, the Pratyabhijna School and the Kula School either no longer exist or exist nowadays in a bare trickle. They are historical curiosities. Shaivism has changed shape since the 11th century, and seems to be developing into a new but related teaching that has little to do with the old schools. Of course, elements from each of these schools have found their way into this syncretic Shaivism. One could say that Consciousness Itself has reshaped Shaivism into a form that is practical for contemporary understanding.

As you will see, I define two contemporary schools of Kashmir Shaivism, one more scholarly, the other more experiential. My Guru, Baba Muktananda, was the great master of the latter school. Accordingly, my approach will tend to be experiential. I will not, however, neglect the rich tapestry of Shaivite ideas; they are interesting and valuable especially when they aid and illuminate the inner quest.

At the time I am writing, there seem to be two sorts of readers associated with these two schools. On the one hand, there is a relatively small group of scholars based in universities in India, America and Europe. On the other, there is a much larger group of meditators throughout the world that draws inspiration from the teachings of Kashmir Shaivism.

The scholars are proficient in Sanskrit and have done important work in translation and exegesis. They have presented these ancient teachings to the modern world. The meditators are, typically, students of contemporary spiritual teachers who make use of these teachings.

To the scholars, I say thank you for your groundbreaking work. This present work could not exist without you, since I am no Sanskritist. Please be kind to it from a scholarly perspective. In my younger years, I was a literary scholar so I know the methods of that world. For the past 30 years, I have been a working yogi. My teaching work is to awaken students and encourage them to practise and grow spiritually.

In my reading, wherever I saw an inspiring quote, I wrote it on an index card and filed it in my box of quotations. I might have written the name of the author but neglected other scholarly details. Hence, my footnotes are only partial. Since I have leaned entirely on sources in translation (in other words, your books), the information could, in principle, be recovered with a monumental effort. My goal not being scholarly, however, I have not undertaken that work.

To the meditators, I say thank you for your interest. I place this book at your feet as an offering. May you gain inspiration and instruction from it. It would be good if your interest in Kashmir Shaivism grew and deepened as a result of reading this book. It would be even better if your interest in and knowledge of the Self grew and deepened as a result of reading it.

To both groups I say 'Salutations to you', and also to my teachers, students and friends. None of us could be where we are, doing what we do, without the grace of Shiva.

Frankly, I am surprised that I myself will supply the book I sought. At the same time, I am deeply honoured that the Shakti seems to be asking me to provide a book on so noble and exalted a subject as the yoga of Kashmir Shaivism. May the spirit of Abhinavagupta and my own Guru support me in this work!

Chapter 1

The Grace of Shiva

> In You, the Supreme who transcends the abyss, You without beginning, the unique one who has penetrated the secret depths, You who rest in everything, You who are found in everything, both mobile and immobile, in You, Shambu, I take refuge.
>
> Abhinavagupta, *Paramarthasara*, Verse 1

I n the late sixties, I taught literature at a midwestern university in the United States. I was beginning what promised to be a successful career in literary studies and teaching. Destiny had other plans, however, and by early 1971 I was living with Baba Muktananda at his ashram in Ganeshpuri, India. It was a whole new life of intense discipline, meditation and service.

Many ingredients go into such a radical transformation. Some of them are subtle, emotional and nonrational. There are many ways I could speak about the salient feature of my biography— the profound change of direction that I underwent. Here let me talk about it in terms of three ideas.

I. SADHANA

I studied philosophy during my college and graduate school days, but I was not familiar with Eastern thought. After meeting Ram Dass in early 1970, I became aware for the first time of the possibility and availability of the path of yoga. A *path* is different from a *philosophy* because it implies a practical methodology. Here the method was yoga, which included meditation, postures, breathing exercises, Self-inquiry and contemplation. The goal was personal transformation from head to toe, not just intellectual transformation. This whole process taken together is called *sadhana*, and it exposed what was lacking in Western philosophy.

To be fair, on re-examining Western thinkers, the best ones do have at least some notion of personal growth and transformation. They understand that thought has something to do with being. But for me in 1970, the idea of *sadhana* was revolutionary. I saw that our educational system was without punch. It was airy with little capacity for transformation. I acquired a deep admiration for the yogic system, which had a highly developed and sophisticated technology of transformation.

I call *sadhana* Second Education. First Education, our conventional education, is the education of our intellect and our personality. Here one can put on and take off ideas and keep them at a distance. Many years ago, I gave a seminar at a university in New Zealand. Members of the department of religion met with me and I shared my experience in India and outlined the principles of Kashmir Shaivism. One of the professors was introduced to me as an expert on Christianity, another on Buddhism, another on Islam. During the course of our conversation, I said to the Christianity expert, 'As a Christian, you probably—'. He quickly corrected me. 'I'm not a Christian, I'm a *Christianist*'. No such distancing is permitted in *sadhana*. Here one stands inside the philosophy and allows it to work on his being through wisdom and technique.

In *Siddha Meditation*, I wrote about this distinction with the passion of new discovery:

> Now, what do we have here? It springs to mind that this is Muktananda's 'philosophy', but nothing could be further from the truth. Philosophy in the West is generally limited to the mental realm alone, reflecting a chronic split between thought and action. The professional thinker is interested in producing an original and clever intellectual system; he rarely sees any connection between his theories and his life. Thus a socialist may consider himself to be very different from a conservative, or a logical positivist may feel superior to a metaphysician, yet they are likely to share the same lifestyle, the same middle-age paunch, the same frequent one martini too many.

I was keenly aware that Baba was a Guru in the time-honoured Indian tradition and not a philosopher at all. He was not interested in stimulating us mentally, but in producing a change in our whole being leading to the realisation of the inner Self. For Baba, an idea must relate directly to *sadhana*.

The book was not Baba's 'thought' but his experience, a description of his actual state of Consciousness.

In the rest period after lunch at the ashram, I read widely in spiritual literature. As I read Baba's writings, I recognised two distinct strains. One was familiar to me and one was not. The former was Vedantic. He wrote of Brahman, maya, and Satchitananda, and used Vedantic stories and illustrations. I was familiar with the language of Vedanta from my first encounters with Indian thought.

The ideas of Advaita Vedanta, nondual Vedanta, are usually associated with the great sage, Shankara (788–820 A.D.). They have been widely known in the West since the first Indian swamis, Vivekananda and Rama Tirtha, toured and lectured on these ideas around the turn of the 20th century. The ascetic tone of the Vedantic teachings is the one that Westerners usually associate with Indian spirituality.

But it was the second literary strain that riveted me. Here Baba spoke of kundalini, Shakti, and *Chiti* (universal Consciousness). While the Vedantic universe seemed flat to me—this whole world is seen as an illusion—this second vision, the vision of Kashmir Shaivism, was full of fire and life. Here the world is not seen as unreal, but vibrating with conscious energy. It is the dynamic unfoldment of the Divine and every atom of it is sacred and mysterious. Indeed, the profane is nowhere to be found. *Na shivam vidyate kvachit*: There is nothing that is not Shiva.

II. EVERYTHING IS CHITI

In the afternoons we would gather in Baba's apartment for question-and-answer sessions. Baba taught us to meditate in a way that I had never before heard. He told us, 'Look at the mind as the play of *Chiti*. Whatever thoughts arise, good or bad, regard them as the play of *Chiti*, the play of Consciousness'. When I sat to meditate, the phrase, 'It's all the play of *Chiti*', echoed in my brain. I saw this implied not taking my thoughts so seriously. Thought was just thought. Everything was Consciousness, and my mind was just the sport of Consciousness.

I came across two books in the ashram library. One was *Kashmir Shaivism*, by Chatterji, the other was Kshemaraja's *Pratyabhijnahridayam*, edited by Jaideva Singh. I began to understand that when Baba said, 'Everything is *Chiti*', he was speaking the language of Kashmir Shaivism.

Baba himself had been profoundly affected by the understandings of Shaivism. That was reflected in the title of his autobiography *Chitshakti Vilas*, or *Play of Chiti (Consciousness)*. In its pages are numerous rhapsodic hymns to the Goddess Chiti. Particularly significant is Baba's chapter called 'Sexual Excitement', in which he receives a Shaivite initiation. He learns not to fight against the sexual impulse in the dualistic manner of the yogis and Vedantins (the followers of Patanjali and Shankara), but to accept it as the play of *Chiti* in the Tantric manner of Shaivism. Years later, I would see that in the experience recounted in that chapter, Baba moved decisively from a yogic/Vedantic world view to that of Kashmir Shaivism.

The Shaivite sage Abhinavagupta warned against forcibly restraining the mind and senses:

> My revered preceptor advised many times, 'The emotional functions of one's senses and organs calm themselves through spontaneous indifference (when the Self is known). But, on the other hand, these become liable to adverse reactions as long as they are forcibly repressed'.

'All is *Chiti*' gives us an acceptance and unified vision of the manifest universe. At its highest level it intoxicates us with the divine vision of the omnipresence of God.

III. I AM SHIVA

The world view of Kashmir Shaivism is compassionate in the extreme. Baba was, like many Indian swamis, reticent about giving too many details of his personal history. There was one story, however, that he told over and over again, with so much delight that I knew it had been a transforming experience for him. As a wandering monk, he had visited the city of Allahabad, where three holy rivers meet and the massive religious festival, the Kumbha Mela, is periodically held. Baba sat down at this auspicious site to meditate.

Soon he was approached by a priest who offered to do a ritual on Baba's behalf. Baba was not interested, but the fellow, determined to extract a fee, would not be dissuaded. Finally, Baba thought, 'I'll do the ritual, give him some *dakshina*, and get rid of him'.

The priest was mollified, and told Baba, 'Repeat after me, *papo ham, papo ham*, I am a sinner'.

Baba was outraged. He yelled at the priest, 'I am not a sinner. I am a pure being who is sitting to meditate on the Self. I see no sin anywhere, but only pure Consciousness. You are a sinner for making good people say that. Now leave me in peace!'

Indeed, Shaivism does not recognise the concept of sin. That which separates us from God is ignorance. Far from thinking of a human being as a fallen creature, Shaivism holds that in our innermost being, each of us is divine.

The single biggest factor that turned me towards spirituality was a nightmare vision of ego that developed in me in the late sixties. I saw ego everywhere. All my actions seemed motivated by selfishness or self-concern, and I also saw the same was true of others, all others. This was an 'awakening', but an awakening to hell.

Baba often encapsulated his teaching with the aphoristic instruction, 'Kneel to your own Self. Worship your Self. Meditate on your Self. Love your Self. Honour your Self. God dwells within you as you'. While I loved the thought of loving myself and felt relief when I heard this teaching, it was clear that my obsession with uncovering my ego moved in a very different direction. On 5 November 1971, I addressed these issues in a question to Baba. I asked:

> You often stress that we must love ourselves and only then will we be able to advance in *sadhana* and love others. I have made many unpleasant discoveries about my own ego. How can I avoid the tendency toward self-hatred?

Baba answered:

> You feel self-hatred when you are face-to-face with your own ego. Why don't you make yourself aware of egolessness? When I say that you should love your own Self, I mean loving the Self, which is beyond ego, not your ego. You can spiritualise your ego by identifying it with the Self. Instead of saying I am this or that, say I am the Self. The ego is nothing but a sense of Self. How much better to say, I am the Self, than I am a sinner or I am a king. Then the ego, too, becomes helpful. Continually repeat, I am the Self. We used to recite a hymn whose refrain was *Shivo'ham, Shivo'ham* (I am Shiva). That provided a healthy channel for the ego. For a great seeker the best thing is to identify the ego with the soul. If you were to look at it subtly, you would find the ego, too, is a stirring of the soul. We fall into misery because we do not know how to use the ego. If we were to repeat to ourselves, I am the Self, I am truth, I am perfect, the ego would be of great help. It would become a powerful mantra.

Scripture says that the Guru can awaken the seeker by word, look, touch or thought. Here *word* usually refers to the mantra. There are many stories, particularly in the Zen tradition, but in yoga as well, in which a spiritual teaching delivered at the right time to the right student, has a transforming and enlightening effect.

As Baba spoke these words to me, I felt his wisdom-Shakti enter me. It was almost as though his mind inhabited my mind. I saw things through his eyes. In that moment I saw that my whole conception of spirituality had been limited. My model had been one of building a structure by slow degrees. You work hard and, at some future point, you achieve enlightenment (although I had no idea what that meant). When he said the words, 'Then the ego, too, becomes helpful', he smashed down the walls of my obsession. The ego was not the enemy, the serpent in the garden, but a stirring of the Self. My mind cracked open.

In Kashmir Shaivism, different types of *sadhana* are listed under the four *upayas*, or methods. In the most basic method, a seeker, who considers himself separate, does yogic practices, like postures and service, with a view to connecting with God. A higher method is concerned mainly with the mind. The seeker tries to move his mind from negative to positive, getting rid of bad tendencies and allowing divine ideas to penetrate his awareness. Higher still is the method of awareness. Here the seeker plunges directly into Consciousness Itself, ignoring all mental forms, whether positive or negative. He exerts his will hoping to maintain contact with pure awareness.

In Baba's answer, all these methods flashed in front of my mind's eye. I felt as though I were moving at great speed, receiving a subtle but powerful initiation. His answer said, 'Don't think I'm a sinner, or a king'. It called on me to go beyond the ego (the mind) and plunge into the Self, with the noble cry, 'I am Shiva, I am the Self'. And his answer went beyond the three methods into the mysterious realm of *anupaya*—the fourth method. Shaivism describes this elusive method as the 'pathless path', or the 'null way'. Here is the ultimate Tantric view of the world: nothing has to be done, nothing has to be attained. Everything is already perfect. The Self is already realised and can never be anything but realised, since it lies behind every thought, every breath, every moment and every experience of life. Everything is Shiva and Shiva alone.

I saw in those moments that my true path was this *anupaya*, living life as already divine. But I saw also that there was one key to this magnificent kingdom and that was to live in relationship with the Guru. I saw as well, that this rarefied terrain was my birthright, not a mountain that I had to climb. I had been airlifted to the summit. I could be shaken by the winds of my own ignorance, self-hatred and bad tendencies, I might even tumble down the mountain, but somehow I had a safety belt that would never permit the ultimate disaster to happen. I simply had to stand that ground and claim it amidst the howling of the wind. The room seemed illumined to me, and a great joy surged in my heart. The session ended and I wandered out for my afternoon work in the garden, the mighty statement 'I am Shiva!' ringing in my mind.

A few minutes later, I was doing my usual job of watering the plants in the lower garden. My head was spinning with new thoughts and understandings and I was in a state of bliss. Suddenly Baba appeared on the path. He seemed remarkably happy and spritely. He said, 'Ah, Shankar, you liked that answer, didn't you?'

I said, 'Yes Baba, that was great'.

'Mmm . . .', he said and danced off.

I had never felt closer to him and he seemed to have gotten as much joy from what had taken place between us as I had. 'It must be tough', I thought, 'to have so much to give, and no one to take it'. When someone can open, even a little bit, to the Shakti of supreme Consciousness, what joy there is for the teacher as well!

I went back to the dorm and reported to my friends that Baba's answer had 'changed my life'. That was normal for me since I was so absorbed in every nuance of the inner process and relished every new insight. In fact it became a bit of a running joke. I would say, for example, that lunch was great today, and Ram or Larry would say, 'Did it change your life?' But this time, it had.

My perspective had shifted permanently. My understanding had become congruent with the sublime perceptions of Kashmir Shaivism. I was centred in the present. There was essentially no problem. Any problem that arose in the moment was simply a wrong movement of my mind or emotion. I merely had to discard the wrong movement and find the perfection that was already there. I am Shiva!

I had already received *shaktipat*, the awakening transmission from the Guru, earlier in my stay at Ganeshpuri, but the experience seemed to come and go. This event was different. My Consciousness was permanently altered. Certainly, afterwards the emotional winds did blow—on some occasions with the force of a hurricane. However, something was now established in me that had not been there before.

Shiva Sutras I.17 says:

> *Vitarka atmajnanam*
> The knowledge of the Self is conviction.

When a yogi holds the idea, 'I am the Self of the universe, Shiva', with unwavering conviction, he is established in the Self. One may have heard and understood the teaching but residual doubt and negative emotion can wash it away. *Sadhana* then becomes a process of strengthening the hold of 'I am the Self', and weakening the hold of doubt. As *sadhana* progresses, conviction gradually overcomes the latter. I certainly had my own generous portion of doubt and negativity. For Baba's words to have had the lasting effect they had on me, they must have been charged with grace.

The sage Abhinavagupta, whom I will quote again and again, pointed out that *anupaya* can refer to 'no means' or 'slight means'. A ripe seeker who comes into the presence of a realised being, may instantly be transformed. Or, more likely, a single spiritual instruction, accompanied by a powerful descent of grace, can effect a transformation that is both profound and permanent.

Baba had transmitted the direct experience of Kashmir Shaivism to me. The audacious equation, 'I am Shiva', is its essential insight. The first aphorism in the first text of Kashmir Shaivism, the *Shiva Sutras,* proclaims, *Chaitanyamatma:* The Self is Consciousness. In my innermost nature, I am my own awareness. That awareness is nothing but the Self and it is also Shiva or universal Consciousness and universal love. My personal awareness is the same stuff as universal Consciousness. I am Shiva and Shiva alone, though I may find it hard to grasp and hold this notion.

Maheshwarananda, the 12th-century Shaivite master, says:

> The most beautiful of rubies is veiled by the brilliance of its own rays. Thus, although it shines forth the greatest light for the entire world, the Self is not manifest.

Like a gem, hidden by its own brilliance, Consciousness is hidden by all the mental and emotional manifestations that are its own creations. The yogi has to cut through these delusions to find the underlying truth.

Shaktipat, the gracious awakening that a seeker receives from a perfected master, tied Baba to Shaivism as well. He had been a passionate spiritual seeker from an early age. He left home at 15 and wandered from ashram to ashram, from sage to sage, throughout India. He studied every spiritual philosophy and technique he could find. By his mid-thirties, he was considered a wise and holy man in his adopted town of Yeola in Maharashtra State. People flocked to him for teachings and blessings. Yet, in his heart of hearts, he knew he lacked an essential something. His search was not over, and he continued to meet saints, hoping to find a teacher. One of them, Bhagawan Nityananda of Ganeshpuri, impressed him and he spent time in his presence. But he was not prepared for the events of the morning of 15 August, 1947.

He had spent the previous night meditating in Bhagawan's ashram. In the early morning, Nityananda came out. He crossed in front of Baba and looked into his eyes, transmitting the force of his Consciousness into Baba. Instantly, Baba was lifted up to a direct experience of God. He left and walked up the road, experiencing cosmic Consciousness, the realisation of Brahman that Vedanta describes. He saw that the whole universe, including himself, was alive with God-Consciousness and shimmered with love and intelligence.

Soon Nityananda sent him off to meditate at his own place. Now powerful experiences followed one after another. Some of them were frightening, some intense. All this was new to Baba. Nothing he had read or studied prepared him for this. There seemed to be no road maps. Was what was happening to him correct and safe? He became filled with doubt and fear as this unknown force took him over.

He writes in *Play of Consciousness*:

> I sat down on my *asana* and immediately went into the lotus posture. All around me I saw flames spreading. The whole universe was on fire. A burning ocean had burst open and swallowed up the whole earth. An army of ghosts and demons surrounded me. All the while I was locked tight in the lotus posture, my eyes closed, my chin pressed down against my throat so that no air could escape. Then I felt a searing pain in the knot of nerves in the *muladhara*, situated at the base of the spine. My eyes opened. I wanted to run away, but my legs were locked tight

in the lotus posture. I felt as if my legs had been nailed down permanently in this position. My arms were completely immobilised. I was quite aware that everything I was seeing was unreal, but I was still surrounded by terror.

After struggling with such terrifying experiences for some time, he came across a text of Kashmir Shaivism. It detailed exactly what he was going through. Nowhere else was he able to find such an accurate picture of the process of *shaktipat*, the awakening by Guru's grace. Indeed, Shaivism describes 27 varieties of *shaktipat* in great detail. From that period, Kashmir Shaivism was close to Baba's heart, and he spoke most often from the point of view of Shaivism. Of the three ideas I have been discussing, *the idea of sadhana* belongs to all traditions of Indian spiritual philosophy, but the latter two ideas, *everything is Chiti* and *I am Shiva*, are particularly associated with Kashmir Shaivism.

SELF-RECOGNITION

In connection with the idea, *I am Shiva*, I discovered the teachings of the Self-Recognition School of Shaivism. As I will discuss in the next chapter, in the early days of Shaivism, there were two main schools: the Spanda School and the Pratyabhijna School. These are reflected in two aspects of contemporary Shaivism. *Spanda* has to do with energy: the *spanda* teachings point to the divine energy that is present or potential in every moment. The *spanda* yogi tries to enhance his experience of Shakti. He studies in himself which thoughts and actions deplete his energy, and which ones uplift it. His ultimate goal is the experience of divine bliss. *Pratyabhijna* refers to Self-recognition and has to do with the path of wisdom. The yogi of recognition tries to understand the Shivaness of everything, especially himself.

In the play *The Bald Soprano* by the Romanian writer, Ionesco, there is a scene in which two people meet at a party. They discover that they live in the same town. 'How remarkable', and 'What a coincidence', they say.

Then they discover that they live in the same suburb. 'How remarkable', and 'What a coincidence'.

Then they discover that they live in the same street and even the same building. 'How remarkable', and 'What a coincidence'.

'What apartment do you live in?' one asks.

'2F', says the other.

'Why, so do I! You must be my wife!'

'Darling!' And they embrace, to the delight of the audience.

The joke, of course, is their total lack of recognition of each other and their silly process of discovering who they are. Of course, you know your own husband or your own wife unless you are going to appear in Oliver Sacks' next book. How absurd is it, then, that we don't know our own Self? The Self is even more intimate to us than our spouse.

Yogis of the Recognition School illustrate Self-recognition with a story something like this: a young girl has a long correspondence with a male pen-pal. Over time, she falls in love with him and yearns to meet him and marry him. She tells her best friend about all his divine qualities. He is so loving, so kind, so intelligent.

When she tells her friend his name, the friend exclaims, 'Why, I know him, and so do you!'

'No, I don't.'

'Yes, you do. He's the young man that sells you your groceries at the market.'

The teaching says that even though she knew him, she had not *recognised* his divine virtues in their face-to-face encounters. But she had recognised those qualities in her pen-pal. In the same way, scripture tells us about the virtues of the Lord and we don't associate those virtues with ourselves. Now the Guru (the friend) tells us that we have those virtues ourselves but we have to recognise them. (The boy at the checkout counter is the same as our pen-pal but we have to recognise him.) The story concludes happily: the girl gradually comes to associate the qualities of her pen-pal with the checkout boy, until she sees they are the same person. In the same way, through Self-recognition, we discover our identity with Shiva.

Utpaladeva says:

> Just as an object of love, who has been brought to the presence of a slim lady by her various entreaties, cannot give her any pleasure, though he may stand before her, so long as he is not recognised, and therefore not distinguished from common man; so the Self of all, which is the Lord of the world, cannot manifest its true glory so long as its essential nature has not been dealt with.

When a yogi of the Recognition School says, 'I am Shiva!' he is not making an affirmation about what he wishes to be, rather he is acknowledging his recognition of what is actually the case.

The practice of Self-recognition combined with the yoga of *spanda*, the enhancement of energy, is a complete and dynamic *sadhana*. It combines knowledge with will and activity in a comprehensive way. One without the other can be limited.

LORD SHIVA

It should already be clear that I use the word Shiva synonymously with universal Consciousness. Of course, in the myths and scriptures of India, one will encounter a personal form of Shiva, covered with ash, the Ganges spouting from His head, entwined with cobras and wearing *rudraksha* beads. That Shiva is a colourful deity: a Bohemian yogi of awesome power. While in devotional moods, the Shaivite masters no doubt visualised *that* Shiva, in these pages I am essentially referring to the impersonal one.

Jaideva Singh derives *Shiva* from the root *shi*, 'to lie', and the root *shvi*, 'to cut asunder'. Thus, Shiva, as Consciousness, is the ground of reality. All things lie in Him. He is also the one who cuts asunder all bonds.

Baba writes, 'Parashiva is full of affection for His devotees. He destroys their sorrow, poverty, ignorance and darkness, and He helps them through crises'. Shiva is thus both the fundamental stuff of the universe and the agent of grace and liberation.

Singh continues, 'The name Shiva for the Highest Reality is a very happy choice. Shiva is the Highest Reality as well as the Highest Good'.

One of the sutras tells us that Shiva is always plainly visible and that nothing can veil Him. From the point of view of wisdom, this is completely and simply true, however, only the eye of an *initiate* can see him.

Shiva's hide-and-seek can be a humorous sport. In my childhood, on the street where I lived, there was a Jewish school. I passed it everyday, always reading the sign which said, *Yeshiva*, or 'school'. Meditating once in Ganeshpuri, the realisation came to me that Shiva had been nodding and winking to me all those years. The sign really said, *Yes! Shiva!*

THE DIVINE SHAKTI

O Lord, how fruitful can this neuter Brahman be without the beautiful female of Your devotion which makes of You a person? (*Bhatta Nayaka*)

The Kashmir Shaivite masters did not reject the world. They were not elitist. Their emphasis was on love and devotion. At the centre of Kashmir Shaivism is the opening of the heart to the divine Shakti. The world is seen as the embodiment of the divine Mother, the eternal feminine who is always one with Shiva.

Maheshwarananda says:

> Shiva Himself full of joy enhanced by the honey of the three corners of His heart (knowledge, will and action), raising up His face to gaze at His own splendour is called Shakti.

The proper attitude towards Her is devotional: to love and adore Her, not reject or control Her as in some forms of yoga and Vedanta. Focusing on the heart, the yogi of Shaivism sees the Mother, the Shakti, everywhere, and celebrates Her sport. An old Shaivite aphorism says that 'Without Shakti, Shiva is *shava,* a corpse'.

Scripture says:

> The Goddess Shakti is always engaged in enjoying the taste of manifestation and yet She is never depleted. She is a wave on the ocean of Consciousness, the volitional power of the Lord.

Shakti and *Chiti*, the ever-sporting Goddess of divine Consciousness are not different. Few of Her devotees reach the lyrical heights of my Guru in his frequent hymns to the Goddess:

> *Chiti* is supremely free. She is self-revealing. She is the only cause of the creation, sustenance and dissolution of the universe. She exists, holding the power within Her that creates, sustains and destroys. The prime cause of everything, She is also the means to highest bliss. All forms, all places and all instants of time are manifested from Her. She is all-pervading, always completely free and of everlasting light. Manifesting as the universe, still She remains established in Her indivisibility and unity. Within the Blue Light, She pulsates with ambrosial bliss. There is only one, the supreme witness, the One who is called cosmic Consciousness of Supreme Shiva. She is ever solitary. In the beginning, in the middle and in the end, only *Chiti* is. She does not depend on any agency; She is Her own basis and support. As She alone exists, She is in perfect freedom.

Shakti is always one with Shiva, She is never separate. The divine pair, *yamala*, like the yin-yang, incorporate all the dualities within them: heaven and earth, matter and Consciousness, world and spirit.

The Tantras are usually in the form of a dialogue between Shiva and Shakti. Shakti asks questions and Shiva gives the answers. At the highest level, the reader understands the oneness of Shakti with Shiva. She is supreme Consciousness, His own power of Self-reflection.

Abhinavagupta writes:

> Self who is the natural state of all existents, who is self-luminous, amusing Himself with question-answer which is not different from Himself, and in which both the questioner (as Devi) and the answerer (as Bhairava) are only Himself, enjoys Self-reflection.

Shakti is the active, manifesting aspect of the Lord. That She is revered by the Shaivite sages gives Shaivism its warmth and quality of heart. Such a 'this-worldly' approach resonates with the modern Western sensibility. Notice also, Baba's use of the word *freedom* (*svatantrya*), in the last sentence. The Shaivite masters emphasise this characteristic of Consciousness. Consciousness freely creates and freely sports. As we liberate ourselves from our dependencies, more and more we take on the characteristic of *Chiti*, this sportive, Self-generated freedom.

THE SHAPE OF SHAIVISM

The essence of the Shaivite world view is easily understood. First we look at universal Consciousness, Shiva. Shiva's creative and active aspect is Shakti. Shakti can manifest as *spanda*, the blissfully aware cosmic vibration of the divine. *Spanda* is described as a throb, a quiver, a pulse or a tremor. The dynamism of *spanda* manifests at the highest level as the bliss of the divine.

Consciousness, in its most expanded state, is perfect in peace, energy, love and Self-awareness. Shiva can create anything. He can become anything. He is perfectly free and empowered. In a paroxysm of creative frenzy, He creates a universe in his own being. He manifests the levels of creation. The Buddha said, 'Life is suffering'. Shaivism says, 'Shiva undergoes contraction via three impurities'. Thus any study of Shaivism must say a few words about the nature of Shiva, the Absolute, and also about the process of creation and contraction.

Shiva's will, Shiva's love, Shiva's wisdom, Shiva's bliss, Shiva's activity, even Shiva's language, all become limited in the process of contraction. Hence, a student should know something about how Kashmir Shaivism looks at contraction. We are the end product of the process of contraction: the limited individual soul, the *jiva*. Shaivism says that the *jiva*, us, is a limited form of Shiva Himself. Our discussion has to explore this unique perspective.

Shaivism takes an extraordinarily detailed look at language. While describing bondage, Shaivism says that language, misused language, is bondage, there is no other. You cannot say that a dog or a cat is bound; only a human being is bound. He is bound not by chains but only by language, by his own thoughts, his own idea of himself. This is the absorbing topic of *matrika*, or how language works. The Shiva Process Self-inquiry finds its source in the Shaivite understandings of *matrika*, inner speech.

Sadhana is the movement from being a contracted individual back to our essential divine essence. It is the return home, from *jiva* to Shiva. This aspect of Shaivism includes contemplations and meditative techniques. This yogic technology constitutes the real wealth of the Shaivite approach. Behind the process of *sadhana* and completely necessary to it, is the grace and compassionate teaching of the Guru. The Guru's grace and Shiva's grace are the real motive force of *sadhana*.

The whole drama is Shiva's and Shiva's alone. He begins in ecstasy and freedom, undergoes limitation and suffering out of His own free will, and then yearns for and achieves the recognition and attainment of His true nature, His former status as Shiva Himself. He takes the form of the Guru and teaches Himself in the form of the seeker the path to Consciousness. The central theme of this book is this process: the movement down and the movement back.

SHAIVA MANDALAS

As I worked on this book, a simple visual summary of what I have just been talking about took form for me. It is a Shaiva mandala, an encompassing symbol of the *darshan*, or philosophical system, of Kashmir Shaivism. Many of the concepts of Shaivism can be expressed by this mandala.

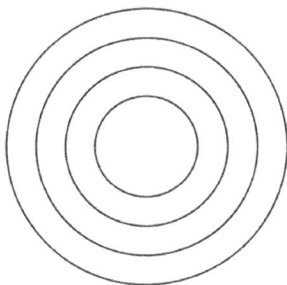

Basic Shaiva Mandala. *Simple concentric circles illustrate levels of reality issuing out of and back to the core, which is always Consciousness Itself.*

This simple form of the mandala can be elaborated in various ways to show complexity or dynamism:

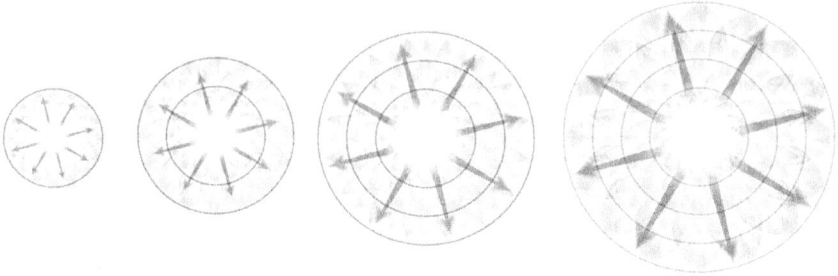

Creation

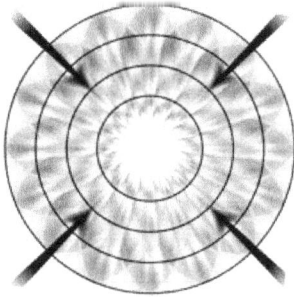

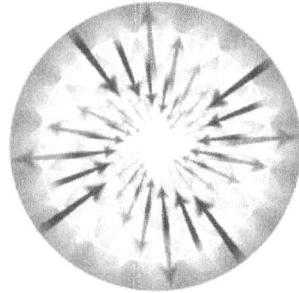

Dissolution   *Vibration of Spanda*

Vibration of Spanda Mandalas. *Pure Consciousness continually pulses from the centre, creating the universe and the densest matter on the periphery, then dissolves back into Consciousness through the process of* sadhana, *or* grace.

The universe beats like a cosmic heart. The pulsation is on the macrocosmic level, in which it unfolds our universe, holds it in place and then withdraws it after many millions of years; and on the microcosmic level in which the same pulsation takes place in every nanosecond with the creation of every thought and the beating of the human heart. In meditation this profound vibratory movement can be contacted in the stillness.

Chapter 2

The Origins of Kashmir Shaivism

> When one follows this path of the transcendental Reality according to
> the teaching of the master, suddenly by means of extremely intense
> *shaktipat*, one certainly becomes Shiva Himself.
>
> Abhinavagupta, *Paramarthasara*, Verse 96

J ust as in Western art there seems an eternal polarity between the
classical and the romantic sensibilities, or in Nietzsche's terms, the
Apollonian and Dionysian, so too, Indian spirituality has its own polarity:
Veda and Tantra. Perhaps these two represent two chambers of the human
heart or the two hemispheres of the human brain.

TWO APPROACHES: VEDIC AND TANTRIC

While the historical facts are obscure and debatable, the Vedic culture is
associated with the Brahmin caste and, in the popular mind, with the light-
skinned, Aryan settlers from the north. At the same time, Tantric culture is
originally associated with the dark-skinned, Dravidian peoples who were
disenfranchised by the Aryans. There is great debate about whether or not
there was an Aryan invasion and if there was one, what exactly it was. But
even without entering that debate, Veda and Tantra present us with world
views that are revealing in their differences.

Open only to Brahmin males, Vedic spirituality was intellectual,
philosophical, orthodox and prescriptive. It embodied the archetype of
male intellectual elitism, so much so, it has become symbolic of that: the

American intellectual elite of the 19th century, for example, was referred to as the 'Boston Brahmins'.

The Vedantic sages taught a yoga of understanding and detachment. Their groundbreaking insight, described in the *Upanishads*, was of the primacy of the inner Self. Through a highly sophisticated and meticulous process of discrimination, an unusually qualified and evolved seeker might bring enough mental discipline, control and insight to his quest that he could realise that Self. Rare was the person who qualified to study Vedanta, rarer still, the one talented and intelligent enough to succeed.

The Vedic path was a strict and orthodox father, with very high standards. Its teachings came down from on-high, from the *shruti*, the sacred *Vedas*, the infallible word of God. The written *Veda* was seen as only a material expression of the eternal Veda that was a self-existing reality, the eternal space in Consciousness where divine spiritual wisdom is sourced. Predictably, there had to evolve a more forgiving methodology for the masses. Tantra was the mother, accepting everyone else, the low of birth, the dark-skinned, the female.

Tantra made a place for the emotional and vital person. It was devotional and also practical. Its yoga was experimental and inductive. It offered techniques that, if adopted, would give results: states of higher Consciousness. Where the Vedic path, as also the path of Patanjali Yoga, called for renunciation and control of the desire nature, Tantra discovered a different method. Rather than suppress, it sought to sublimate—to use and redirect existing impulses and energies, not supress them. For the Tantric, the world was not the enemy but the embodiment of God. Every manifestation in the world was God playing hide-and-seek in that form. So for the Tantric, anything and everything was a potential doorway to the infinite.

Brahminism makes a strong dichotomy between pure and impure. The caste rules are strict and inflexible and ritual impurity, as in marrying a person of the wrong caste, or even eating food prepared by a lower caste, is social/religious suicide. The Tantric view, on the contrary, finds nothing impure, since everything is Shiva, and makes no distinction between the secular and the religious, seeing everything as one.

The stronger and the more intense the worldly energy, the more the potential it offers for realisation. If the Vedic student flees in terror from sexuality, the Tantric might embrace it as a method or *upaya*. If the Vedic approaches his spirituality primarily with his intellect, the Tantric approaches it with his whole body, bringing his mind, heart and gut into action. This visceral yoga claims that it is possible to have not only *yoga* (liberation) but *bhoga* (pleasure) as well.

Among the Tantric paths, Kashmir Shaivism is the crest-jewel. For Westerners, being denied entry into the pristine temples of the Veda, the Tantric path is the most welcoming. It becomes the Way of the West by default. Even apart from that, it more innately suits the Western mind and temper.

The *Shiva Sutras* date to the ninth century. Long before that, Tantric scriptures called *agamas* existed. The *agamas* were based on the actual and repeatable experience of the sages and therefore come from the 'bottom up'. The *Vedas*, of course, were regarded as coming from above by divine revelation.

Tantrics must have had a difficult time authenticating themselves. On one hand, the Brahmins claimed a tradition based on divine revelation. On the other hand, the Tantric yogis must have seemed, by comparison, a low-born tatterdemalion lot. To counter this, they also insisted on the divine origin of their scriptures.

The word *Tantra* itself means a rule, a teaching or a technical system. Its root meaning is to 'control', or 'harness', therefore, it teaches the seeker not to suppress the forces of reality but to control and harness them. Every Tantric text will have three elements: it will give a philosophical overview, perhaps a depiction of the human condition and human suffering; then it will talk about the spiritual goal, Self-realisation: bliss and wisdom; and finally and most importantly, it will offer a *sadhana* manual: specific yogic methods and techniques for attaining the goal.

KULA AND KRAMA SCHOOLS

The Kashmir Shaivism of the ninth or 10th century is usually associated with four schools: the Kula, the Krama, the Spanda and the Pratyabhijna. Of these, the Kula and the Krama are actually older Tantric schools, dating to perhaps the fourth century. The two others came into being as a direct result of the new insights provided by the *Shiva Sutras*.

Kula means 'family' and the name has two possible explanations. It emphasised the union of Shiva and Shakti, hence, family; and a spiritual group or *satsang* is family-like.

A famous aphorism says, 'Be a *Vaishnava* by day, a *Shaiva* at home and a *Kula* in the night'. The Kula School is notorious for the secret sexual ritual. It aimed at Self-realisation through the practice of the five 'm's' (meat, fish, wine, parched grain and sexual union).

Since the sexual ritual was central to the Kula School, and would necessarily have to be kept secret, it would give the members of the circle a keen sense of being apart from the larger society and a strong family feeling.

Although the sexual ritual was by far the most sensational and controversial aspect of the Kula School, there was more to the school than that. It had knowledge of kundalini yoga and, at the higher end of Kula practice, the sexual act was seen as a metaphor of inner union.

Abhinavagupta, seeking direct instruction in every dynamic form of yoga available, travelled from Kashmir for initiation into the Kula School. He seems the first of the Kashmir Shaivite sages to have brought the Kula teachings into Kashmir Shaivism.

The Krama School, like the Kula, existed independently of Kashmir Shaivism proper, though many of its teachings were later included in the Trika. *Krama* means 'stages', or 'gradation'. The Krama system said that realisation happens only through successive stages. Its sages did an epistemological analysis of experience, defining each discrete moment in the perception of anything. They spoke of 12 Kalis or goddesses that governed this movement and also the *shakti chakra*, which I discuss in Chapter 22. Like the Kula School, it emphasised worship of the goddess.

THE ORIGINS OF KASHMIR SHAIVISM

Legend has it that Kashmir Shaivism was born when the ninth-century Kashmiri sage Vasugupta had a dream of Lord Shiva. In it, Shiva told him that the world had lost its way and needed a restatement of the true teaching. If Vasugupta would go to a certain large rock and touch it, the rock would roll over and reveal the teachings beneath it. The sage did and uncovered what is now called the *Shiva Sutras*, a set of 77 aphorisms on yoga. They are the seed of the philosophy and discipline of Kashmir Shaivism. The corpus of work in Kashmir Shaivism is a commentary on these sutras or an expansion of them.

It is worthwhile to consider this story. We have every right to be sceptical. Having spent many years in India, I have heard many like it. While some of these stories may be factually true, most often they are a code in which something is hidden. What could Vasugupta (or his follower) be telling us? He might be saying, 'These writings came to me from divine inspiration. I did not create them personally. They are "channelled" from my higher mind'. Or, 'I have an insight I feel is a spiritual breakthrough. I want you to take it as seriously as you do the *Vedas*. Indeed, I feel it should have as much authority as the *Vedas*'.

It is true that anyone who works intimately with these sutras will be convinced that they do come from a higher source. Great sages like Vasugupta had access to that source.

Prior to the eighth century the valley of Kashmir was a centre for Buddhist studies. It was cosmopolitan and multicultural: Hindu, Buddhist and Mediterranean. It is a place of great beauty and in my early days in India, many people rented houseboats on Lake Dal and stayed there. Now, of course, there is war between the Hindus and Muslims.

In the eighth and ninth centuries a number of kings fostered culture. They patronised the arts, drama, music and poetry. They built temples and brought in Brahmins from all over India to perform rituals. One of them brought the ancestors of Abhinavagupta, the greatest of the Shaivite sages.

Tibetan Buddhism traces its spiritual roots to Kashmir. There is a tradition, possibly apocryphal, that Shankaracharya also visited and debated various Buddhists there.

The earliest sages of Kashmir Shaivism were sometimes scholars but always yogis. Each was involved in the process of transformation. Each had disciples. After Vasugupta, two main traditions emerged: Spanda Shastra and Pratyabhijna Shastra. The *spanda* tradition concentrates on divine energy. It says that the universe is nothing but vibrating awareness. Western physics also acknowledges that the basic stuff of the universe is vibrating energy, but regards it as material and therefore not conscious. The masters of the *spanda* tradition sought to find that energy in every moment of life. The main text of the *spanda* tradition is the *Spanda Karikas*, written by Vasugupta or his disciple, Kallata.

Pratyabhijna means 'recognition'. The Pratyabhijna tradition says that since we are Shiva, all we have to do to know Shiva is to recognise or 're-cognise', *know again*, that we are Shiva. As soon as we recognise our Shivaness inwardly our spiritual search is complete. Thus the Doctrine of Recognition is a wisdom tradition reminiscent of some of the teachings of the Vedantic sages. 'I am Shiva' is clearly consonant with the Vedantic, *'aham Brahmasmi'*, 'I am Brahman'. Somananda and Utpaladeva were two authors in the Pratyabhijna tradition.

Utpaladeva, in his massive work *Ishvara-Pratyabhijna Karika*, begins with the charming statement:

> Having somehow realised my identity with the Supreme and wishing to render service to humanity, I am establishing 'Self-recognition', which is a means of attaining all that is of value.

In the 10th century looms the massive figure of Abhinavagupta. Many times in these pages I will write, 'Kashmir Shaivism says . . . ' Most often (but not always) it would be accurate to substitute 'Abhinavagupta says . . . ', so pervasive was his influence. His great work, *Tantraloka*, is a magnificent achievement and a burgeoning scholarly industry that makes Indologists' mouths water.

Equally, his yogic insights are relevant to seekers today. Abhinavagupta created a Shaivism that was a synthesis of the Spanda, Krama, Kula and Pratyabhijna schools. He also wrote on the *agamic* sources of Shaivism like the *Malini-Vijaya* Tantra, the *Vijnanabhairava* Tantra and the *Svacchanda* Tantra. These are earlier authoritative texts considered to be 'revealed', that is, of divine origin. His extensive writings gave Kashmir Shaivism its modern shape. He was encyclopaedic; he wrote definitive works on Self-recognition, as well as on the Tantras, and he also wrote on Sanskrit poetics and aesthetics.

THE TRIKA

Kashmir Shaivism is often called the Trika or the Trika System. Historically, the term Trika had a specialised meaning, but more and more it has come to be synonymous with nondual Kashmir Shaivism as a whole, and I will use it that way. The historical issues are rather complicated. Anyone interested in exploring them might begin with the interesting discussion in Mark Dyczkowski's *Doctrine of Vibration*. Certainly, as Dyczkowski says, it was Abhinavagupta 'who made Trika the focal point of nondual Kashmiri Shaivism'.

Trika means 'the three', and Kashmir Shaivism is, as we will see, filled with triads. The primary triad is that of the three goddesses: *para, apara* and *parapara,* who represent three levels of reality. *Para* is nondual, *apara* is dualistic, and *parapara* is unity in duality. Another threesome is *pati*, the Lord; *pashu*, the individual; and *pasha*, bondage, or the 'noose'. The noose is the force that binds the Lord and the individual together.

I think the most significant Trika for the yogi is the *Shiva-jiva-sadhana* triad, which could also be called the *Consciousness-bondage-yoga* triad. It holds that there are three topics for us to explore: first is the nature of Consciousness and the creation of the universe within Consciousness. Second is bondage, the contraction of Consciousness and the rise of limitation and suffering. The third is *sadhana*, the way out of bondage. Trika suggests an emphasis on *sadhana*, the yogic or practical aspect of Kashmir Shaivism.

As a yogi, my main interest is in the *sadhana*. However, there are many wonderful ideas in the other aspects of the Trika that are useful in *sadhana*. Thus, in this book, I will explore all three in a number of different ways. The chapters on the *tattvas*, the *malas* and the *upayas* will begin the discussion. The *tattvas* are a description of the creation and structure of the universe and therefore deal with the nature of Shiva or supreme Consciousness. The *malas* describe the process of contraction—how Shiva becomes a limited individual. The *upayas* are the methods of *sadhana* and include the whole range of meditative, contemplative and yogic techniques.

TWO CONTEMPORARY TRADITIONS

Following Abhinavagupta, his disciple Kshemaraja is a significant figure. But from the 11th century to the present day, Kashmir Shaivism essentially disappears, or at least goes underground. One of the contributing factors to the break in the lineage was doubtless the intrusion of Islam into the valley of Kashmir. Until the 20th century, Kashmir was essentially cut off from the rest of India by tribal warfare. There are a few significant figures like the 12th-century Maheshwarananda, but it is only in recent years that it has again come to prominence.

I: THE SCHOLARLY TRADITION

In the 20th century, two significant streams of Kashmir Shaivism have emerged, centring around two great contemporary teachers. One of these was established by Swami Lakshmanjoo (1907–1991) of Shrinigar, Kashmir. He began his Shaivite studies at a young age. He mastered Sanskrit to the extent that he could speak this ancient sacred language fluently. He learned the ancient texts of Shaivism— some of them profoundly esoteric— under the guidance of local scholars who were in touch with the oral tradition. Thus Lakshmanjoo early on had a strong scholarly connection with Kashmir Shaivism.

The young scholar was not content with mere intellectual knowledge, however. As the texts and teachings permeated him, they detonated an inner explosion. Lakshmanjoo was transformed, so much so that those who studied with him later experienced him as an enlightened master.

Scholars flocked to him to study with the man they considered to be the last living representative of the oral tradition of Kashmir. They included Bettina Baumer, Mark Dyczkowski, Pandit Rameshwar Jha, Gerald Larson, Andre Padoux, Lilian Silburn and Thakur Jaideva Singh. All of them wrote on Shaivism and some produced useful editions of texts in English, French or Italian. All of them found Lakshmanjoo to be not only a scholar, but also a yogi.

Lilian Silburn said:

> Thanks to him the oral tradition, after an apparent eclipse, has been securely renewed, because the swami, a very learned scholar but also a real yogi and *jnani,* has mystically lived that which the old Shaiva masters of Kashmir, and in particular, Abhinavagupta, brought to light.

II: THE SHAKTIPAT TRADITION

The second stream of Shaivism has emerged under the inspiration of my teacher, Swami Baba Muktananda (1908–1982). I am not aware that the Lakshmanjoo tradition has taken a specific name but it could be called the 'scholarly'. Baba's line, I call the *'shaktipat* tradition' of Kashmir Shaivism. He has had an immense impact among spiritual seekers because he was able to transmit the *experience* of Shaivism. He delivered the *Shakti.* He awakened the kundalini energy of thousands of seekers.

A number of his disciples have become spiritual teachers in their own right, and all of them have been deeply affected by Baba's Shaivite vision. Swami Chetanananda of the Nityananda Institute, has a specifically Shaivite approach. Others like Gurumayi Chidvilasanada of SYDA, Swami Nityananda of Shanti Mandir, Master Charles Cannon of Synchronicity, Swami Gurupremananda of Gurudev Ashram, California, and Da Avabhasa (Franklin Jones) were all trained in the *shaktipat* tradition and make implicit use of many of the Shaivite teachings. In the Shiva School of Kashmir

Shaivism here in Melbourne, practical and theoretical studies in Shaivism are pursued.

Truly speaking, Shaivism cannot be understood inwardly or spiritually without *shaktipat*, real spiritual awakening. By this, I do not mean to imply that the scholarly tradition is devoid of spiritual awakening. There is ample evidence that Swami Lakshmanjoo did awaken a number of his students via *shaktipat*. Of course, it is possible to turn Kashmir Shaivism into merely an academic and historical subject, but that should not be mistaken for spiritual authenticity.

Baba had *initiating power:* in his presence thousands had the direct *experience* of the Self. His Shaktipat Shaivism will continue to drink from the living waters of the Shaivite vision. Gurus in this school may not care too much for intellectual and historical niceties. Rather, they will be concerned with transmitting the power and wisdom of the Shaivite world view to seekers in order to uplift them and connect them to the Self. Nonetheless, the scholarly approach performs a vital function and can help ground contemporary Shaivite visionaries. Study of the ancient texts should be an essential part of today's Shaivite *sadhana*, and scholars perform a significant service as they make more of these texts available in translation in lucid modern editions.

SCHOLAR AND YOGI

Perhaps a way of defining these two Shaivisms is to observe that the two Gurus came to the tradition in different ways. Lakshmanjoo always operated within the philosophical domain of Kashmir Shaivism. First he acquired the knowledge, and that knowledge led to experience. Baba Muktananda began with the experience and came to Shaivism because it gave an intellectual structure that explained the kundalini experiences he was having. Thus for Baba, the experience would always hold primacy over traditional material.

When the Shaivite ideas are regarded as facts and theories to be compared and analysed, they remain as limited knowledge. The true Shaivite application of these principles is to use them to increase Shakti or the mystical awareness of the Self. The goal or purpose of what we do defines what we do. A scholarly quest is designed to unearth the historical truth. In it one idea is linked to another in a horizontal way. The founding sages of Shaivism did not plan for their ideas to be compared to each other, but to give 'vertical access', to provide a means to higher consciousness. Scholarly Shaivism will always be horizontal but never vertical. Experiential Shaivism, on the other hand, can sometimes be horizontal and scholarly, but it will always use the ideas vertically as an *upaya* or 'means' to know the Divine.

Ideas are seductive. Coming from an academic background I am susceptible to their allure. This came home to me vividly while I was writing the chapter, Being Present. I wanted to write something on the rather esoteric Shaivite theory of the *sadadhvas*. No matter how I struggled with the material I felt a block. Finally I saw that I was taking the ideas as somehow real and terribly interesting in themselves. I had the insight that I had to use the ideas vertically, as tools for spiritual upliftment. I had to write in the manner of the *shaktipat* tradition, from the point of view of yogic practice. The chapter reformed itself radically, and the block released.

The two traditions have occasionally undervalued each other, the yogic side thinking of the scholarly side as mere academics. Even Lakshmanjoo's scholarly students generally say that he is the last of his tradition. But they would be in an academic line rather than a disciplic tradition, and they might not be aware of the latter. It is likely that such a great being would have left initiates as well as scholars to carry on his tradition.

On the other side, the scholarly world has overlooked Baba's contribution. I have several times heard it said that he 'popularised' Kashmir Shaivism or spread a 'popular' and therefore less authentic form to the masses. I would contend, on the contrary, that he didn't simply popularise Shaivism, he *verticalised* it. He inspired thousands to actually do the practice, and in this way he gave an authentic form of Shaivism that Vasugupta and Abhinava would have saluted.

The large Indian publishing house, Motilal Banarsidass, has published most of the key books in English on Kashmir Shaivism. While in the process of publishing the Indian edition of my book, *Happy for No Good Reason*, the publishers told us that many years ago, Baba had strongly urged them to publish Jaideva Singh's translations of the Shaivite sutras. Out of respect for Baba, they complied, and were pleased because all of those editions have sold steadily. Baba's devotees bought, and still continue to buy, a high percentage of the books.

Similarly in America, State University of New York (SUNY) Press has been the main publisher of Shaivite texts. Bill Eastman, for many years the head of SUNY Press, was a devotee of Baba and published Shaivism at Baba's suggestion. Scholars are sometimes a generation behind, and they may not be in tune with Baba's approach to Shaivism. Baba was not afraid to rework it and cared little for pedantry. I have no doubt that future generations of scholars will give appropriate weight to his contribution and stature, as the passage of time makes him suitable material for scholarship.

It is an interesting, harmonising footnote to add that late in his life, Baba took some devotees on a pilgrimage to Kashmir. They visited the holy sites around Shrinigar and chanted the *Guru Gita* on top of the rock where Vasugupta discovered the *Shiva Sutras.* On Wednesday, 22 September, 1982, Swami Lakshmanjoo and some of his students visited Baba where he was staying. They chatted with great affection. Swami Lakshmanjoo held Baba's hand during the photo session.

Baba said, 'Holding your hand, I feel that I am holding Vasugupta's hand because you are in his lineage'. Ten days later, after his return to Ganeshpuri, Baba passed away.

Swami Muktananda (left) and Swami Lakshmanjoo. The two great masters of modern Shaivism meet in Kashmir in 1982.

Theory and practice are two wings of the bird of spiritual development. For thousands of years, people have done spiritual work with the aim of finding their own inner greatness. All who have pursued the path with any dedication have progressed; many have reached the final goal. So yogic theory is a way of talking about what we, as a community of seekers, have learned from each other's experience. One of the beauties of the path of yoga is that there is an internal alarm that does not allow either theory or practice to go too far without the other. Too much theory can feel dry, and automatically directs the seeker to practise the teaching; and intense practice impels the seeker to read, reflect and contemplate what he has experienced.

READING SHAIVISM IN ENGLISH

The situation for the non-scholar or the non-Sanskritist is already much better than it was a few years ago. There is enough material available in English to satisfy the Shaiva yogi, and there is more appearing all the time. Basic to any library are the excellent translations by Jaideva Singh of the *Shiva Sutras, Spanda Karikas, Pratyabhijnahridayam* and the *Vijnanabhairava*. These are widely available, published by Motilal Barnarsidass, and are the fundamental texts. Mark Dyczkowski has also done editions of the *Shiva Sutras* and the *Spanda Karikas*. These are also well worth having, and use different sources.

Worthwhile secondary sources by modern scholars include Dyczkowski's *Doctrine of Vibration*, Mishra's *Kashmir Shaivism*, Muller-Ortega's *Triadic Heart of Shiva*, Sharma's *Philosophy of Sadhana* and Silburn's *Kundalini*. There are a number of excellent studies by Indian scholars, published in India, which are more difficult to obtain. Among them, I recommend Pandit's *Specific Principles of Kashmir Shaivism* for the new student.

More yogic works are Swami Lakshmanjoo's *Self Realisation* and *The Secret Supreme*, Swami Chetanananda's *Dynamic Stillness I and II*, and, of course, *Siddha Meditation* by Swami Muktananda.

I should also mention Bailly's translation of Utpaladeva's poems, *Shaiva Devotional Songs of Kashmir*, which show the devotional side of Utpala and a different face of the tradition.

A number of other wonderful texts are either difficult to obtain or hardgoing for new students. But others will certainly appear as interest in Kashmir Shaivism continues to grow.

Chapter 3

A Shaivite Overview

> Shiva pervades everything without being different from anything. How can anything be other than Shiva?
>
> Baba Muktananda, *Siddha Meditation*

V asugupta's text, the *Shiva Sutras*, describes a mystical pathway to enlightenment. At its centre is the ideal of the Shaivite sage, the yogi who has attained the goal. Having conquered errant tendencies by arduous spiritual practice, he lives in the world as a beacon for humanity. His orientation to suffering is different from that of ordinary people:

Sukha-duhkhayor bahirmananam
The experiences of pleasure and pain in the life of such a Self-realised yogi are confined to the periphery of his Consciousness and do not affect his inner being. (*Shiva Sutras* III.33)

Tat pravrittau api anirasah samvetri-bhavat
Even though he is engaged in activity he is totally unattached to it and remains unmoved because he is established in the awareness of the supreme Self. (*Shiva Sutras* III.32)

We might think that such detachment is austere and life-denying. To be 'unmoved' is to become a dry stick, with emotions programmed out, cold and hyperrational. The Shaivite sage is not that. He loves the richness of life as the arena of the divine. He has purified his mind and heart of anger, jealousy, fear, greed, and the like, not out of a puritanical urge, but because these emotions destroy the love and joy of one who suffers them.

The sage is a hero who lives the highest understanding of Shaivism: all forms in this universe are made of the one substance, Shiva. And the very fabric of the universe is endless joy, endless abundance and endless peace and satisfaction. Only the creations of our own minds keep us from this knowledge.

Baba wrote of this knowledge and this state in *Siddha Meditation*:

> The sage rests in the realisation of pure knowledge, 'I am Shiva'. He is in bliss. This is the highest *samadhi,* the perfect state of enlightenment. The yogi who looks upon the universe as his own body, drinks the nectar of ecstasy. He sees the vast variety of objects, shapes and forms, the endless modifications around him, as diverse and yet one; for they all appear in his own Self trembling with bliss. To him all the worlds are vibrations of the one Being, expansions of the one Consciousness.

This state is the goal of Kashmir Shaivism. The great Shaivites always have this goal in mind. The yoga of Shaivism joins right understanding to right action, and joins philosophy to yoga *sadhana.* A powerful practical technology of self-transformation is harnessed to achieve the goal.

Shaivism describes the creation and order of the universe, the process of *involution*, whereby original divine pure Consciousness materialises, vibrating at grosser and grosser frequencies. Once conscious beings find themselves in manifestation they ask: Who am I? What am I doing here? What is this universe? Why do I suffer?

The Shaivite yogi reverses the process of creation within himself, he *evolves.* He reclaims the source of joy and destroys the illusion of duality. This feeling of duality, 'I am a separate individual at war with the world', he regards as the source of all suffering.

KASHMIR SHAIVISM AND THE MODERN WORLD

In the years I have been teaching Kashmir Shaivism and meditation, I have seen a significant awakening of interest in holistic knowledge. This constitutes a shift from exclusive concern with conventional education to a new emphasis on, or discovery of Second Education. Our view of life, reflected in medicine, psychology, religion and the arts, has become more spiritual. Though the roots of such a change are ultimately found in divine will, culturally it might be traceable to the counterculture of the sixties. For the first time, the materialistic and mechanistic thinking that underlay the older culture was opposed on the mass level.

Today there is a growing interest in meditation and spiritual development and it is no longer a counterculture. Many people have contact with Eastern practice and philosophy, the concepts of reincarnation, liberation and yoga. People are simply more open to meditation and more interested in looking within themselves. This opening is no longer accompanied by a spirit of revolution or extravagant lifestyle as in the sixties, and so it is perhaps less visible.

Among Eastern philosophies, Kashmir Shaivism is uniquely suited to the Western mind. It validates the material universe. It adds insight and a wider context, expanding but not contradicting the scientific view. Modern physics has penetrated behind appearances and found a common substratum: cheese and aluminium are both made of the same subatomic particles. Today, physics tells us that the substratum of the universe is vibrating energy. Kashmir Shaivism agrees with this strikingly monistic view—and asks further questions: what is the mind? Who is the observer of this energy? Are we forever trapped in a basic duality: mind and matter, the viewer and the viewed? Kashmir Shaivism provides an illuminating answer: mind and matter are one. The energy that underlies the universe is conscious energy, Consciousness Itself.

No matter how fastidious a scientist may be, his quest for complete objectivity is undercut by his very presence. The *subject* is always part of the picture. Heisenberg's famous Uncertainty Principle says that the mere act of observing something changes the nature of the object observed. Shaivism contends that this universe is us, experiencing ourselves in different ways. Or more precisely, it is me, myself (Shiva) as matter, as dream, as the waking state, as separate from others, as love, as knowledge, as many, as one. Behind all these modalities and experiences of life lies one Consciousness. The scientist hard at work at being objective is actually enjoying his own splendour. The world and our organs of perception fit together so neatly, not because of natural selection, but because they are one and the same thing.

If everything is made of the same Consciousness then every part recapitulates the whole. As above, so below; whatever is true of God is also true of us. If we want to understand God or the universe then we would do well to understand ourselves. A human being is a hologram of the universe. The ocean is contained in the drop. This mystery transcending time and space is the essence of Consciousness.

THE HUMANISM OF KASHMIR SHAIVISM

Humanism suffuses Shaivism in a way that is different from some of the other philosophies of India. Vedanta is a discipline for the few. Only the Brahmin male youth of exceptional intelligence and purity can practise it. Shaivism, however, historically has had no restrictions of caste, creed or gender. 'Even women and untouchables', says the scripture, 'can practise the Shaivite Yoga'. This language may be offensive to the contemporary ear, but it was not meant to be. Women have absolute equality in Shaivism. The path is open to all, the only variable being the earnestness of the seeker.

Also in the spirit of humanism, is the emphasis on yoga in the world as opposed to a monastic approach. Gurdjieff spoke of a method of *sadhana* he called 'the fourth way', the way of the sly man. Gurdjieff's sly man did not have to go to a monastery or ashram to perform special practices and isolate himself. He found the natural flow of ordinary life to be filled with transforming possibilities. Yoga can—and should be—practised amidst the ordinary circumstances of family life. It is a simple and spontaneous refining of the spirit, attuning the mind and heart to the divine presence, even in everyday life. The Shaivite approach is not to forsake the world in search of the spirit but to bring the world into the spirit, to discover, in fact, that the world *is* spirit.

In the inner world of every person there are two phenomena: thought and feeling. These two are inextricably related—positive thoughts invariably accompany positive feeling and negative thoughts go with negative feeling. Spiritual paths that emphasise a set of ideas tend to make practitioners strong and stable, but they often lose touch with their humanity. In ordinary life, a person is concerned with the feeling experience but may lack the strength given by a powerful set of spiritual ideas; hence he goes up and down with the flow of events. True spirituality, Shaivite spirituality, is therefore a blending of strong thought with positive, strong feeling.

ARGUING WITH VEDANTA

Kashmir Shaivism is tolerant of differences of personality and style. It tempers the strength of noble spiritual ideas by equally valuing the warmth of the heart. In both Vedanta and Patanjali Yoga, the individual is largely ignored. Vedanta, with its emphasis on the unreality of the world of the senses, and its uncompromising intellectual austerity, reads like a foreign language and has never found a large audience here. Similarly, Patanjali Yoga, with its physical, emotional and mental austerity, with its tendency to reject life in quest of hoped-for inner states of being, presents some difficulties for us.

All personalities are placed into the same grinding machine, to be transformed into a superconscious, impersonal sage. Shaivism, with its compassionate view of human personality, is closer to the modern spirit. This is not simply 'something for everyone', but a respect for human differences, even a relishing of them as a manifestation of the variety-within-unity that adds savour to life. Such an approach fosters and demands self-acceptance.

Shaivism, unlike Vedanta, says that this world is not an illusion. Rather, everything we see is God. Vedanta is world-denying in its tone. Vedanta claims that the world we see does not exist. It says it is an illusion and tells us to renounce, give up and reject. Its approach is *neti-neti*, 'not this, not this'. Shaivism, on the other hand, is life-positive. Perhaps a philosophy that says everything is God could be used to justify sloth and indulgence. A tendency might be to say, 'This mud is God, so I will wallow in the mud for a long time'. Maybe someone has used Shaivism this way.

As philosophies, both Shaivism and Vedanta have significant strengths but each has a potential weakness. The weakness of Vedanta is a certain coldness, arrogance and denial of life. It is strong in discrimination and renunciation. Shaivism's weakness is the possible justification of self-indulgence and sensual attachment I have just mentioned. Its strength is in its power of love and acceptance: Shaivism divinises life; it affirms the world as the arena of God.

As students of Shaivism we should be aware that some of its rather puzzling ideas came about because of the historical context—the philosophical situation of the time: what the Buddhists were saying, what the Vedantins were saying and what other dualistic philosophies were saying. One section of every learned text was expected to deal with and refute rival positions. So be aware that a certain line of reasoning may be dealing with a contemporary rival. When you understand that, many things begin to make sense.

Strictly speaking, Shaivism is beyond good and bad. But since good and bad also come from God one would have to acknowledge them. A great being sees it all as part of the play of Consciousness. For a Shaivite, good is that which moves him towards oneness and bad is that which moves him towards separation or delusion. That which moves towards depletion of Shakti is bad. But then from an even higher perspective, the play of depletion is also part of the dance.

A Zen master wittily said, 'There is no good or evil, but good is good and evil is evil'. In the same way a Shaivite has the capacity to hold apparently opposite truths in his understanding at the same time. Truths that refer to different levels of reality sometimes appear to be contradictory.

When a master attains the highest state, even the distinction between apparently opposed philosophies, like Vedanta and Shaivism, disappears. My teacher occasionally said that Vedanta and Shaivism were essentially the same. He lived in a place beyond intellectual differences. As did the great *advaitin* Ramana Maharshi whose teachings were often indistinguishable from Shaivism:

> Thus God is not only in the heart of all, He is the prop of all, He is the source of all, their abiding place and their end. All proceed from Him, have their stay in Him, and finally resolve into Him. It does not mean that a small particle of God separates from Him and forms the universe. His Shakti is acting; as a result the cosmos has become manifest.

The eighth sutra of the *Pratyabhijnahridayam* tells us that all the different philosophies are all different roles or attitudes of the Self.

Abhinavagupta says:

> There is only one tradition and all is based upon it, starting from the popular doctrines, to those of the Vaishnava and Buddhists up to those of the Shaivas. The ultimate goal of this (tradition) is the abode known as Trika. . .

Thus, in the spirit of *sanatana dharma,* universal spirituality, Abhinavagupta saw all other paths not so much as rivals, but as less realised forms of Trika. As a seeker matured in his quest, he would ultimately come to Trika.

Still, the ancient Shaivite masters spent a lot of energy disputing the Vedantins. One of the main issues was that the Vedantic picture of the Absolute had only *jnana* (knowledge) but not *kriya* (activity). That is, Brahman shone like a light but did not have the capacity to act. The Shaivite Absolute, on the contrary, had both *jnana* and *kriya*. It was not only light, but also mind and activity. In the Vedantic universe, the world is a false appearance on the Absolute, while in the Shaivite universe, the world is real and is nothing but the embodiment of the Absolute.

Abhinavagupta says:

> But if you say 'indeterminate knowledge is true knowledge, while determinate one is false', I would question 'Why this distinction (why one is right and the other is wrong), because both of them are equally shining?'

That is to say that both Brahman—the formless, thought-free Absolute ('indeterminate knowledge')—and the manifest universe of thought and form ('determinate knowledge') shine equally within Consciousness. Where else can they shine?

Swami Muktananda writes:

> According to Vedanta, Brahman is the cause of the universe; He is ever pure, awake and free. He is bliss but the world is false, the result of ignorance. Only Brahman is real, and one becomes Brahman when false knowledge is replaced by true. On the other hand, the philosophy of Self-recognition teaches that the world is not false. Emanating from supreme Shiva, it runs by His will. By His will also He withdraws it one day.

The Shaivite master would say that each of the classical yogas by themselves, *bhakti* yoga—the path of devotion, *jnana* yoga—the path of wisdom, and *raja* yoga—the path of mental and physical control, is incomplete. Shaiva yoga is a combination of all of these yogas. It includes will, knowledge and action in a comprehensive whole.

YOGI AND BHAKTA: TOTAPURI AND SRI RAMAKRISHNA

These issues and polarities are neatly embodied in a vignette from the life of the 19th-century Bengali saint, Sri Ramakrishna. Ramakrishna was a highly accomplished mystic of the path of devotion. He was in constant mystical union with the divine Mother, Kali.

He received a visit from a powerful yogi named Totapuri, who was a spiritual strong man having been raised from birth in an environment of austerity, renunciation and wisdom. He saw immediately that Sri Ramakrishna was a spiritual genius, but was stuck in devotional duality. He wanted Ramakrishna to go beyond worship of the form to merge in *nirvikalpa samadhi*, unitive awareness. After inner consultation with Mother Kali, the childlike Ramakrishna agreed. Totapuri told him to slice Kali in half with the sword of discrimination in meditation. He did and he merged in Consciousness where he remained for days.

On his side, Totapuri also received a teaching. Plagued by dysentery, he decided to discard the 'bag of dust' (his body) and merge in Brahman by drowning himself. At the crucial moment, his inner being erupted: he had a vision of the Goddess. Shakti was everywhere and in all things. What had previously been the realm of maya and dry objects was now infused with divinity. His understanding of the world changed utterly and he could not kill himself.

Human personality is given space to grow in Shaivism. The mind and emotions are not forcibly repressed, the senses are not starved. Shaivism never advocates self-torture. Instead, the personality is polished. Negative aspects of the ego-mechanism are transformed: anger, desire and fear hinder the free flow of the divine personality. But, in Shaivite surrender, the human being becomes a joyful expression of his own essential nature. A leaf remains a leaf, a cow remains a cow, and a person remains a person. But self-will, ego, unproductive and painful parts of the personality are eliminated. The Shaivite sees God in full measure in every object, animal and person. He worships and respects everything as a form of Shiva.

Chapter 4

Self-Realisation

> Nourishing Himself with whatever He finds, wearing anything at all, full of peace, living anywhere, He is liberated. He, the Self of all beings.
>
> Abhinavagupta, *Paramarthasara*, Verse 69

I was raised in a family and culture that placed enormous importance on education. Of course, I mean First Education. In that world you moved higher and higher on the scale of worth as you acquired degrees—B.A., M.A., Ph.D. You could make a lateral move towards a professional degree—medicine or law—but always self-worth and status came, not from money, but from education. There were loopholes for artists and other 'noble primitives', but the sure path was by means of steady progress through the educational system.

About the same time I realised that my own academic progress was bringing me disappointingly little personal satisfaction, I became aware of the other educational hierarchy. In this second system you do not progress via degrees granted by universities, but by inner landmarks known only to yourself, in which you grow in wisdom and joy. The Ph.D. in this inner education is called by different names in different schools of inner (Second) education—Self-realisation, enlightenment, Buddhahood, *satori*, *samadhi*, God-realisation and so on. But every school agrees that the goal is some form of higher awareness.

One of the major turning points in my life was a meeting with the American spiritual teacher Ram Dass at a dinner party in Chicago in early 1970. That night I first heard about yoga in a meaningful way. What I took away from my discussion with him was this: there are enlightened beings on the planet, now. This struck me as a shattering, life-transforming idea— to feel certain that such beings were here now, not five thousand years ago. Beings like Jesus and Buddha were on earth and had attained that state. They understood the purpose of life and how to live.

I knew that I did not have that understanding. I also knew that even though I moved in academic circles, among people who were extremely well-educated, and had spent a lot of time thinking about things, I knew that not one of them had it either.

There was an indefinable conviction in the way that Ram Dass told me his story. He had gone to India and found a great Guru, Neem Karoli Baba (whom I later met). I was convinced that he was telling the truth. That evening changed the direction of my life. Suddenly there was a real answer. I was determined to find a teacher, work with him and discover the truth.

THE GOAL: SELF-REALISATION

To be a yogi, to search for Self-realisation, is not one of the widely held goals of our culture. I was voted 'most likely to succeed' by my high school class, but I wonder what my old friends say behind my back about the odd (to them) choices I have made in my life. Nonetheless there are many cultures in which goals in Second Education are acknowledged and understood. Still, in today's world, it remains an esoteric goal.

Every strong spiritual path has the ideal of enlightenment or Self-realisation at its core. An Islamic scholar writes:

> The perfected Sufi is great, exalted. He is sublime. Through love, work and harmony he has attained the highest degree of mastership. All secrets are open to him and his whole being is suffused with magical effulgence. He is the guide and the traveller in the way of infinite love, beauty, power, attainment and fulfilment. He is the guardian of the most ancient wisdom, the trailblazer to the highest secret; the beloved friend whose very being elevates us, bringing new meaning to the spirit of humanity.

The master is guide and friend. Here the words *suffused, magical effulgence, love, beauty, power and fulfilment, most ancient wisdom, trailblazer, beloved friend,* and *elevates* illustrate the Sufi's predilection for affect, the Sufi path is devotional, inspirational and romantic.

Gampoppa, a Tibetan master in Milarepa's tradition, says:

> For him who is established in the Self, it is the same whether he refrains from worldly activities or not. For him who is free from attachment to things it is the same whether he practises asceticism or not. For him who controls his mind it is the same whether he partakes of worldly pleasures or not. For him who is unshakeable in his love for his teacher, it is the same whether he lives with him or not. For him who has attained the ultimate it is the same whether he is able to exercise *siddhis,* psychic powers, or not.

When a being realises the Self he transcends the path. He is free. Gampoppa tells us that great beings come in all styles and personalities. They may be immersed in the world or not, they may be ascetic or not: the attainment is inside, a state of being.

Tukaram, the great poet-saint of 17th-century Maharashtra, was a humble grocer living in the dusty town of Dehu. He used to sing his ecstatic poems called *abhangas* in the temple every night. He echoes the paradox of Gampoppa:

> I speak and yet I am silent. I have died but I am alive. I live among people but in truth I do not. I appear to enjoy but in fact I have renounced. I am in the world, yet out of it. I have broken free of all bonds. I am not what I appear to be says Tuka. You want to know? Ask the Lord what I really am.

No appearance or concept can limit the perfected master—he transcends the mind.

Whenever a holy man or Jesus is depicted in a Hollywood movie a stereotype emerges. He is usually portrayed as ponderous and portentous and given to oracular utterances. If you met such as person in real life, you might suspect him of being a serial killer. On the contrary, real masters are vivid, spontaneous and full of life, and cannot be categorised. They are light, not heavy or pretentious. They are real human beings. It is told of the 19th-century saint Sri Ramakrishna that he once took on his devotee, the flamboyant playwright Girish Ghosh, in a competition to decide who knew more risqué words. At the end Girish bowed down and told Ramakrishna, 'You are my Guru in this also'.

My teacher used to quote the poet Bhartrihari about the natural state of enlightenment:

> *Siddhas*, realised beings, behave in countless different ways. They teach scholars and learn from fools. They fight with heroes and run away from cowards. If people give them gifts they renounce everything. If there is no one to give them gifts they go begging. Those in whose heart the master of the world has taken residence behave in contradictory ways. *Siddhas,* enlightened beings, do not have to pretend because they are saturated with divine bliss. Their senses fall slave to them; they don't fall slave to their senses.

> There is no distinction for them between self and other, between sin and virtue; between great and small. They may live like beggars but they are not, they are kings. A *Siddha* is drunk on the knowledge of the spirit. He knows, *'Aham Brahmasmi'*, I am God, I am the Absolute reality, while also knowing that everyone is God also. Knowing this he soars with intoxication.

No passage I know better describes the paradoxical nature of the Great Being. Freedom ultimately is freedom. It is not an act or pretence. It is not predictable or limitable.

Baba's Guru, Bhagawan Nityananda, was in an extraordinary state of divine detachment. He was enigmatic and completely indifferent to worldly power and splendour. When the governor visited he was as likely to roll over and present his rear end, as he was to speak to him. Nityananda was so anchored in the Self that he could not be swayed by the outer world.

Baba had his own ways, too. My former brother-in-law, Rishi, met Baba and became transfixed as he watched him meet hundreds of people. If anybody told him something he would say, *'bahut acha'*, very good. Rishi was amazed that to Baba everything was 'very good'. Rishi started saying *'bahut acha, bahut acha'* also. It uplifted him tremendously.

That was Baba's vision, the vision of perfection. In that state even the harsh realities of life are understood from a higher perspective. When we understand things only from a personal perspective, our life is filled with tragedy and misery. The more expanded our awareness becomes, the more acceptance we have. A *Siddha* sees everything as the will of God or the play of Consciousness. He is at peace with this human condition.

In my Guru's ashram in India there was one meditation room that was extremely powerful. It had no windows—it was below ground level—and we called it 'the cave'. After doing ashram work I would shower and go there for pre-dinner meditation. It was my refuge. One day as I was meditating peacefully, the lights were suddenly thrown fully on. Visitors were being shown the ashram and the guide was proudly showing off the cave—never mind that 30 of us sat there meditating. The guide, in a loud voice, told the visitors all about the room, who we were, what professions we followed in the West, and what we did in the ashram. I was livid. I complained to Baba and it stopped, but only for a week or two. Eventually I had to surrender and incorporated these disturbances into my meditation. I began to see them as extremely funny and in the end would almost be disappointed if they did not happen often enough.

The 13th-century Zen master Daikaku, who brought Buddhism from China to Japan, says:

> If you take peace and quiet to be bliss, all things are afflictions. But when you are enlightened all things are enlightenment.

If you have a strong preference for peace and quiet then you are always in a control battle with your world. The world is unpredictable and unruly. But if you regard everything that arises as a spiritual opportunity, or as God coming to you in that form, everything is enlightenment. This is the vision that sees Shiva everywhere.

GURDJIEFF'S SEVEN MEN

Gurdjieff gave one of the most lucid maps of the stages of inner evolution. In his teaching there are seven levels of spiritual development: man number one, man number two, man three, up to man seven. Man seven is a spiritual master at the level of Jesus or the Buddha. The first three are ordinary people and spiritually equal. Gurdjieff said that everyone is born man number one, two or three. Man number one is action-oriented, the *doing* type; man two is emotional, the *feeling* type; and man three is intellectual, the *thinking* type.

It is only when a person consciously begins to evolve spiritually through 'school work' does he become man four and beyond. School work refers to esoteric schools or schools of Second Education. A person may reach the summit of First Education—hold a Ph.D. or even be a Nobel Laureate—but he will remain man number one, two or three if he hasn't entered Second Education.

Kashmir Shaivism can be looked at from the perspective of both First and Second Education. Under the lens of First Education, Kashmir Shaivism is a philosophical system that gives unusually convincing perspectives on fundamental questions.

From the point of view of Second Education, Kashmir Shaivism is a way of *sadhana*, a path of enlightenment that provides yogic techniques designed to expand awareness.

A Shaivite master would not disagree with Gurdjieff when the latter says, 'The knowledge of man number seven is his own knowledge, which cannot be taken away from him; it is the *objective* and completely *practical* knowledge of all'. A master is anchored or established in the highest truth. He doesn't have glimpses only to lose it, nor does he go up and down according to his moods. His knowledge is 'objective' in the sense that it is not an emotional position. It is held in his being. It is practical: it flows into every aspect of his physical, emotional and worldly life.

It is interesting to notice that Shaivism also defines seven different 'experients', seven knowers at different levels of evolution. The level of man one to three, which is the level of ordinary life in Gurdjieff's system, I would call the level of religion. Here there is no commonly held understanding and consequently, strife and misunderstanding among different groups, which are actually more alike than they think.

At the level of man four, spirituality or true Second Education begins. Now a seeker does *sadhana*. His religion becomes practical and transforming. The influence of man seven is more keenly felt. The seeker studies the spiritual ideas and G-Statements (noble understandings) that come from man seven, submits himself to the discipline given by man seven, practises the contemplative techniques of man seven, and perhaps repeats the mantra received from man seven.

The more directly the influence of man seven (who is the agent of the Absolute, and indeed, is not different from the Absolute) is felt, the more powerful are the transformational possibilities. That is why a living Guru, and also the proximity to such a Guru, are both highly desirable. At the level of ordinary life (man one to three), the ideas of man seven show up in church homilies, scriptural stories and ethical codes. The key turning point happens at the level of man four, when one embraces the teachings of man seven as a practical path or *Way*.

Gurdjieff says that man four has begun to balance his centres so there is a blend of feeling, thought and activity, or in Shaivite terms, *iccha, jnana* and *kriya*. Also, he has a 'permanent centre of gravity', which means that he is consistent in his spirituality; not spiritual on his good days and afflicted by spiritual amnesia on his bad days. In our terms, Shaivite man four would deeply value his *sadhana* and be constantly contemplating and rotating the Shaivite G-Statements in his mind, trying to uplift himself.

Gurdjieff says that man five has reached unity and man six has reached full development, though under certain circumstances, he could still suffer a fall. That is not possible for man seven, who is established permanently in the Self and in objective wisdom. From a Shaivite perspective, man seven has attained a state of complete inner freedom and connectedness with universal Consciousness.

At the higher levels there is common discourse and mutual understanding. For example, the Buddha would understand the Christ more truly than a Christian at the level of man one, two or three. As evolution continues, understanding increases and discord diminishes. It is clear to everyone that the current level of spiritual evolution on earth leaves much to be desired. We should not, however, be blind to the increasing influences from higher Consciousness that are filtering into the general culture, such as yoga and meditation, and even alternative therapies.

THERE IS NOTHING THAT IS NOT SHIVA

I grew up in Brooklyn surrounded by communities of Hasidic Jews. I do not know if any of them were spiritual masters, but a few hundred years ago there was a great master in that tradition named the Bal Shem Tov. He was truly a God-intoxicated being.

A scholar says:

> The mystical ecstasy of Hasidism flows from the rediscovery that God is present in all of human life. All things and moments are vessels that contain divinity. 'There is no place devoid of Him' was the ecstatic cry of early Hasidism. There is neither place nor moment that cannot become an opening in which one may encounter Him.

This is pure Shaivism, too. The *Svacchanda Tantra* says, *Na shivam vidyate kvachit:* Nothing that is not Shiva exists anywhere. There is no thought, no feeling, and no event that is not Shiva. When our minds, through practice, through meditation, through contemplation, become subtle then we experience that Shiva, Consciousness, is everywhere. The ground of our vision has changed.

Spiritual practice unfolds our understanding. We see the pattern of meaning in our life. We see that events teach us and make us grow. Things happen for a reason. As we grow we begin to see divinity at the core of everything. We catch a glimpse of the wonder of existence. We have the intuition, *Na shivam vidyate kvachit*: Nothing that is not Shiva exists anywhere.

The *Shiva Sutras* say that when a seeker attains the *turiya* state, the state of enlightenment, his senses become powers intent on abolishing all sense of difference and are no longer mere senses. A change takes place in the way we view things. Instead of our previous predilection for separation and negativity, in that state everything is directed to Consciousness.

Yogis think of the mind as the sixth sense, so when the sutra says, 'senses', we can include the mind. Imagine how it would be if instead of seeing differences or threat, you saw oneness and love everywhere. Imagine if you always had the uplifting vision of harmony and peace. Whatever arose in your life, your mind would have the tendency to return to peace. Now sometimes when good things happen, our minds make them into negatives.

Another significant sutra (III.13) says:

> Siddhah svatantrabhavah
> A *Siddha* is supremely free.

Siddha means a perfect yogi, *svatantrya* means freedom and *bhava* means attitude, or the state. Taken together it means that a *Siddha* has the attitude of perfect freedom. It can also be translated as 'the state of freedom is achieved'. A *Siddha* is a realised soul, one who has attained the ultimate, and is supremely free. He is man number seven.

My teacher writes:

> A *Siddha* lives in total freedom. The state of a *Siddha* is the state of freedom. Freedom is his very nature. He knows everything and can do anything.

A two-year-old wants to do what he wants and hates it when he does not get his way. We have to distinguish the state of a two-year-old from that of a *Siddha*. Self-realisation is not a state of ultimate self-indulgence.

We have strategies for getting what we want. If you are rich enough you can buy whatever things you want. Failing normal methods of fulfilling desire, some people use intimidation and terrorism. By the judicious use of anger they strike fear in people and get them to do what they want. Another time-honoured method is pouting and sulking. Withdrawal and manipulation are also good strategies. You can work inwardly and outwardly. These are all methods. However, the *Siddhas* have taken a different point of view. They recognise that your outer life will never be exactly the way you want. They suggest that surrender is the way. Zen adherents would say they conform to *what is*. They teach us to mould ourselves to what is, and surrender.

In what way then, do we say that a *Siddha* is supremely free? Isn't a *Siddha* the biggest puppet of all, since he is totally surrendered to the Divine? Such surrender is true liberation. The *Siddha* has merged in God's will. He is free to act spontaneously, not scheming to achieve some end or concerned with consequences. He acts out of inspiration in immediate and direct response to situations.

Once, I visited the ashram of a great sage who had died. I meditated near his shrine. He spoke to me in my meditation with force and clarity, saying, 'Teach independence!' Indeed, independence and freedom are the essential ingredients of enlightenment. The Shaivite sages emphasised the quality of *svatantrya*.

The divine will is at the core of our being. Our personal will, when it is out of harmony with the Divine, is misguided and a superimposition. If we peel away our ignorance and reveal what is underneath, we reach a place of peace within. When instead we exert our personal will and fight against outer circumstances there is a tension. Letting that tension go, we attain peace. Of course, that is not easy or automatic. It requires yoga, disciplined inner practice.

CONTEMPLATING BONDAGE

The realised sage lives from the point of view of unity awareness. He knows that supreme Consciousness, the One Self, pervades everywhere, within and without. In every moment there are two roads, two doors in our minds. One leads to heaven: it is inscribed, 'I am Shiva!' The other leads to suffering and is inscribed with our tearing thoughts, thoughts that diminish and constrain us. It says, 'I am small, I am weak, I am bad, I am a loser, I am unlovable', or 'I want this, I want that'.

These statements of limitation are not superficial mental ideas, they are held deep within. But Shaivism tells us that they do not reflect our deepest truth. When we know our true Self we discover that these tearing thoughts, these shrinking negative thoughts, are untrue. Though they are ingrained in us, the good news is that there is a still deeper truth.

With our ordinary mind we meditate on and ponder bondage. We contemplate lack. We feel we are being cheated. We believe that people are cruel and unfeeling to us. We feel overlooked. We pursue this negative vision from every angle. In this way we make a case for bondage and strengthen it. Each of us has our own characteristic methods of contemplating and increasing our own disempowerment.

What a strange perversity! We act consistently against our own best interests. We have bad habits only because we have not been properly trained. We have been trained by people who themselves contemplate bondage, so we have learned to contemplate bondage also.

As Philip Larkin says in his poem, 'This Be the Verse':

> They fuck you up, your mum and dad.
> They may not mean to, but they do.
> They fill you with the faults they had
> And add some extra, just for you.
>
> But they were fucked up in their turn
> By fools in old-style hats and coats,
> Who half the time were soppy-stern
> And half the time at one another's throats.
>
> Man hands on misery to man.
> It deepens like a coastal shelf.
> Get out early as you can
> And don't have kids yourself.

Forgive me for Larkin's language and his dark humour. Things are not as bad as his witty poem would have it. We simply need to meet someone who contemplates enlightenment and can teach us how to do it ourselves. Such a one is the realised sage, the Guru.

Shaivism gives other answers to the question of bondage. The Shaivite understanding is that here and now—as we are—*we are Shiva*. With that understanding we can relax and live our lives. To understand Shiva we have to understand ourselves. Whatever we find in ourselves is also contained in God or universal Consciousness in a perfect way. By becoming us, God has become less (at least apparently). Since He is God He must have done it out of His own free will.

God created the world. He said, 'I will create Atlantis'. And there was Atlantis. Then He thought, 'I will create Lemuria'. And there was Lemuria. Whatever He thought was created.

Then He got the idea, 'I will create bondage. I will forget who I am'. What a great idea! (I can hear you thinking, 'Baaad idea!') He must have felt like Einstein. He was enjoying His game of hide-and-seek with Himself. He forgot who *He* was, and here *we* are: Shiva with amnesia. Nonetheless, the state of total freedom always, in every moment and under all conditions, exists as a possibility. In that state there is total mastery and union with God.

To ask why Shiva would create the universe and undergo contraction and suffering is a serious question. There are many possible answers. The one just given ('Shiva made a terrible mistake') is not very popular with the Shaivite masters. You could say that given infinite time and space, infinite Consciousness would explore every possibility. In an infinity everything happens . . . infinitely.

When the Shaivite masters were in lyrical moods, they said things like, 'Shiva, out of abundance of joy, overflowed and poured forth his love in creation'.

Maheshwarananda says:

> When Shiva turns towards the world still in seed form to desire it, to know it and to manifest it, He feels a great bliss enjoying His own heart which is sweetened by the spontaneous gushing forth of His inner joy.

The 20th-century sage Acharya Amritavagbhava says that the whole cycle of creation, ignorance and ultimate rediscovery of the truth is the *vilasa* or play of the Lord. He says that the highest joy for the Lord is to rediscover Himself after having been bound in impurity, in the same way that we feel keen relief after the dentist stops his drilling. It certainly is true that we have memorable spiritual experiences per contrast when the grace touches us when we are most contracted.

There are many theories about the creation, but as Shaivites our method is to look into the human experience to discover an analogy. There is one. Shakespeare said it, 'Enjoyed no sooner but despised straight': the orgasm. Shiva is filled with the invincible desire to pour Himself forth into His creation. Nothing can stop Him. Afterwards, though, He might usefully ask,

'Was that really such a good idea?' And if He doesn't ask it, we might ask it of Him! Just as in the creation of an individual, so in the creation of the universe, abundance, climax and depletion is the rhythm. But Shaivism says that depletion is temporary and illusory. Shiva is always present.

THE SACRED TRIANGLE

The Tantras say that there are three sources of wisdom that need to come together for Self-realisation to take place. They are scripture, guide and Self. Just as you need two coordinates to locate something precisely on a map, so you need the conjunction of all three to locate you in the Truth. One or two of them is not enough. Using all three coordinates ensures there is balance.

A seeker has to be grounded in scriptural understanding that is traditional and objective. He does not have to have a scholar's knowledge of scripture, but he must have a basic understanding. Scripture by itself is not sufficient for liberation because unaided interpretation by the seeker is likely to be faulty, distorted by ego or lack of mental clarity. Baba's version of this teaching was, 'God, Guru and Self are one'. In this case, 'scripture' is 'God' (God's word).

Along with scripture, he needs a guide, a true Guru. Such a one must be established in the state of Self-realisation and be able to clarify and illumine the scripture. He will make it a living document and show aspects and nuances that the seeker, left to himself, would never find. He must also have the power of *shaktipat*, the ability to awaken the Inner Power. In truth, the Guru is a living scripture and embodies the unwritten text that lies between the sentences of the written scriptures. While the Guru is undoubtedly the rarest, and, for that reason, the most important of this triad, reliance on the Guru alone is not enough. There will always come a time for any seeker to study scripture and practise Self-inquiry.

Even having a true Guru and knowledge of the scriptures is not sufficient. The seeker must assimilate the teaching and make it his own. His spiritual intuition must become alive. The same voice that speaks in the pages of the scripture and from the mouth of the Guru, he must also find in his own heart. Thus, a strong sense of Self is necessary. But a strong sense of Self without the Guru and scripture, becomes simply ego. Thus, all the three angles of this triad must work together. Together they create an objective and powerful framework that ensures that realisation is not partial or specious.

A SIDDHA'S VISION

In this life I have had two fathers. My physical father used to argue that the world is a vale of tears. He would become joyful when he talked about how the world was full of sorrow. I would quote Shaivism to him: 'Pop, Pop, this world is a play of Consciousness'.

'No, no, no!' he would say. 'Look at all the suffering, the poor children, suffering humanity.' That was his sport. He was a man of warm humanity and he taught me to cherish the follies and foibles of human beings.

My spiritual father taught me another way of seeing. He was a man of divinity, though he never lost touch with his personal heart. Speaking of the state of a *Siddha*, Baba says:

> He has rid himself of notions of acceptance and rejection, and he has burnt away the imaginary distinctions of virtue and sin, enjoyment and liberation, worldliness and spirituality, in the fire of inner knowledge. He goes beyond all conceptual differences. He regards all the thoughts that arise within him whether good or bad as the stirrings of the Self.

A *Siddha* lives in an expanded state. He is not on one side of any pair of opposites. He sees all of life as a play of Consciousness. To regard all of our thoughts as the play of *Chiti*, Consciousness, is a fine way to meditate. Normally we pay attention to good thoughts and bad thoughts. Bad thoughts shrink us and good thoughts expand us. However, in this technique we regard good and bad as equal, even meaningless. It is simply a play. Now good thoughts arise, now bad thoughts, now good, now bad. And, we just watch them all. We let the mind unfold its dance. We sit as the witness.

My Guru was a supreme example of this awareness. He was intensely active doing his work and yet he was always *arrived*. He was not in transit going somewhere. There was growth and expansion but he was also completely where he was and fulfilled at every stage. We live according to goals and expectations. We think, 'If only we could get to this point or that point everything would be okay'.

It is not bad to have a goal and accomplish it. But to be content and fulfilled at every step, not living for the future, is freedom. Being present in this moment is the secret that Baba embodied. He was completely present. He brought his full beingness and energy to every moment, not in a state of enthusiasm or passion, but as radiant awareness. You could feel it. It was as though his every action was a kind of play. Nothing mattered too much in itself. He was simply there, with us, a stillness amidst the whirlpool of activity. Many a time I would arrive for the evening programme frazzled with the stress of the day. Then, sitting in Baba's presence, it would fall away. I would remember, 'Oh yes, that's it again. Everything is okay'. That is the state of a *Siddha*.

In Baba's words a *Siddha* is 'his own path and his own destination'. He is aware, 'I am supreme Shiva'. It is not that he flouts human law and human morality—to be *against* something or passionately *for* something is surely to be ensnared by it as well. A *Siddha* responds to a higher law and a higher morality. In direct contact with the Divine, he is responsible to Shiva alone. Indeed, he has become one with Shiva.

MEDITATION: THE POWER OF CONSCIOUSNESS

Pratyabhijnahridayam Sutra 15 says:

> *Balalabhe vishvam atmasat karoti*
> By acquiring the inherent power of *Chiti*, the aspirant assimilates the universe to himself.

The power of *Chiti* is endless expansion, endless abundance. That place exists within us. If we can touch it, 'We assimilate the universe to ourselves'. We live in union and ecstasy.

Meditate on the abundance of the power of Chiti, *Consciousness within. Look for a place within where there is life-force, a vibration, an upliftment, an expansion. It may be hidden and faint within you, but search for it and locate that current, however slight, and be with it. See if you can coax it to become larger and stronger. Meditate for 10 minutes.*

Chapter 5

You Are Your Awareness

> Having apprehended the transcendent Lord, Supreme Truth, free from origin and destruction, all duty completed, He dwells here below according to His wish because He has had the revelation of the state of the perceiving Subject.
>
> Abhinavagupta, *Paramarthasara*, Verse 81

L ike most philosophies in India, Kashmir Shaivism is both a philosophy and a yoga. It is a philosophy of salvation—not just an intellectual system but also a method designed to attain liberation or Self-realisation. And so, it discusses *sadhana*: meditation techniques and understandings that are useful today.

I have said that Kashmir Shaivism can be summed up in one sentence: 'Everything is *Chiti*, everything is Consciousness'. The first Shiva sutra, *Chaitanyamatma*, which I have already translated as 'The Self is Consciousness' can also be translated as 'The nature of reality is Consciousness', or, 'Everything is Consciousness'. Let us consider that for a moment. It may not be immediately obvious that everything is Consciousness. Our culture is not predicated on that notion but on its opposite.

The normal Western position is that everything is matter. A scientist might say that at some stage of evolution, through natural selection and a random combination of amino acids, Consciousness occurred. This understanding seems reasonable in the West, though under scrutiny, I think it is wildly implausible.

Where does Consciousness come from? How does it come about? Is it a mutation? Once there were just a couple of rocks sitting around and then things started to boil for a while and suddenly there was Consciousness . . . and then here we are?

Shaivism says that Consciousness underlies all creation. It was there in the beginning, it is there in the middle and it will be there in the end. It is the fundamental stuff of the universe.

Now think about your own experience. Shaivism encourages us to move contemplatively from the divine experience to the individual experience and back. It says that if you want to understand God, then know yourself. If you want to understand yourself, then understand God. But always look to your own experience first.

So consider your own Consciousness for a moment. See how luminous it is. It can entertain any thought. It reflects sensory information. It governs your life. Consciousness is not ordinary, like a jar or a clock. It is hard for me to accept that it is the product of random mutation. Examine your experience of life. Is there anything apart from Consciousness that you know?

In the *Brihadaranyaka Upanishad*, there is a dialogue between King Janaka and his Guru, Yagnavalkya:

> Janaka: Yagnavalkya, what serves as the light for man?
>
> Yagnavalkya: The light of the sun, Your Majesty; for by the light of the sun man sits, goes out, does his work, and returns home.
>
> Janaka: True indeed, Yagnavalkya. But when the sun has set, what serves then as his light?
>
> Yagnavalkya: The moon is then his light.
>
> Janaka: When the sun has set, O Yagnavalkya, and the moon has set, what serves then as his light?
>
> Yagnavalkya: The fire is then his light.

Their dialogue regresses through a series of lights, resolving itself in the ultimate and irreducible light, the light of the Self. That Self is the conscious heart of the universe.

> Yagnavalkya: Pure like crystal water is that Self, the only seer, the One without a second. He is the kingdom of Brahman, man's highest goal, his supreme treasure, his greatest bliss. Creatures who live within

the bonds of ignorance experience but a small portion of His infinite being.

Consciousness is unique because every atom, every molecule—if you can talk about Consciousness that way—replicates the whole. It is a hologram of everything. 'As above, so below'. Shaivism says, 'As here, so elsewhere. As elsewhere, so here'. Everything is contained in the most minute part. Abhinavagupta neatly expresses this idea by saying, 'Everything is the epitome of everything else'. Everything is awareness. Everything is included. Equally, the whole universe is contained in you. You may think, 'I am a small creature', 'I am a separate atom', but in fact the whole is contained in your awareness. I can understand the whole by understanding, in a profound way, the smallest part.

Shaivism, the Trika, focuses on three main universal issues. First, it inquires into the nature of Consciousness, the nature and oneness of reality and of God. Next it talks about contraction, the material world, that which separates us from Consciousness, and finally it sets forth the means of *sadhana*, the method that liberates us from suffering and returns us to oneness.

If there were only God, and no tension, then we would be sporting in constant bliss. Alas, life is full of tension and struggle. We may feel that we lack something that would improve our situation, or maybe we feel we have lost something that was necessary. Both conditions create conflict and contraction. As soon as Consciousness becomes contracted there is suffering. If we are Shiva, we are Shiva in prison. Shiva became intoxicated with His creation and managed to forget His true nature.

The third aspect of the Trika is *sadhana*, yogic practice. The great Shaivite yogis developed a methodology to get rid of our metaphysical bondage. *Sadhana* is the path back to our original condition, back to Shiva. It culminates in Self-realisation. Thus Shaivism has an interesting discussion of realisation and the state of a realised being.

THE CAUSE OF THE UNIVERSE IS CONSCIOUSNESS

Let us look at some of the sutras of the very useful *Pratyabhijnahridayam*, which means 'the heart of the doctrine of Self-recognition'. (See Appendix B.) *Pratyabhijnahridayam* is a later text, not one of the foundational texts of Shaivism. It is the work of Kshemaraja, a disciple of Abhinavagupta, who came late in the line of Shaivite Gurus. The tradition began in the eighth or ninth century and he appeared about the 11th century. Kshemaraja was a commentator, not one of the founding sages or great innovators.

The original Shaivite texts, such as the *Shiva Sutras* and *Spanda Karikas*, are strange and numinous. It is hard to wrap your mind around them. That is one reason why Kshemaraja's text is so helpful. His text is highly structured and logical, with a beginning, a middle and an end. It has a plot. By contrast, the *Shiva Sutras* and *Spanda Karikas* are hard to categorise. They are mysterious and wonderful, but the *Pratyabhijnahridayam* is more manageable. In Chapter 12, I will discuss the *Pratyabhijnahridayam* as a narrative. For now, let us look at its broad movements.

Pratyabhijnahridayam begins with God and the creation of the universe. The first sutra says:

> *Chitih svatantra vishva-siddhi-hetuhu*
> Supremely independent *Chiti*, universal Consciousness, is the cause of the universe.

The cause of the universe is Consciousness. Notice how different this is from the scientific view I have already mentioned. There Consciousness is a byproduct of the evolutionary process, not the fundamental cause. Here Consciousness is fundamental and matter evolves from it. My friend, Dr Gary Witus, a cognitive neuroscientist, tells me that science doesn't actually address the issue of Consciousness. He says that science is based on reductionism, and Consciousness is 'too big a question'. Science acknowledges that Consciousness is here, but avoids the question of what it is and where it came from. It is certainly true that Consciousness is a big question. I would say it is the biggest question for the obvious reason that all questions appear in Consciousness and nowhere else!

The second sutra says:

> *Svecchaya svabhittau vishvam unmilayati*
> Of Her own free will, *Chiti* unfolds the universe on Her own screen.

Consciousness creates the universe of Her own free will. No one made Her do it. She wanted to do it and She did it. *Chiti* unfolded the universe on Her own screen, which means on Herself. Western religions think of God as creating the universe over there. Shaivism says that there is no place outside of God where that can occur. There is no material other than God that He can use. He cannot say, 'I am God and I will go to a lumberyard and get some lumber. I am God and I will create a universe over there in New South Wales'. He cannot do that because there is no other 'there' besides

Himself. In the beginning there is only God. God has to create whatever He creates inside Himself. Thus the second sutra: Consciousness is free and Shiva unfolds the universe within Himself.

Notice by the way, I am saying Shiva: He; Chiti: She; and Consciousness: It. In the Absolute there is no gender distinction. It is She, He and It, both Shiva and Shakti, male and female. As we will see, the subjective side of supreme Consciousness is usually referred to as Shiva and the objective side as Shakti. In fact they are one. *Chiti* is sometimes considered the Goddess and is sometimes referred to as neutral Consciousness.

I AM THE SUBJECT OF MY UNIVERSE

Shaivism homologises cosmic processes with personal ones. Consider the world you create while dreaming. You create a universe within yourself that seems objective. You feel that you are just one character in your dream and your world is filled with other people. When you wake up you discover there had been no one but you. It all took place within you. Shaivism says that one day we will awaken from the dream of our waking existence to discover the same thing. There is no one else here but me. All this, this whole universe, is the play of my awareness. And even though I see many, there is only one of us here.

Usually, we say that there are two sorts of things in our world, matter and Consciousness. Matter is inert and passive while Consciousness is active and can understand, analyse, think and feel. Matter is 'out there', Consciousness is 'in here'. But in a dream, what seems to be matter is revealed upon awakening to be Consciousness. In the waking state, science has shown that by splitting the atom, an enormous amount of energy is revealed to be latent in matter. Likewise, when our vision becomes subtle we discover that not only is energy latent in matter, but Consciousness is as well.

The *Upanishads* say: 'Wake up O man, wake up from the dream of separation'. Let us go one step further. Everything in your life that you know, you know through your own awareness. Every person, every fact, every thought, every fantasy, every fear, every event, every outside object, is always registered in your awareness. You cannot know anything outside of your awareness. Thus there is no universe outside of your own awareness. Wherever my awareness falls, those objects it perceives exist. Whatever my awareness does not perceive does not exist for me. If I try to imagine something outside my awareness, my awareness is imagining it.

A Shaivite sage said:

> Nonexistence is contained in existence and is not other than it, given that there is no trace of anything outside of it.

The sage Kshemaraja says, 'In this world, nothing exists which is outside the range of Consciousness'. Consciousness is the supreme light by which everything else shines; it holds everything within itself.

In devotional yoga, the *bhakta's* attitude is that God is great and he is small. That is a perfectly legitimate attitude. But Shaivism's stance is much bolder, much more outlandish. It says that you are not the little *bhakta* who says, 'God is great, I am small'. You are Shiva Himself. Shaivism invites you to contemplate 'I am Shiva', here and now. (Let me add that, as we will see later, there is also space for the *bhakta's* attitude within Shaivism's large and compassionate borders.)

This room I am in exists for me because I am here. When I go to sleep at night my outer world ceases to exist. When I open my eyes the world exists again for me. When Shiva opens His eyes, the universe is created. When He closes His eyes it disappears. You will never have a universe beyond your own awareness. Thus, you are the aware subject of the universe you experience. You are Shiva.

AWARENESS IS THE HIGHEST GOOD

Awareness is much more than a luminous screen on which we record things. Everything that we want in life, whether it is success, money, love or health, is held in our awareness. The irony of the situation is that it is awareness itself that we seek. These external goals are each reducible to an inner world goal, an attribute of awareness. More fundamental than our desire for money, fame and relationship is the feeling that these things give us: the feeling of importance, of love, of security.

When a baby does not get the loving attention of its mother, it develops personality disorders. If a child were deprived of all human contact for an extended period, it would probably die. Human attention is love: an infant basks in it, a performer or an artist craves it. Human attention is the highest good. When it is brought to bear on any problem in the world, eventually it can solve it. And it is only human attention that can solve it. Human attention is what we seek from our loved ones. When we feel distraught we seek the comforting presence of a loving person.

Nisargadatta Maharaj says:

> Do not undervalue attention. It means interest and also love. To know, to do, to discover, or to create you must give your heart to it—which means attention. All the blessings flow from it.

A few years ago, when they landed an unmanned spaceship on Mars, they sent a little camera on wheels running along the surface of the planet. The images it sent back were striking. I found myself riveted by them. Here was a terrain that no human eye had ever seen. It seemed lifeless and inert. In its coldness and stark quality, I felt sure that I could see this lack of human attention.

In India, they put a statue in a shrine and thousands of pilgrims come and worship it. In Pandarpur, in the state of Maharashtra, there is an image of Lord Vitthal in a temple that has been a place of pilgrimage for over a thousand years. That same image was glimpsed by Jnaneshwar, Tukaram and Eknath. They wrote devotional poems to it hundreds of years ago.

When you see today the very same image that they looked at, you can feel the vibrations of all the love and human attention over the course of many years. That image, and many others that are similarly regarded, have come alive with Shakti. The secret lies simply in human attention.

For the same reason, famous landmarks and buildings, and places where significant events happened, have a special energy. This is why, also, famous people have an unmistakeable charisma. They are not solitary individuals, like the rocks on Mars, but are a centre of many peoples' awareness.

In 1990, a friend invited me to attend one of the games of the World Championship chess match between Garry Kasparov and Anatoly Karpov. It was held in a theatre in midtown Manhattan. I had watched grandmasters play many times before, but this one was very different. The moves were being broadcast to thousands of people around the world on the Internet. Beyond them, they would be analysed by chess players in future magazines and books. The game was being played in chess history, which meant before unnumbered observers, many of them not yet born. I felt a different kind of resonance and depth of interest, which was a direct result, I thought, of the focus of all that human attention.

When, in meditation, we turn that blessed attention on ourselves, we nourish ourselves profoundly. In human attention there is love, luminous intelligence and energy. It has more vitamins than vitamins, more protein than protein and more restorative power than the latest new remedy. Awareness itself is the most nourishing substance in creation. It is the Fountain of Youth that Ponce de Leon was searching for.

It is said that we are what we eat, but much more so, we are the thoughts and impressions that we entertain. The *Shiva Sutras* say, *Jnanam anam*: Knowledge is food. How we use and where we put our attention is decisive in defining the quality and profundity of our lives.

HEADLESS SHIVA: FIRST PERSONISM

Many years ago the English architect Douglas Harding was in India in the mountains. He looked across a vast expanse in the Himalayas. One moment he had the conventional understanding that his head was a small circle in a larger circle (that vast scene) which contained it. The next moment he had the experience that the scene he was looking at was actually inside his head. He had no head: awareness was a blazing entity that sat on his shoulders and contained everything he saw. For him on that day it was not a theory or an insight; but a direct experience. This experience changed him forever and he wrote his famous book, *On Having No Head*, which is a witty treatise whose essential point is that nothing we see, hear, feel or think is outside our awareness. Harding had performed the action of *anusandhana,* or unification of everything with the light of Consciousness. He had united the subject and the object or, perhaps more properly, had absorbed the object into the subject.

Contemplating a vast open space, as in the mountains, is a meditation technique known to the Shaivite sages. In this circumstance, thought-forms, *vikalpas,* end, and the mind opens to Consciousness. Jaideva Singh calls this *drishtibandhanabhavana,* or the 'visionary attitude in which all things are related'.

Based on Harding's insights, I wrote the following tale:

Once, Lord Shiva was between creations. He was considering manifesting a new universe and He called in His advisers to discuss the possibility. They were delighted, but they strongly objected to the fact that He was apparently absent from the last universe He had created.

'You must guarantee', they told Him, 'that You will not be so remote this time'.

'Don't worry', Shiva said. 'I recognise my mistake. This time I'll be obviously manifest. Wherever people are, I will be. And there will be an easy way to find me.'

'And what is that?'

'I will be manifest as a body without a head!'

This universe is the one He was creating. And He made good on His pledge. Look around you now. Actually follow Shiva's direction. Perhaps there are people nearby as you read this. Or perhaps you are alone. Notice that each body you see has a head—except one.

Headlessness. The headless author sees his own head 'over there' in the mirror.

The headless one is always me. This is everyone's experience. I can't say that the headless one is you, because to me you have a body and a head when I see you. But from your point of view, the headless one is you.

Other people have heads and bodies. One person, however, has only legs and a torso which culminate 'up here' in a space of blazing Consciousness. It is seen as a head in a mirror. But that is 'over there'. When experienced 'over here', it is not a head but the place of subjectivity, 'I am', the Self. This is, of course, a yogic joke. But like some jokes, it contains a profound understanding.

Harding took it as his life's work from that moment to express and share his experience. He developed a humorous technology of putting people in touch with their own subjectivity; 'I AM'. He called this the experience of the 'headless one' because when we know ourselves as subject, we are headless.

We have a head for ourselves only as object, in a mirror or a photograph. Living as object (third person) is the source of all our pain. We experience ourselves not as we are but as we think we are perceived by others. We allow ourselves to become objects 'over there', in others' eyes. The headless one is full and complete; the person as object is always vulnerable to the judgment of others.

This view of ourselves as object, Harding says, is learned behaviour. As infants we are headless. We are unselfconscious and uncontracted. To be headless means to be in the *avikalpa*, or thought-free state. As we learn to live in the mind we 'acquire a head'. The mind is a small head floating in a larger universe. Let the mind go and the universe is perceived as springing up from our shoulders. The room is in us, we are not in the room.

Learning to perceive ourselves as object is the real fall of man. It is the process of shrinking and diminution that Wordsworth laments in 'The Ode to Immortality':

> Whither is fled the visionary gleam?
> Where is it now, the glory and the dream?

By gradually absorbing a social awareness we establish ourselves in the third-person mode. We acquire a biography, a sense of personal dignity, a personality to develop, a reputation to defend. We enter the mundane drama of life. We become actors in the play, relatively indifferent to the performances of others but terribly attached to the outcomes of the one we call 'I'.

The headless one is different. He is supremely detached from those dramas. He knows himself to be the formless Consciousness that is the context of the play of life. He is not an actor in the play: he contains all the actors. He is aware that two arms, two legs and a trunk issue outward from this formless Consciousness, but he is not fooled into thinking he is a person.

Spanda Karikas I.14 says:

> Two states are spoken about, the subject (the doer) and the object (the deed). Of these two, the object decays but the subject is imperishable.

The yogi thus must remember the subject, the headless one.

Washington Irving's story, 'The Legend of Sleepy Hollow', always resonated powerfully for me. The main character is pursued by the image of a headless horseman, which is terrifying and final. He is a primal figure evoking the myth of Yama, Lord of Death. But as in the *Katha Upanishad* where the terrible Yama becomes the Guru and gives instructions on the Self to young Nachiketa, so death is always the friend of the yogi. If there were no death there would be no yoga. Yoga conquers death by conquering that which is temporary. It lops off the head of the temporary personality and the finite mind. It puts us in touch with what is eternal and ever-present behind the endless succession of personalities and events. The headless horseman is not only the threat of death but also the threat of enlightenment. It is not only the cruel enemy trying to humiliate the personality but also the benevolent Guru trying to slaughter the ego. And beyond that it is the Self—for the headless one is me—and you.

Just as I am the 'I', so each of you is the 'I' too. There is only one 'I' in your universe and the way to find it is by looking inward. There is one subject, but many objects. When we look around from the point of view of the headless one, we feel certain that each of the other people is also the subject of his own universe. You are the Shiva of your own universe; you are the subject of your own universe.

I am intuitively sure that you others have interior worlds. My inner world is the major fact of my experience and no one but me is directly privy to it. I am the only one who is there. My thoughts and feelings are my own subjective reality. Notice that since I am the only one who lives inside it, I am the only one who is directly concerned with investigating and uplifiting my inner world. That is why each of us has to take responsibility for our own spiritual growth.

MEDITATION I: HEADLESSNESS

If Douglas Harding had looked in the Shaivite text *Vijnanabhairava,* he would have found Dharana 62:

> *Linam murdhni viyat sarvam bhairavatvena bhavayet*
> *Tat sarvam bhairavakaratejastattvam samavishet*
> The yogi should contemplate the entire open space (or sky) under the form of the essence of Bhairava and as dissolved in his head. Then the entire universe will be absorbed in the light of Bhairava.

Practice headlessness this way. Look at your Consciousness. Harding says that it is a luminosity on top of your shoulders that looks out and sees and records everything. He says that you only apparently have a head, what is really there is this formless luminosity. You see your own head only in the mirror or in a photograph. From the point of view of awareness of the Self you are headless!

Look around you. Notice that the room and everything in it is recorded in your awareness. Try to see from Harding's or Shiva's perspective: everything is held in my awareness. Ultimately the only thing I see, hear, sense or feel is my own awareness. Let your head open up and accept everything you see within itself. I am Shiva, the Headless Being. There is no separation between me and my experience. It is all held in my awareness. Meditate this way for 10 minutes.

MEDITATION II: CONTEMPLATE YOUR OWN AWARENESS

With eyes closed, contemplate your own awareness. Contemplate that within your brilliant awareness there is boundless love and luminous intelligence. You hold your whole universe within your awareness, and awareness itself is the great healing power. Awareness is a deep ocean that contains all things. Meditate for 10 minutes.

Chapter 6

The Contraction of Consciousness

> By focusing on the revelation of supreme Consciousness he unveils the inner Self. Thus great Shiva unfolds His prodigious game of bondage and liberation.
>
> Abhinavagupta, *Paramarthasara*, Verse 33

Remembering the headless one is an instantaneous method of Self-remembering. Have you noticed that in the movies when the director wants to give a particularly powerful experience of the subjectivity of a character, he uses point-of-view photography. He will use a handheld camera in which the camera becomes the eyes of the character. You see just what the character sees. You don't see the character in the scene. You never see his head, though an arm may come up. This is a cinematic presentation of the headless one. You see the scene as he sees it, so you are put in the scene too. Such moments are uncommonly intense and dramatic.

Whenever in life we come from a third-person or mental perspective—no matter how subtle—we lose touch with the Self. The headless one is ever the Self, beyond all the dramas of third-personism: fear and desire, fame and calumny, pleasing and displeasing others. Shiva is always the subject. Because of that He has complete freedom.

Clearly then, the subject is of permanent significance. What of the object, which, though of perhaps less importance, is undeniably present?

The third sutra of *Pratyabhijnahridayam* says:

Tan nana anurupa grahya grahaka bhedat
The universe is manifold because of the differentiation of reciprocally adapted objects and subjects.

Once the cartoonist Leunig did a cartoon in which a round creature split in two and became a TV and a fellow sitting on a couch watching it. This was the mutually adapted subject and object of the modern world.

I am the subject and my whole world is my object. It is clear that the subject (me or you) has always been the same, but the objects we perceive continually change. From another perspective you could say that the objective side remains the same. Your objective world gets filled with different things all the time, you are in this room or that room, you see different people. But the shape of it, the form of it, is always the same. The sutra says that every one of us as a subject has his own objective reality. It comes with you. You have an objective field, a world that always goes around with you.

We have different worlds depending on what kind of subject we are. The world of my dog Bhakti is different from your world. The world to an antelope is different from Bhakti's world. It means that the object is suited to the subject. The world you perceive is exactly suited to the perceiver, to you, to your awareness. It is shocking sometimes when you think you are having the same experience as someone else and then you discover that he or she had a completely different experience.

Coming out of a movie the husband says, 'That was one of the worst movies I have ever seen'.

'Really?' says the wife. 'I loved that movie!'

It happens all the time.

Shiva may be our true nature, but on a personal level our awareness is limited. At lower levels of awareness the world looks different to each of us. But the world of a realised being is very different from that of an ordinary person. It is integrated, harmonious and drenched in Consciousness.

BECOMING THE MIND

With the fifth sutra we meet the contraction of Consciousness. The text describes how Shiva becomes us:

Chitireva chetana padadavarudha chetya sankochini chittam
Chiti Herself descending from the plane of pure Consciou_
becomes the mind by contracting in accordance with the object
perceived.

Chiti, which is pure awareness, descends from its expanded state and
becomes *chitta*, the mind. Pure Consciousness becomes the individual
through a process of contraction. Now the plot thickens.

Shaivism agrees with Douglas Harding that the answer to the
quintessential spiritual question, 'Who am I?' is 'I am my awareness'.

When a person's awareness leaves his body that person is gone. The
body is still there, but his essence is no longer there. When we feel we
know a person, it is really the awareness of that person that we know.

Our essential awareness is always pure, but the physical-mental-
emotional sheath that overlays it has acquired knots and contractions. Our
vision has to be cleansed so that it may return to pure awareness. That is
the process of spirituality. It is particularly the realm of meditation and
inquiry.

Pratyabhijnahridayam Sutra 6 continues the discussion of contraction:

Tanmayo maya pramata
The empirical self governed by maya, consists of *chitta*.

Loosely translated, this sutra says, you are your mind. As an individual,
jiva, you are the sum total of your attitudes, your emotions, your experiences
and your likes and dislikes. You are a programmed mind. This is the story
of the bound soul. Our bondage is our programming.

It is an heroic act to crawl inside your own mind and deprogramme
yourself! What a noble enterprise! How ecstatic when you actually do a
little bit of it, when you untie a knot.

The mind is not the true Self. The Self, awareness, is prior to the mind.
The mind is an object, the Self is the subject. We identify with our mind
much more closely than we identify with our body. We think our attitudes
are us. But the Self is beyond the mind. We can observe our mind from the
witness perspective and see that our thoughts are simply output that our
minds produce.

To be fully in the spirit of Kashmir Shaivism we have to start from
Shiva and keep going back to Shiva. We assume the point of view of Shiva.
Shaivism says, *Shiva Shivena sadhana:* The *sadhana* of Shiva is Shiva. We
become Shiva by being Shiva.

There is only one person here: it is Shiva, and He plays all the roles. You are that Shiva. Shaivism is impressively lacking in the concepts of guilt and sin that Western religious thought so dwells on. We have simply forgotten who we are, and we have to work to return to our essential nature. Ignorance is the deluding force, not sin.

The ninth sutra of *Pratyabhijnahridayam* provides the definitive analysis of contraction:

> *Chidvat tacchakti sankochat malavritah samsari*
> In consequence of its limitation of Shakti, Reality, which is nothing but Consciousness, becomes the *mala*-covered transmigrating individual soul.

Reality, which is pure expanded Consciousness, becomes limited in power, in energy, and becomes the ignorant individual soul. This is called poverty of Shakti, poverty of divine energy. The only difference between us and Shiva is that Shiva is empowered and we are not. We have become disempowered. Shiva had the desire to explore disempowerment and He got his wish.

If you look at your life as a movement of energy you will notice that you are sometimes energised and sometimes depleted. In some situations and relationships you are empowered and in others, speechless and disempowered. With some people you really feel good, uplifted and strong. With others you feel contracted and heavy.

We show the scars of many hurts, wrong movements or choices and understandings that have led to disempowerment. Imagine a completely empowered version of yourself, a you who knows what to do in every situation; one who is free from fear, one who is masterful.

We look back at situations and say, 'I wish I had said that'. The *empowered you* would have said it. Or maybe the empowered you is saying it in an alternate universe. Why is it that we do not speak up, or speak inappropriately, and regret it later? Contraction blocks our expression. When we are fully empowered the words come unfailingly. Even now, we get glimpses of empowerment. It is good to acknowledge them and say, 'Ah, a glimpse of my divine nature'—and let it uplift you. Do not tear into yourself because you are not your best Self all the time.

To be a perfect Shaivite is to apply Shaivism moment to moment in your life. Remember, Shaivism always looks from the microcosm to the macrocosm.

Look first at your mundane experience if you want to understand cosmic mysteries. On a cosmic level the same drama that is unfolding in the personal realm, is also eternally being played out.

Why would Shiva, in perfect bliss, choose limitation and contraction? The sleep state may give us a clue. You fall asleep all at once. You are awake one moment and in the next moment you are in a different state. It might be that from Shiva's point of view the creation of the realm of illusion is like falling asleep and dreaming this world.

BECOMING SHIVA AGAIN

Pratyabhijnahridayam Sutra 9 says that because we have lost Shakti we have become the individual soul. But Sutra 10 says:

> *Tathapi tadvat pancha krityani karoti*
> Even in this limited condition the individual performs the fivefold act as Shiva does.

Here is hope! This sutra is archetypal Shaivism. Even in our limited condition we do the same sorts of things that Shiva does. Divine in nature, we are still divine, even in limitation. Whatever we do Shiva does, whatever Shiva does we do. We are just a contracted form of Shiva. We already have everything we need, Shiva represents our perfection.

A Hasidic source says:

> God is present in all of human life. All things and moments are vessels that contain divinity. There is no place devoid of Him. . . There is neither place nor moment that cannot become an opening in which one may encounter Him.

Shaivism says that Consciousness is the core of everything. Everything— whether it is a person, a sport, an organisation, a stone—the essence of everything is divine. The core of every conversation and every relationship is divine. Every part of the universe has been formed from the one Consciousness. However, we should not lose our discrimination.

There was a great Shaivite Guru called Ramdas whose main teaching was to see God everywhere. He would say, 'See Ram everywhere. See Shiva everywhere'. He had a disciple named Kalyan Swami who was eager, but not overly intelligent.

One day he was walking down the road rehearsing his master's teaching, 'All this is *Chiti*. All this is Consciousness. All this is Ram'.

Three men ran by with terrified looks on their faces. 'Oh Kalyan Swami', one of them shouted. 'Run for your life. A wild elephant is loose and is destroying everything!'

Kalyan Swami reflected, 'If everything is *Chiti* then the elephant is *Chiti*, too. Why should I worry?' He watched the elephant bearing down and shouted, 'All this is *Chiti*. The elephant is *Chiti*. You, O elephant, are *Chiti*. You are Consciousness!' The elephant picked him up with his trunk and dashed him to the ground, breaking quite a few bones. Kalyan Swami lay moaning in a despondent heap.

Eventually word reached Ramdas and he hurried to the side of his stricken disciple. 'How are you?' asked Ramdas.

'O master, I'm not doing too well, and also I think I have to leave you. Your teachings are quite false.'

'Why, what happened?' asked Ramdas.

Kalyan Swami narrated the events. 'You see', he said, 'this is the result of following your teachings and contemplating that everything is Consciousness'.

'You are a fool', said Ramdas. 'It is completely true that everything is *Chiti*. The elephant is *Chiti*, too. But weren't those men who warned you also *Chiti*? Why didn't you listen to them?'

So meditate on the world as a play of Consciousness, but also use your intelligence.

Baba says:

> Shiva pervades everything without being different from anything. How can anything be other than Shiva? The *Parashakti Chiti* spreads everywhere in the universe. She is matter in material objects and Consciousness in conscious beings. She takes on attributes, yet is without attributes. It is She who is sporting everywhere. How can there be anything different from Her? In the universe that is only *Chiti's* play, what can be impure or unclean?

If we don't see the Shivaness of this universe we deny divinity to ourselves. We live in a world of depletion and limitation. Our ego has to fight a continuing and hopeless battle to be heard. We see threat and fault everywhere, drying up our hearts and plunging ourselves into depression. This world of ignorance is nothing but hell on earth.

Baba continues:

> That which the ignorant see as the phenomenal universe is in reality the playful outer manifestation of Consciousness. What can be done if a deluded person thinks that a rope is a snake? The snake, and the fear, the trembling, the stuttering speech, the palpitation of the heart caused by its appearance, are illusion. The rope alone is the immutable truth. The imagined snake is part of the rope.

The reference is to a well-known Vedantic analogy of a man who sees a rope and thinks it is a snake. His heart starts thumping, his blood pressure goes up and he has a fear reaction. Then he looks again, sees it's just a piece of rope and calms down. It was always a piece of rope and was never a snake. Because of wrong understanding, wrong identification, he felt afraid. Vedanta says that we react to the universe in the same negative way because we have wrong understanding.

Baba writes:

> The imagined snake is the sport of the rope. Shiva is the 'is-ness' of everything. Shiva is real. Shiva is all-pervading. He never ceases to exist. He never vanishes. He is eternal whether or not He is perceived to be so. He is everything. He is in the fallen in the same measure as in the redeemed. He is as much in the wicked as in the enlightened, as much in the sinner, as in the saint, as much in an atom as in the vastest cosmos, as much in a drop, as in an ocean. He is beyond all limitation of space, time and substance. He is everywhere. He is everlasting. He is in all. He is ever perfect. Indeed to think that nothing is without Shiva is to see Shiva.

We externalise everything. We think God creates something apart from Himself. But Shaivism says that this universe is within God's being. We are never separate from God's being.

Shaivism can be summed up in a few principles: one is that everything is Consciousness; a second is that you are literally Shiva. You are a contracted form of Him, and through inner means you can win back your Shiva status. You can do that by Self-recognition. Let me give you a practical tip. The *Vijnanabhairava* taught me that the best way to deal with a spiritual idea is not to argue with it, but to contemplate it and see if it resonates inwardly as peace. That is the criterion. If you tackle it mentally, you never get to the end of doubt. You have to see how such ideas affect you experientially. Work inwardly with these ideas.

MEDITATION I: CHAITANYAMATMA

The first Shiva sutra says it all: Chaitanyamatma. *Contemplate the following possible translations:*

- *The Self is Consciousness*
- *Consciousness is the Self*
- *Reality is Consciousness*
- *Consciousness is reality*
- *Everything is Consciousness*
- *Consciousness is everything*

Do these one by one, giving each enough time so that its nuances emerge. If one or more is powerful, do more work with it.

MEDITATION II: CHITI

Contemplate, with eyes closed, 'My body is Chiti'. *Every feeling and sensation is* Chiti. *This is a Shaivite spin on Vipassana's meditation on impermanence.*

Chapter 7

The Tattvas I: Shiva, the Divine Being

> Resplendent, perfect, enjoying great happiness because He rests in his own Self, abundantly provided with willpower, consciousness and instruments of action, full of limitless *shaktis*, free of all dualistic thought-constructs, pure, peaceful, free from appearance and disappearance, it is in Him, Paramashiva, the supreme *tattva*, that the world of 36 principles appears.
>
> Abhinavagupta, *Paramarthasara*, Verses 10-11

I n India a philosophy is called a *darshan*, because it is not merely a mental construct but a way of 'seeing' ultimate reality. The vision of Kashmir Shaivism is more than optimistic. It says you can overcome suffering by yoga, meditation and right understanding. Beyond that it says that even when we feel most in bondage, most dragged down by the suffering and insecurities of life, even then, we are still Shiva.

The Shaivite sage Utpaladeva wrote a series of exalted poems called the *Shivastotravali* from the perspective of nondual Kashmir Shaivism. In one of them he writes:

> Because, Lord, I cling intimately to Your universal body, far from the ills that afflict me, not only do my fears disappear, but my joy is in exaltation!

By clinging to the true form of Shiva, Consciousness Itself, Utpala finds that his psychological suffering has vanished, replaced by abundant joy. He sees Consciousness everywhere, permeating all of creation. Our Shiva nature is obvious once you start to search for it. Kashmir Shaivism embraces the world as the arena of God and as God Itself.

THE TATTVAS AND THE GREAT CHAIN OF BEING

Shaivism meticulously describes the process whereby the one undivided Consciousness (Shiva) opens out and becomes the universe. This process has 36 stages or *tattvas*, each one a little denser than the one before. The first *tattvas* have the highest, purest vibration. They are unobstructed Consciousness and light. Descending through the *tattvas*, the light darkens, things become more veiled, dull, ignorant and heavy. At the conclusion of the process, we have a material universe. Maya, the mysterious principle of veiling and separation, has full sway.

Here you might ask why 36 *tattvas*? Is that precisely the correct number? A little historical knowledge illumines this point. Shaivism adopted an already existing analysis made by the Samkhya tradition, which outlined 25 *tattvas*. Samkhya, which traces itself to the sage Kapila who lived at the time of the Buddha (500 B C), is neither materialist (everything is matter) nor idealist (everything is Consciousness). Instead, it is dualist: it says that the universe is made of matter *and* Consciousness. This is an intuitively defensible position, since on a practical level there is a clear dualism between the outer world of materiality and the inner world of awareness.

The Shaivite masters acknowledged the truth of this dualism, but contended that there was a higher monistic truth. To describe it they added 11 more levels at the top of the chart, *beyond* Samkhya. It is appropriate to ask where these extra *tattvas* came from. A number of answers are possible. In Western philosophy, succeeding philosophers try to think harder and deeper than their predecessors. Their new ideas come from the intellect and from logic and insight. We like to think that in yogic paths a sage receives a higher visionary experience in meditation. Lord Shiva might have entered Somananda's meditation and revealed 11 new *tattvas*. I think in the case at hand, both of these possibilites were at play combined with a third one: the positions taken by contemporary rival philosophies. All three of these possibilities, namely intellect, mystic vision and apologetics, were enlisted to take the Shaivite *darshan* into new territory.

This cosmology is close to the so-called Great Chain of Being, a medieval world picture based on Plato adopted by Christian thinkers. The Great Chain of Being portrays a hierarchal universe from God to inert matter in which every possible niche is filled by some form. Correspondences exist from each part of this universe to all other parts. Man's place in the chain is crucial and dramatic—the angels are above him, the animals below. He decides his fate by cultivating his divine or his bestial qualities.

In the Great Chain of Being, man has a central and important place in the chain of creation. In the Trika, man's place is even more central. It could be said that the *tattvas* occur *within* man. The higher states of Consciousness are actually found within in deep states of contemplation, beyond the mind. The reducing valve of maya turns pure Consciousness into egoic Consciousness. The mind, including the ego, comprises three *tattvas* for the different functions of mind, and the senses comprise five *tattvas*, one for each sense. As Consciousness moves from the inner to the outer, we come down the *tattvas*. The centre of the process is the individual human Consciousness glancing at the divine within and the material without. Man, in Kashmir Shaivism, is thus not a mere link in a great chain; the chain itself is a description of man's Consciousness. The whole event occurs *within* man himself. This is an essential difference between the subject-oriented, human-centred view of Kashmir Shaivism and the objective and linear view of Western thought.

Since Trika holds that there is only one substance in this universe, then each of the 36 *tattvas* is nothing but the one Consciousness vibrating at particular frequencies and behaving in specific ways. Trika emphasises that even at the most dense stages, all the previous, higher *tattvas* are still present, though not explicit. The divine realm of grace is never remote. Shaivism has no dualistic notion of 'fallen matter' as found in so many Christian writings. At every point and in every condition man has access to higher Consciousness, higher *tattvas*, by an *inner* movement of his attention. This is an important point—the creation of the universe is conceived of as an opening out—not a linear movement, but a movement from the centre to all points on the periphery. Shaivite meditation is thus a glance towards the centre, a 'getting in touch with' the purest vibrations of Consciousness.

In its usual Trinitarian way, Kashmir Shaivism divides these 36 *tattvas* into three main parts: the pure, the pure-impure and the impure *tattvas*. The impure *tattvas* relate to that level of experience based on duality. This is the normal experience of a human being. The pure-impure *tattvas* relate to a higher order of experience. Differentiation and multiplicity exist—a world of forms—but the underlying unity is clearly intuited. The Shaivites describe this as an experience of the universe as one's own body. It is not the experience of a separate person—but of God—God in a mood, as it were.

Finally, the pure *tattvas* refer to Consciousness in its pristine form. Here the world of objects has totally disappeared. There is no world, but only vibrating Consciousness. This level is attained by yogis who reach *nirvikalpa samadhi*. When a realised yogi operates in the world, however, he remains in a middle state in which duality is perceived but rendered harmless. This is *sahaja samadhi,* natural samadhi. The world of objects exists, but absolute peace, joy and unity hold sway. The attainment of this state is the goal of the Shaivite yoga. A person who has attained this state is called a *Siddha* or perfected master.

THE TATTVAS

By direct experience, the founding Shaivite yogis had *realised* Consciousness as the primary stuff of the universe. Kshemaraja says:

> The knowers of Trika philosophy . . . maintain that the *atman* (Self) is both immanent in the universe and transcends it.

Looking around they saw that other schools did not agree. In the Shaivites' eyes the other schools fell short of their noble and comprehensive vision. Thus in the higher 11 *tattvas* they positioned the levels of realisation offered by these schools. For example, they say that some Buddhists do not go beyond *tattva* 14. Some Vedantins and other Buddhists reach the sixth *tattva*. The followers of Samkhya, they say, go beyond the sixth *tattva* but don't reach the fifth one, while the Grammarians go as high as the third *tattva*, and so on. A student interested in these distinctions could study Sutra 8 of *Pratyabhijnahridayam*.

While you could view this system as a kind of spiritual one-upmanship, I think it is more accurate to say that the Shaivite masters were attempting to move seekers past their limitations.

In science or philosophy when a new paradigm is created, what usually happens is that the old view is thrown out and replaced by something entirely new. Here, Shaivism says, 'You got part of this right—at least right enough not to argue with. Look to my new ideas to see where I go beyond you'. We would be right to assume that Shaivism's unique point of view is fully expressed in the new 11 *tattvas*, which are *tattvas* one to 11.

PARAMASHIVA

1. Shiva *Chit Shakti*
2. Shakti *Ananda Shakti*

3. Sadashiva
Iccha Shakti

4. Ishvara
Jnana Shakti

5. Shuddha-Vidya
Kriya Shakti

6. Maya
Veil of Limitation

Kanchukas	7. Kalā	8. Vidya	9. Raga	10. Kāla	11. Niyati
Limitation of:	*Omnipotence*	*Omniscience*	*Completeness*	*Eternity*	*Omnipresence*

12. Purusha
Individual Subject

13. Prakriti
Objective Experience

Manas 16. 14. Buddhi
Mind *Intellect*

15. Ahamakara
Ego

Jnanendriyas
(Powers of Perception)
17. Shrotra (hearing)
18. Tvak (touch)
19. Chakshu (seeing)
20. Jihva (tasting)
21. Ghrana (smelling)

Karmendriyas
(Powers of Action)
22. Vak (speaking)
23. Pani (grasping)
24. Pada (locomotion)
25. Payu (excretion)
26. Upastha (procreation)

Tanmatras
(Subtle Elements)
27. Shabda (sound)
28. Sparsha (touch)
29. Rupa (form)
30. Rasa (taste)
31. Gandha (smell)

Mahabhutas
(Gross Elements)
32. Akasha (ether)
33. Vayu (air)
34. Agni (fire)
35. Ap (water)
36. Prithivi (earth)

The 36 Tattvas of Kashmir Shaivism

TATTVAS ONE TO FIVE: THE DIVINE EXPERIENCE

Tattvas one to five, above maya, represent the divine realm of perfect experience, pure Consciousness. There are different changes that happen within that realm, but unity and divinity are never lost. Shiva, *tattva* one, is transcendent Consciousness. He is the Brahman of the Veda, pure light. *Tattva* two is Shakti, Shiva's consort. Here the pure light becomes active, creative and self-reflective. Without Shakti, Shiva is incomplete and ineffectual. With Shakti, the universe teems with creativity and abundance. By seeing Shakti as the dynamism of God, Shaivism separates from Vedanta whose highest principle is inactive.

Shiva and Shakti are not really two. They are God and His power, the light and self-awareness, yin and yang, male and female. You could say that these first five *tattvas* are different roles or aspects of God. Still, there is only One. He is not lost; He has not forgotten who He is. He is not miserable. He is not neurotic. He is there in all His energy, light and power.

By enumerating five divine or pure *tattvas* instead of one, the Shaivite masters give us a fuller and more varied portrait of the Absolute. Here are the different moods of Shiva: Shiva as perfect will and feeling (*tattva* three), Shiva as pure wisdom and light (*tattva* four), Shiva as omnipotent activity (*tattva* five).

The first five *tattvas* represent divine Consciousness. Then there is the dotted line. Something bad happens. Something goes terribly wrong at the dotted line. The dotted line is maya, or contraction. Shiva, who is perfect oneness, suddenly becomes separate. At *tattvas* one and two, Shiva and Shakti are joined in a perfect, harmonious dance. But down at *tattvas* 12 and 13, we have *purusha* and *prakriti*. Each of us is a *purusha* and each of us has a *prakriti*, or a world. *Purusha* and *prakriti* are really Shiva and Shakti in disguise. When maya impacts Shiva and Shakti they become *purusha* and *prakriti*. This is revealing: Samkhya begins with *purusha* and *prakriti*. Shaivism tells us the hidden history of the pair by bringing in the new *tattvas*. In a kind of prequel to their earthly career, we learn that this somewhat distressed couple is of divine birth. How did they get the way they are now? It is the effect of maya.

LANGUAGE AND THE FIRST FIVE TATTVAS

In the highest *tattva*, were God to speak, He would say, 'I am That'. That has always struck me as a richly resonant statement. Especially the 'That', which refers mysteriously to the 'other', the objective world. Of course, 'I am That' is a coded symbol of divine speech.

The *Vedas* say:

> *Tat tvam asi*
> You are That (the Absolute).

When Shiva is Shiva He knows 'I am That'. It means that whatever He sees is part of Himself. There is only one and that is Himself. 'I am That' has both a subject and an object, but they are tied together by the copulative verb, 'to be', which operates as an equals sign: subject = object, I = That. The first five *tattvas* are called the 'pure creation' because duality has not yet entered the picture. The subject and the object are one and the same: Shiva.

I call these upper *tattvas*, 'moods of God'. At this level there is still only God, but they are different aspects of God. They are not, strictly speaking, five different things.

Tattva three, the *Sadashiva tattva,* can be described as *'I* am That'—the emphasis on 'I'. Here, God looks around at Himself with His emphasis on 'Self'. In mundane reality we say things like *I* own that car—emphasis on 'I'.

In the fourth *tattva,* the *Ishvara tattva,* the emphasis is on the object, not the subject. I painted *that.* I own that *car.* Instead of calling attention to myself as in *tattva* three, I am pointing out the car. You can see that it is a different mood.

In the fifth *tattva, Shuddha-vidya,* there is a mutual emphasis, an equal emphasis, between subject and object. The attention goes back and forth between the 'I' and the 'That'.

THE FIVE SHAKTIS OF SHIVA

God has five main powers, or *shaktis* that accompany the first five *tattvas*: they are *chit, ananda, iccha, jnana* and *kriya*—Consciousness, bliss, will, knowledge and action. The last three correspond to our emotional centre, intellectual centre and physical centre. We are feeling, thinking, doing mechanisms. Hence we have the yoga of devotion, the yoga of intellect, and the yoga of action. The three moods of God, described in *tattvas* three to five, correspond to will, knowledge and action at the divine level.

Intellectuals absorb themselves in study. They investigate the *other.* The emphasis is on *That.* An emotional person is more involved in his own process, his own emotions and feelings, his own being. His orientation can be indicated by *I am That*. He is absorbed in himself. Finally, the active or vital type of person is always doing, doing, doing. There is so much to do and he does it. He is poised between *I* and *That*.

The Shaivite equation is: Shiva equals *jiva*, *jiva* equals Shiva. To know God or universal Consciousness we imagine an expanded version of ourselves. You might call this extreme anthropomorphism: the god of caterpillars is a gigantic caterpillar, but I don't think so. Shiva is not a big person, an old man in the Michelangelo model. He is not a human being at all, but Consciousness Itself.

Just as we have the three *shaktis* of will, knowledge and action, so God also has them, though in an expanded state. What would God's perfect *iccha*, perfect *will*, be like? Will is related to desire and emotion. Perfect will implies both perfect intentionality and also perfect contentment and bliss. The lower emotions are permutations of will. Perfect will is a powerful feeling, a pure feeling. It is perfect love and peace. It is also *svatantrya*, perfect freedom.

God has perfect knowledge. He knows everything since the world only exists in his knowledge. He knows the past, the future. He understands how everything works. He sees it at every level, intuitively, fully. He has perfect mastery of language. He can express and create. He also has perfect power of *action*. Whatever He wants to do, He can do. He says, 'Let there be light' and there is light. He creates the whole universe. He has complete freedom of action. He has *mantra siddhi*, the creating word.

The three *shaktis*—will, knowledge, and action—are always related. First you want to do something, then you figure out how, then you do it. The movement is from the interior to the exterior.

TATTVA SIX: MAYA

In the sixth *tattva*, maya, we encounter contraction for the first time. The principle of limitation dramatically takes the stage, changing everything. Shiva, perfect and free, now goes through a painful diminution. Maya is a black hole from which He emerges in a new form at *tattva* 12. Maya is not something separate from Consciousness. Kashmir Shaivism is a perfectly monistic philosophy. There are not two things, there is only one thing: Consciousness. When Shiva manifests the world, He Himself is not changed by that, but creates phenomena as a kind of reflection inside Himself.

What happens at the dotted line on the *tattva* map is very strange. My goal is to talk about liberation, but for the moment we are stuck in bondage.

According to Kashmir Shaivism, Shiva's perfect will, perfect knowledge and perfect action become limited. *Pratyabhijnahridayam* Sutra 9 says:

> *Chidvat tacchakti sankochat malavritah samsari*
> In consequence of its limitation of Shakti, Reality, which is all Consciousness, becomes the *mala*-covered *samsarin*.

Consciousness (Shiva), which is perfectly powerful, loses touch with its Shakti or power and becomes us. We are perfect Shiva having lost Shakti. This is something like Superman having been given kryptonite. We all know that there is a piece missing. Shaivism insists that everything is within us, but that something is obscuring it. If we could only find that obscuring factor and get rid of it, we would experience our natural state.

The essence of our predicament is externalisation. We are bewitched by the outer world. We look at other people, we look in the mirror, we worry about our image, we worry about how other people perceive us. We judge ourselves, we compare ourselves to others and we put ourselves down. Gurdjieff called this tendency to see ourselves through others' eyes, *internal considering*. It simply disempowers us. We lose touch with the Shakti. Every moment in which we worry about our image or we seek fulfilment via some external thing, is a movement away from the Self towards our bondage. A friend of mine told me that he got free of his tendency to internally consider by reflecting that since everybody is so worried about themselves—how they look to others—nobody really cares about how he looks!

Here is Kshemaraja, an 11th-century Kashmiri sage and great yogi, writing in his peculiar style, and here we are at the turn of the millennium in our Western world with our cable TV watching 'Oprah'. There is a big gulf culturally, but still the heart speaks to the heart universally. When we parse Kshemaraja's language we find he speaks directly to our condition.

Kshemaraja writes:

> When the highest Lord, whose very essence is Consciousness, by His free will assumes duality all round, then His will and other powers, though essentially nonlimited, assume limitation.

He chooses to do it! We don't know why, but we can attest to the experience of limitation. The Lord decides to conceal His oneness and assume duality and separation. Then His powers become limited, although they're essentially nonlimited. You see the emphasis is on the freedom and the glory of it still.

TATTVAS SEVEN TO 11: THE KANCHUKAS

Tattvas seven to 11 are called the *kanchukas* or 'limitations'. They are aspects of the reducing function of maya. In each case the individual has a similar power to Shiva, but in a much reduced version:

KANCHUKA	INDIVIDUAL SOUL	SHIVA
7 Kalā	Limited ability to do things	Omnipotence (All powerful)
8 Vidya	Limited knowledge	Omniscience (All knowing)
9 Raga	Desire (Sense of lack)	Completeness
10 Kāla	Time	Eternity
11 Niyati	Space and causation	Omnipresence (Everpresent)

The *kanchukas* (literally 'clad in armour') are coverings. They are different ways that the force of maya affects supreme Consciousness. When Shiva plunges into maya, His will, knowledge and happiness all become limited.

Ensnared in time, space and desire the individual soul becomes depleted and handicapped. He becomes a transmigratory being, lacking in Shakti. Abhinavagupta memorably depicts the condition of such a one caught in personhood:

> Thus, the subject, being limited by or intertwined with *kāla, vidya, kalā, raga* and *niyati* and being deprived of divine glory by maya, shines as limited, feeling 'that which knows something now, does this, and is attached to this, am I'.

However, says Kshemaraja, when such a limited individual learns to fully unfold his Shakti, 'he becomes Shiva Himself'. In this view, Shiva is simply a more complete version of what we are.

Paul Muller-Ortega points out that the early sages in the Samkhya tradition had a problem that flowed from the dualistic nature of their system. If only the *purusha* were conscious and everything else were material, how could they give some degree of consciousness to the individual soul? Muller-Ortega says that the Kashmir Shaivite sages had a similar but opposite problem. Since, in their system everything is Shiva, then why isn't the individual soul Shiva, too? To solve this problem, they conceived of the idea of the *kanchukas*. Abhinavagupta describes the *kanchukas* as:

> Powers that maintain the individual soul resting in the middle like Trishanku, which otherwise would fall into the condition of complete inertia like a rock, etc., or would ascend into the sky of Consciousness like the supreme Lord.

The Trishanku story is a Hindu version of the Icarus myth. His ambition was to ascend bodily to heaven. To this end, he had a great ritual performed. But Indra, the God of Heaven, barred his entry, and Trishanku was hurled back earthward from the celestial abode of the gods. The prickly sage Vishvamitra became furious, and finally a compromise was reached in which Trishanku was made immortal by arresting his downward fall midway between heaven and earth. Since then he has been hanging up above the earth as a constellation.

Thus the individual *jiva* hangs in space, not allowed to plunge fully into materiality nor to ascend easily to Consciousness. Muller-Ortega goes on to point out that in one place Abhinavagupta mentions four *kanchukas* and in another six. It has become normal to speak of five *kanchukas* plus maya. So how many are there? Can't someone count them? Of course they can't and that is exactly the point.

These are conceptual entities designed to deal with certain philosophical issues. It is well to remind ourselves not to impute to them ontological status, else we get caught in these intellectual structures rather than keeping our attention on the experience they point to.

I am reminded of an episode from Mark Twain's sequel to his vastly popular novel, *Tom Sawyer*, which was called *Tom Sawyer Abroad*. In it, Huck Finn and Tom are for some reason aloft in a balloon flying across America.

Huck looks down and asks Tom, 'Where do you think we are?'

Tom answers, 'I am certain we are above Kentucky'.

Huck considers this for a while and says, 'We can't be above Kentucky'. 'Why not?' asks Tom.

'Because on the map, Kentucky is red and it's green down there!' answers Huck.

Equally we should remember that the structures of Shaivism are also maps and while maps have something to do with reality they are not the same as reality. Perhaps this also sheds light on how the Shaivites could make use of the 25 *tattvas* of Samkhya.

The *kanchukas* explain what happened to Shiva so that He became us. Since Shiva has five *shaktis* or powers—*chit, ananda, iccha, jnana, kriya*—it is reasonable to assume that the five *kanchukas* are limitations of each of the divine *shaktis*. It is easy to see that *jnana shakti* is limited by *vidya kanchuka* (divine knowledge/limited knowledge); *iccha shakti* is limited by *raga kanchuka* (completeness/desire); and *kriya shakti* is limited by *kala kanchuka* (omnipotence/limited action). It is less obvious that *Chit Shakti* has to do with *kala* or time, and *ananda shakti* has to do with space. However, *Chit* is pure, expanded Consciousness without thought-forms and time begins with thought-forms. And *ananda*, bliss, is the same as *svatantrya*, or freedom, and this is diminished by being closeted in a particular space. I will talk about these last two *kanchukas*, time and space, in the chapter, Being Present.

Chapter 8

The Tattvas II: Jiva, the Human Being

> His temple is his own body which contains the 36 *tattvas* and is perfectly provided with windows which form its structure. It also includes those things which are different from his body, like vases and other objects.
>
> Abhinavagupta, *Paramarthasara*, Verse 74

S hiva, who begins as the impersonal divinity of *tattva* one, now becomes a human individual at *tattva* 12. *Purusha* is also called *jiva*, and he is the individual soul—each of us. The dance of Shiva and Shakti is replicated on a lower level: Shiva becomes *purusha*, the individual, and Shakti becomes *prakriti*, the world.

TATTVAS 12 AND 13: PURUSHA AND PRAKRITI
THE ROCKS AND THE SAND

Shaivism says that *purusha* is no one but Shiva. Maya and the *kanchukas* have done their work on Him. He is limited, insecure and confused. He has been hypnotised, or drugged. He has had an accident, a little brain damage. So, *tattvas* 12 and 13 are Shiva-Shakti in a diminished form. The rest of the *tattva* map is an elaboration of the rest of the created universe. Notice that *purusha* is aloof, like Shiva, while *prakriti* gives rise to everything.

We could say, although I might be pushing things, that *purusha* is your inner world and *prakriti* is your outer world. Subjectivity is *purusha*, your most intimate Self. Even your mind, in this context, is external to who you truly are. Perhaps in Shiva's experience there is no inner and outer world. The split between inner and outer occurs as the result of passing through the doorway of maya. If everything is Consciousness there must always be a subject or an 'experient'. Science imagines a time on earth before human life when there were only objects. Shaivism says, 'Not possible', and asks, 'Who is the subject? Who experienced it?' When Consciousness is the primal stuff, there must always be a subject. Shaivism insists that if a human viewer were not there, then Shiva was the experient of those objects.

In the sentence, 'I am That', we can already see the seeds of separation. We have a subject and an object, which clearly are distinguishable. If 'I' equals 'That', there exists also the possibility that 'I' might not equal 'That' under certain conditions. Maya is the principle of separation and limitation. It is also the principle of negation. Linguistically a 'not' comes in. The new statement is 'I am *not* That.' Going through that tunnel of separation means that the principal of negation comes in. What does that 'not' mean? It means that the 'I' is separate from the 'That'. Shiva now feels separate from His universe.

Utpaladeva says:

> God, Consciousness in essence, like a magician, makes the whole ensemble of things which reside in Him appear outside Himself without using any external cause, solely by the power of His will.

Utpaladeva here vividly describes the moment in which Shiva becomes *jiva*, the *purusha* in *tattva* 12. Let's imagine that a moment before, Shiva had conceived of a universe filled with rocks and sand. He was the experient of that universe, and the rocks and sand He knew as existing within Himself. Perhaps He intuited another way to experience His creation, perhaps the idea of separation dawned on Him, perhaps He was overwhelmed by a frenzy of inspiration: any of these metaphoric scenarios are possible. In an instant, by His will, 'like a magician', Shiva becomes *purusha*.

Now he sees the rocks and sand as outside himself, no longer within the womb of his own Consciousness. He has a dim memory of having seen them before and so he imputes to them a separate and independent existence. He creates a theory of evolution that explains how He came to be there amidst the rocks and sand, but in fact, He was never absent. Originally, as Shiva, He experienced the rocks and sand within Himself. Now he sees them as external and separate. The Shaivites tell us that in truth, these objects are never separate from our own awareness. There never was a material world *separate* from the one who views it.

Utpaladeva says:

> All objects appear outside because they already shine in the Lord's Self. If they did not already exist in Him there would be no desire for manifestation.

Now as *purusha* we feel small and the rest of the universe is very big and rather indifferent. We are in a struggle to be safe or fulfilled. The universe sometimes yields good fruits to us, and sometimes miserable fruits. We are in a struggle, the odds are long against our getting what we want and avoiding what we don't want. This is the condition of 'I am *not* That'. Our spiritual problem is precisely this split between the inner world and the outer world.

Shiva and the *purusha* create two different worlds. Shiva's creation (the outer world) is held in common by all individuals and is never the problem. It is the *purusha's* creation (the inner world), coloured by maya and the *malas*, which creates bondage. The *purusha* experiences attachment and aversion to external objects and this creates a flood of inner thoughts and feelings which confuse and delude him.

When Shiva exercises His power of maya He becomes contracted. As *purusha*, He experiences contraction of will, contraction of knowledge and contraction of bliss. Shiva loses His bliss and becomes unhappy. He loses His perfect knowledge and becomes partial. He loses his will power and becomes impotent. He loses His ability to do things.

THE LOWER TATTVAS—TATTVAS 14 TO 36: MIND, SENSES, BODY, WORLD

The lower *tattvas* 14 to 36 account for the mind, senses, body and the physical world. *Tattvas* 14, 15 and 16 are the mind: the intellect or higher mind, the ego and the lower mind respectively. *Tattvas* 17 to 21 are the senses. Called *jnanendriyas*, or the powers of perception, they are the ways that the Self gains knowledge of the outer world (hearing, touch, sight, etc.). *Tattvas* 22 to 26 are called *karmendriyas*, or the powers of action. They are speaking (tongue), grasping (hand), locomotion (feet), excretion and procreation. The actions performed with these organs have karmic consequences, which are manifested in our present and future experience. The last *tattvas*, 32 to 36 are the gross elements, including the traditional ether, air, fire, water and earth. These constitute physical or material reality.

All these *tattvas* are straightforward and readily understandable. However, the ancient sages of Samkhya muddied the waters with *tattvas*

27 to 31, the *tanmatras* or subtle elements. These are sound in itself, touch in itself, form in itself, taste in itself and smell in itself. They form a bridge between the senses and the physical world and can be considered the general ability that individual sense impressions draw on. The *purusha* is at home in his world and his senses conform to certain manifestations of physical reality so that he can interact with the world. There is sound itself so that he can hear, there is form itself so that he can see. The *tanmatras* are also part of the physical world, though subtle.

UNDERSTANDING THE TATTVAS

The *tattva* map with its 36 levels of creation is somewhat misleading. The cosmology of Shaivism begins with Shiva or supreme Consciousness at the top. Then you have human beings, and then you have the world. That's the basic outline. It looks linear, which can be misleading.

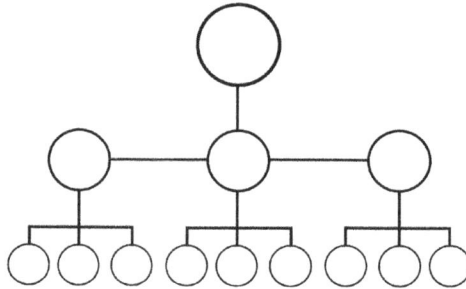

Tree Diagram

In this diagram the principle on the top gives rise to three more principles, and each of them gives rise to three principles. One becomes three, three becomes nine and so on. Another way to draw this same idea is:

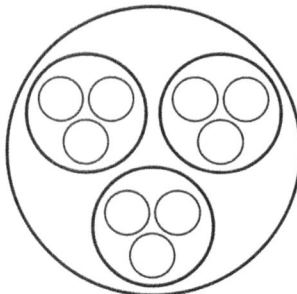

Chinese Box Diagram

This is called a Chinese Box diagram. It is easy for me to draw because it looks like my electric razor. It is a representation of *exactly* the same thing depicted in the previous diagram. In this diagram it becomes obvious that the back circle is behind everything else, and everything else is within it. Each smaller circle that is generated is within a larger circle, which is within a larger circle still. This is a more accurate depiction of how Kashmir Shaivism describes the unfoldment of Consciousness. The upper *tattvas* are always hidden within successively lower *tattvas*.

THE HIGHEST PRINCIPLE IS ALWAYS PRESENT

Vedanta has to assume a second impure principle, which is maya or ignorance. *Brahman*, the Vedantic Absolute, is pure but inert. On the contrary, Shaivism thinks of the Absolute as dynamic, thus the *tattvas* (the created universe) are manifestations of Shiva himself, in the form of *spanda* (divine vibration), not some other thing. Even maya cannot be anything other than Consciousness or, as some would say, the *sport* of Consciousness.

The highest principle is always present. It doesn't become some other thing and disappear. Each *tattva* represents a more gross or slower vibration than the one before it. The whole universe is thus the same material, *Chiti* or Consciousness, vibrating at different frequencies. Let us say a stone is the most dense, inert and stupid thing in the universe. Yet even then, Consciousness and the higher *tattvas* are all present in a stone. *All 36 tattvas are present in the stone.* This is important to understand. Kashmir Shaivism says that Shiva is present in every atom and fibre of the universe. One of the contemplations suggested by the Shaivite masters is to plunge each *tattva* imaginatively into the undifferentiated light of Consciousness. Thus you might contemplate a stone as Consciousness, your mind as Consciousness, your emotions as Consciousness, the whole phenomenal universe as Consciousness.

What is interesting about this scheme is that, again, it comes from *the inside out* rather than from the top down. Where do you look for *tattvas* one to five? Not in heaven, you look for them within yourself. There is nowhere else to look. The universe is the opening out of Shiva, which is the opening out of each of us. To contemplate this understanding and connect with it is to become a real Shaivite. It is to look around and say: *This world is generated from within me.* This is the transforming vision and practice of Shaivism.

SIMPLIFIED TATTVA MAP AND MAYA

Our physical world is filled with objects like cars and people and houses. Seen from outer space, none of these things are visible. A scientist using an electron microscope describes the very same world completely differently. At different levels of magnification we find atoms, subatomic particles and so on. Depending on where the viewer stands, things look different.

Thus the 36 levels that Shaivism gives are not the only possible view of the universe. You could come up with a scheme having more than 36 since the 36 we have are not comprehensive. Some of the *tattvas* could be analysed further, and more fully broken down. On the other hand, a God-intoxicated saint like Bhagawan Nityananda, for example, might recognise only one *tattva*, Consciousness Itself. He might ask us why we are so keen to make all these distinctions that only hurt the brain.

Consciousness

Bhagawan Nityananda's One-Tattva Map. A great being always experiences life in the highest state of Consciousness.

Being less exalted than that, but seeking simplicity, let me suggest a scheme in the spirit of the Trika, that has three *tattvas*. *Tattva* one—universal Consciousness, *tattva* two—maya, *tattva* three—the world of the individual. (See Simplified Tattva Map, opposite.)

First there is God, universal Consciousness. Remember that God says 'I am That'. He's a boring fellow, all he says is, 'I am That; I am That too; That am I'. In some moods he says, '*I* am that', and then he says, 'I am *That*'. He is Shiva-Shakti: God and His own creative power. In *tattva* two we have the veil, maya. It is the principle of negation and separation. This may look like nothing special on paper but it is a serious, serious step down. Oneness and bliss here become multiplicity and suffering. Shiva and Shakti enter one end of the tunnel of maya in all their cosmic glory, their freedom and joy, and come out the other end as the human subject and his objective world, bound and miserable.

1. Universal Consciousness
Shiva - Shakti
(GOD)

Subject and Object
are one
I am That, I am all this
God's thought and experience

2. Maya : The Veil

3. Individual Soul
Man's thought and experience
I am not That, I am separate

Outer World
Mind, Senses,
Body, World

Simplified Tattva Map (Three Tattvas). 1. Universal Consciousness 2. Maya 3. Individual Soul and Outer World

Creation is not coming down from above, it is coming out from within. Consciousness is the first principle which then goes through a loss of memory and metamorphoses into the individual soul and his world. The world comes last in this process as Consciousness opens out from within itself. This is the opposite of the Western idea of evolution which begins with a Big Bang creating the world and human life, with Consciousness coming later. The Shaivite concept is different. In God there is no inner world and outer world. Only with the veil of maya is there a split into an inner world and an outer world. If you imagine living only in your inner world, or, alternatively, seeing all outer phenomena as actually belonging to your inner world, you have an approximation of God's experience.

The veil of maya is no abstraction. You can see it operating in the foolishness of other people and you can see it in your own mistakes and bad choices. And you can see it directly through introspection—the inner experience of contraction, doubt, fear, confusion and agitation.

Maya is ignorance. Shaivism says we don't know the true Self, we have forgotten who we really are. Though we are Shiva, we identify with this limited individual. That is the veil. When you want to meditate, your mind gets distracted and wanders. That is the veil. Or you try to decide what course of action to take in life and you can't get it right. You veer wildly wrong. That is the veil. We all know that principle in operation. Sometimes you make choices that are so stupid, looking back you know you knew better, and you can't imagine why you did what you did.

When I understood the concept of maya, I felt much better. Maya descends. The veil comes down and you blunder. When I was playing tournament chess the veil would descend and I would sometimes play moves that in my wildest dreams I would not make. Later I would wonder how I did that. How did the hand move and the brain think that? It was impossible, and yet undeniably I had done it. Making a bad move in a chess game is one thing, but sometimes the veil descends and people make truly serious mistakes and suffer for them.

Kashmir Shaivism does not postulate a God sitting on high and casting out a universe. Instead, Consciousness Itself opens and manifests in precisely the same way that your dream world is manifested. The outer world is withdrawn when universal Consciousness returns within, just as when you go to sleep at night the outer world disappears as you go within. To get to the pure space of Shiva, we have to go inside ourselves and find it there. The thing that stops us, that makes the process hard, is the veil, maya. We get pulled to the outer, to the material part of creation. The senses get intoxicated by objects and pull us away from focus on the Self. The pull of the world is so strong, the outer is so overwhelming: this is the power of maya.

The interiority of the Self suggests one more map of the *tattvas*: the Shaiva Mandala (see opposite).

The mandala may be the most lifelike depiction of the *tattvas*, showing them issuing forth from the centre, Consciousness. While the Self/Shiva-Shakti appears small at the centre, it in fact is the 'big thing' that underlies everything.

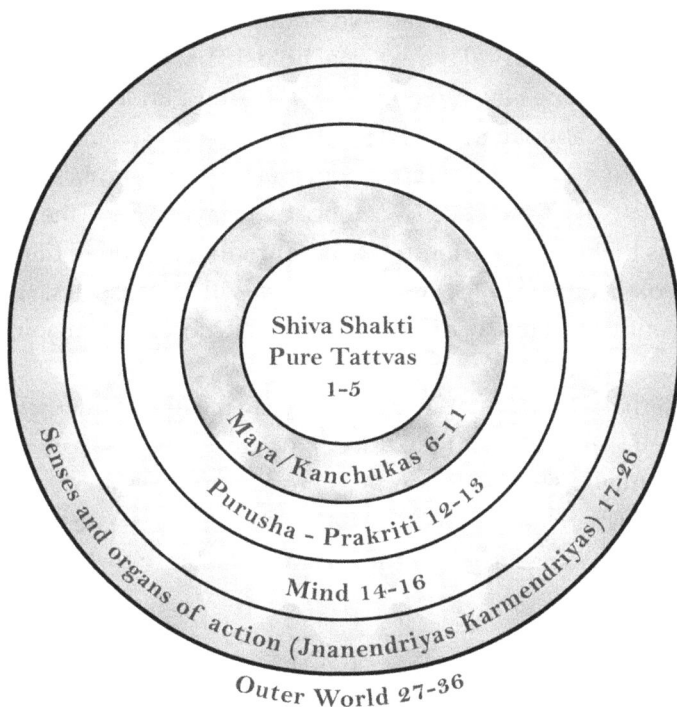

Tattva Map as Shaiva Mandala

For completeness, I will also give the simplified *tattva* map in the form of the Shaiva Mandala:

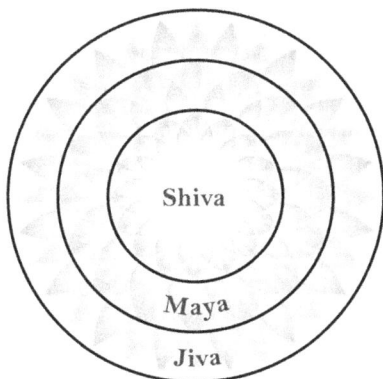

Simplified Tattva Map as Shaiva Mandala

If our true good lies within, why is it that we have such a struggle? Either the spiritual point of view is wrong and our hope lies in objects and we can have satisfaction by acquiring more money and things, or the spiritual masters are right and the good lies within. No doubt the spiritual point of view is correct but still, what a pull the external holds! That is the cosmic principle of maya. How strange it is. Vedanta says we don't understand maya. We can't even speak about it. It just is.

Let me make one more point about maya. Take another look at the Simplified Tattva Map on page 113. Notice that maya is above the individual. That means that maya is prior to the individual or *interior* to him. So if we were to look for maya we would look for it within ourselves, where it is doing its confusing dance of creating attachment, despair, aversion, jealousy and so on.

The external world is fine. We apply maya to it with our minds. Of course, the inner Self is even more interior than maya. In a real sense a meditator has to traverse maya. That is the same as crossing the 'ocean of *samsara*', or going through the 'cloud of unknowing'. It is good to be aware that wherever you go, whatever situation you are in, you carry your own highly personalised maya with you.

MEDITATION: LAYABHAVANA, RESOLVING GROSS INTO SUBTLE

The *Vijnanabhairava* Dharana 31 says:

> If the yogi contemplates that the subtle and subtler *tattvas* of one's own body or of the world are being absorbed in their own respective causes, then at the end, Para Devi or the Supreme Goddess is revealed.

This technique called *layabhavana*, or 'fusion', is based on the Shaivite insight that the more subtle *tattvas* underlie and give rise to the more gross ones. Thus you can begin with physical reality and resolve it imaginatively into the senses, then into the mind, then into the personal self, finally arriving at the transpersonal Self. Behind each manifestation is a deeper one, and underlying the whole is Consciousness Itself.

Let's withdraw the tattvas *into the Self. By turning within, you withdraw the world and the senses into your inner world. Now you are aware of your mind. Turning to the core of the mind, you will become aware of maya, the principle that makes it hard to still the mind and to focus it. Sit in maya as in the cloud of unknowing. You may experience stress, tension, boredom, tearing thoughts. Try to hold your attention there. You cannot control the higher* tattvas, *they are free and show themselves only by grace. However, sitting at the doorway of maya, we make ourselves available to that grace. Make the statement inwardly, 'I call on the Self, I call on Shiva'. You will experience a movement of grace. A light, a flow of energy, a release of tension. Meditate for 10 minutes.*

Chapter 9

Shaivite Yoga:
The Three Malas and the Three Upayas

> There, within the cosmic spheres, the universe resides, a series of worlds, organs and various bodies. It is there that Shiva Himself becomes a patient with a body, clothed in the condition of the individual soul.
>
> Abhinavagupta, *Paramarthasara*, Verse 5

The *tattvas*, the cosmology of Shaivism, form one part of the Trika that also includes the *malas* and the *upayas*. In review:

- *The tattvas:* The 36 cosmic principles that underlie all of reality, the structure of the universe.

- *The malas:* How Shiva becomes a bound soul, the process of contraction, the process *down* into manifestation.

- *The upayas:* The yogic means by which the individual soul returns to his Shiva nature. The process of expansion.

MALA

Shaivism specifically talks about three *malas*, contractions or impurities, that afflict all of us as human beings. Jaideva Singh defines *mala* as 'dust, dirt, impurity, taint and dross':

> Dross is the best English equivalent. *Mala* is what covers and limits the pure gold of divine Consciousness. *Mala* means those limiting conditions, both personal and impersonal, which hamper the free expression of the spirit.

The *malas* are a contraction of *will* (emotion); a contraction of *knowledge* and a contraction of *action*. At the level of Shiva, will, thought and action are simultaneous and inseparable. Shiva can manifest anything. He is empowered and effective. Impure will involves desire: we are not content with our lot. We think we need this or that to make us whole. At the same time, we feel that we can't achieve our goals and are ineffectual.

When we are confused about the direction and meaning of our lives we manifest the contraction of knowledge. Finally, we are tied to our bodies: we do bad things and we acquire bad karma, or we do good things and acquire good karma. Action is limited in that we can do some things, not everything. Shaivism defines the problem we all feel by speaking of these three *malas* or impurities.

Who is it that becomes a bound soul? It is Shiva who becomes a bound soul. Shiva does it to Himself, so each of us has done this to ourself.

In Dickens' *A Christmas Carol*, the enchained ghost of Marley tells Ebenezer Scrooge:

> I wear the chain I forged in life. I made it link by link, and yard by yard; I girded it on of my own free will, and of my own free will I wore it. Is its pattern strange to you?

In just the same way, we also have made choices that strengthened our bondage.

UPAYA

Equal and opposite to the *malas* are the *upayas*, or yogic methods. *Upaya* is from the verb *upa-i*, 'to approach'. Thus an *upaya* is a way to approach the truth, a spiritual means or yogic technique to repair the dimming of our light caused by the *malas*. *Upaya* is the means to approach *upeya*, 'the goal'. All of us have the *malas* as a given part of our predicament, but we have to *choose* to make the effort to help ourselves by applying the *upayas*. *Mala* is the path into contraction. *Upaya* is the path back to wholeness. It is a two-way street, the same road with two directions.

The yogic scriptures describe a human being as a fourfold structure, a series of bodies at the centre of which is the Self. Moving from the outer to the inner or the gross to the subtle, they are the physical body, the subtle body, the causal body and the supracausal body. Their corresponding attributes are *kriya*—or physical action, *jnana*—or knowledge, *iccha*—or will and desire, and the most subtle, the state of the Self.

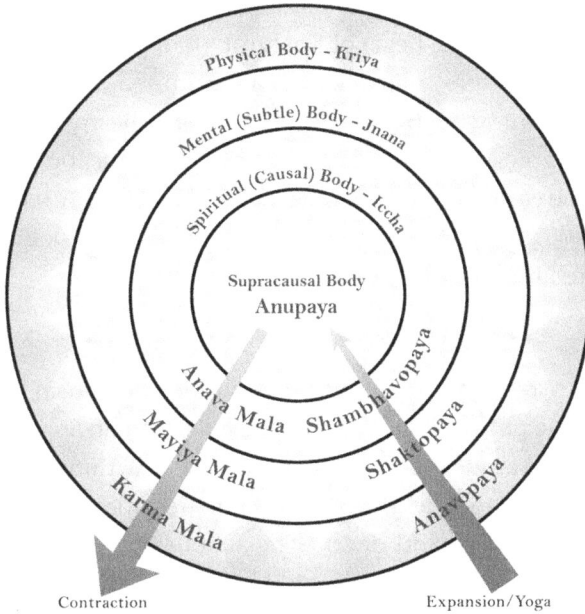

Contraction   Expansion/Yoga

Mandala of the Malas and Upayas. The malas *issue from the centre, causing contraction, while the* upayas *move back to the centre, generating expansion.*

In the state of realisation a person is perfectly balanced in the bodies and energies, with the ability to do, think, generate will, and be centred in the state of the Self. More often, however, a person might be centred in any of the outer layers, producing separation from divine *iccha, jnana* or *kriya*. The *upayas* categorise methods of *sadhana* according to a seeker's centre of gravity in general or at that moment.

In 1914, Chatterji wrote:

> The method of Shaivism consists of self-culture, mental, moral, spiritual and even physical, which constitutes what is called Yoga. It enables a Spirit to shake off the very limitations that makes of the real Experiencer a limited entity and to rise to those regions of experience which the highest *tattvas* are. Those who train themselves by this method of Yoga, can and do realise the *tattvas* by direct experience as clearly as, indeed more clearly than, we perceive the physical and sense-objects, and as they thus realise them, they experience the *tattvas* in their real nature and grandeur, increasingly more, and not less, grand and glorious, than the physical universe in all its grandeur can ever be.

Yoga is Chatterji's word for what I have described as *sadhana*, spiritual practice, or *upaya*. It is the heart of Kashmir Shaivism. We are cut off from the experience of a finer, more vivid, more unified and bliss-permeated universe by the contracting force of maya. Maya is the mysterious principle of duality that gives rise to the *tattvas* or levels of creation that Chatterji describes. In the case of human beings it gives rise to the three *malas*, which define our predicament. To overcome these *malas* is the task of yoga *sadhana* and a separate kind of yoga exists for each *mala*.

KARMA MALA AND ANAVOPAYA

The *malas* correspond to the physical, subtle and causal bodies. *Karma mala* relates to the physical body. It is the result of selfish and fearful actions. While God can do anything, we can only do the few things that our hands and feet, our organs of action, can do. Furthermore, we are under the tyranny of gravity, time and decay. The actions we perform can be good or bad. If they are good we acquire good karma. If they are bad, we acquire bad karma. That is the predicament of limitation—the bondage of karma is that we have to live with the fruits of our actions. Physical karmas can be overcome by good (God-oriented) actions.

Karma can prevent us from discovering the spiritual path. Baba used to say that only when a person's karmas were balanced, that is, when there was roughly an equal amount of good and bad karma, could he receive *shaktipat*, or divine awakening. Too much good karma or too much bad karma creates attachment to the external world. A person with a lot of good karma basks in the good life, while a person with a lot of bad karma completely focuses on his material or physical lacks.

The corresponding yoga is called *anavopaya*, 'the way of the body'. Literally translated this is the 'means' or yoga of the bound soul (the body). *Anavopaya*, therefore, is the cultivation of right actions on the level of the body. It includes karma yoga, which is the yoga of service; ritual worship (*puja*); hatha yoga; and *pranayama*, yogic breathing exercises. All of these sort out the physical body or how we conceive of ourselves *as* the body. *Anavopaya* helps us balance our bodily karmas. Meditation on the chakras or points in the body, on the breath, on objects in the world or deities are all within the scope of *anavopaya*.

MAYIYA MALA AND SHAKTOPAYA

One step more subtle is *mayiya mala*, which refers to the underlying sense of duality. The organ of duality, of course, is the mind (the subtle body). With *mayiya mala*, knowledge (*jnana Shakti*) becomes limited and brings about the thinking mind and the senses that perceive separation and difference. Another way to understand *mayiya mala* is that it is the force which separates the subject from the object. It makes us feel like a separate person in a larger world. As we saw in my discussion of the *tattvas*, it is the 'not' in the statement 'I am *not* That'.

The corresponding yoga is called *shaktopaya*, 'the way of the mind'. It is the *upaya* that uses the power of knowledge. This yoga involves a purely mental effort. Inside our brain unwanted thoughts keep ticking over: tearing thoughts, negative thoughts, foolish thoughts, inaccurate thoughts. To repair the mind we have to bring in appropriate, true thoughts. We have to expand our philosophical awareness and get rid of our negative thoughts, moving to positive thoughts.

Abhinavagupta says:

> Whoever wishes to have access to the divine nature, should first of all purify his thoughts.

This is achieved by contemplation—the old limited concepts are slowly replaced by the higher truths by means of constant contemplation done with imaginative fervour. A spiritual attitude that transforms the aspirant's understanding of who he is, is cultivated. A pure thought that the aspirant adopts as his spiritual means becomes the focus of his interior life. It eradicates false, contracting movements of Consciousness.

Abhinavagupta continues:

> When a thought is purified it engenders another thought which is pure in itself. This thought also produces another thought similar to itself and then this later thought again produces another. This one again produces another similar to itself.

When we indulge impure, that is negative, thoughts, we weaken our minds. We create a greater likelihood for negative thoughts to arise in the future. It is as though the fabric of the mind has been rent and unwanted elements have gained entrance. In the same way, when we choose strong and positive thoughts, we set up a chain within the mind, which strengthens it and heals its weakness. Such a strong mind becomes a vessel of divine Shakti and a fit instrument of higher contemplation.

121

Abhinavagupta says:

> As a result of purification, Consciousness, which is brought to the most evident and elevated condition, attains the stainless state of thought.

Abhinava's striking image of the 'stainless state of thought' may refer to the thought-free (*avikalpa*) state or it may equally refer to that kind of thought in which *vikalpas* occur, but the underlying feeling is so pure and free from ego and negative emotion, that such thought reflects the purity of the Self.

Shaktopaya includes whatever mental means we use in the realm of self-talk. In that sense, Self-inquiry is a form of *shaktopaya*, sorting out concepts, understandings and emotions. Mantra repetition is another powerful means. So are affirmations, prayer, anything in the realm of language, especially inner language, that makes it more intelligent, accurate and God-oriented. In *shaktopaya* the focus is on Shakti, the power or the adjunct of the Self. A Shaivite aphorism says that Shakti is the doorway to Shiva. If the Self is Shiva, the mind and its language is Shakti.

Shaktopaya has to do with understanding. Aspirants at this level are held in bondage by wrong understanding and misidentification. They think they are the mind or the body and not the Self. Or they have experiences of the Self in mundane life but give the credit not to the Self but to the outer objects that seem to have caused the experiences.

In *shaktopaya* the aspirant works with the *contents* of his mind, that is the kind of thoughts he thinks. He tries to improve his understanding, following the teachings of the Guru and the scriptures. He uses positive thinking techniques, working to enlighten his mind by getting rid of heavy, dark thoughts and habituating it to light, pure and noble ones.

Abhinavagupta says:

> Discursive, dualistic thought certainly is discourse, but in its deeper nature, it is awareness (*vimarsha*).

Such an understanding gives us an incentive to look behind thought to find something greater. In the final phase of *shaktopaya* the seeker uses a high thought to carry him out of the realm of thought altogether into the stillness, the Consciousness that is the background of discursive thought. Abhinavagupta explains that the Consciousness of an individual is limited to his mind and therefore functions under the influence of maya, creating separation and duality. He says, however, that if he adopts a thought like:

> 'I am present everywhere, everything is in me', then by means of

persevering determination his thought-form, though dominated by maya, eventually leads him to the thought-free state.

ANAVA MALA AND SHAMBHAVOPAYA

The highest means is called *shambhavopaya*, 'the way of pure Consciousness'. It is associated with *anava mala*, the contraction of will. *Anava mala* is essentially a sense of imperfection and individuality. Even before our minds begin to analyse and differentiate, there is a feeling-sense of separation that is inherent. No matter how well-trained our mind may be, there abides this underlying sense of imperfection and isolation.

Jaideva Singh writes, '*Anava mala* is the primal limiting conditioning which reduces the universal Consciousness to an *anu*, a small, limited entity'. We feel, 'I am imperfect'. This is deep within us, centred in the heart. It affects our causal body. It is the very place in us where our Shiva nature becomes our individuality. Shiva loses the memory of who He is. His first horrible thought, His first *tearing thought*, is something like, 'I am small, I am weak, I am separate'.

It is mysterious and incomprehensible. You could argue that it never happened—that Shiva becoming a limited individual is an illusion. It is not real. Some sages are so intoxicated with divine Shakti they don't bother to give spiritual teachings. Neem Karoli Baba was like that. The most he would do is have some chanting and suggest you say a mantra. Mostly you drank tea and ate sweets. Why worry? The whole play is Shiva and nothing but Shiva.

I'm not surprised that Shiva would explore every possibility in *Chiti*. If you were in the Garden of Eden and you were told about the forbidden fruit, in an infinite expanse of time you would eventually taste it. The fruit is there waiting to be eaten. And given enough time you would eat it. You have to try it; you have to explore the totality.

From *anava mala*, first limitation, limitation of the will, all other limitations emerge. Since will is associated with *affect*, or feeling, *anava mala* ushers in the first negative emotions. Shiva becomes limited. The archetypal statement of *anava mala* is 'I am a person!' This is, unfortunately, not the triumphant shout of a humanist, but the sad cry of one who has been something greater.

Utpaladeva writes:

> The *mala* called *anava* is due to the loss to Consciousness of its essential

nature. It is of two kinds, it consists (i) in the loss of its freedom, *svatantrya*, or (ii) in the loss of the power of knowledge.

God's state is one of complete satisfaction. The human individual, however, is lamentably different. Having become trapped in time, space and causality, he feels the lack of many things. Desire arises—flowing from *anava mala*. He feels an emptiness and a deep need to fill it.

No physical or mental means can correct this condition. In *shambhavopaya* the aspirant focuses on pure Consciousness or pure awareness, free of mental movements. This Consciousness is Shiva (*Shambu* is Shiva, hence *shambhavopaya*). It is silent and vast. In *shambhavopaya* the object of meditation is the thought-free Consciousness out of which thoughts spring. Only great vigilance and steady willpower can prevent thoughts from arising. If you were to sit in meditation and exert your will; be present . . . and present . . . and present . . . now . . . and now . . . and now, staying with the thought-free state, that is *shambhavopaya*. Shiva is the underlying awareness beyond thought, the witness.

Different *shambhavopaya* techniques are described in the Shaivite texts. Krishnamurti called it 'choiceless awareness'. To overcome your *anava mala*, you focus on the space beyond thought. Strictly speaking if you become absolutely thought-free you will pass into a trance, a blank or sleep. Really, you don't have to eliminate all thoughts, simply pay no attention to the *content* of thought, and aim for the *context* of all thought, the background, that is, Consciousness. Thoughts can continue to play, but you should keep your focus on the space beyond thought, the space that contains thought, the witness of thought. The aspirant in *shaktopaya* tries to watch only pure and noble programmes on his television set. The aspirant in *shambhavopaya* wants no programmes at all; he likes the empty screen.

Shambhavopaya focuses on the meditator's own essential nature. He stands in the Self. Nisargadatta Maharaj says that at this level, the meditator has to go beyond definitions and descriptions, which are mental, 'into what is undefinable and indescribable'.

Shiva Sutras I.11 says:

> *Tritayabhokta vireshah*
> The supreme Lord Shiva is the witness or enjoyer of the three states of waking, dream and deep sleep.

The witness is the silent observer of the thought process.

ANUPAYA: THE METHODLESS METHOD

The fourth yoga beyond these three is called *anupaya* or the non-means. This actually is a way of being. It is not different from the state of *samadhi*, the state of enlightenment and the goal of Shaiva yoga. Here, no effort is made since the vision has already been transformed. In *anupaya* the whole world is seen as the sport of the Divine. There is absolute unity awareness, ease and supernal joy. It is not an intellectual position, but a felt state of being. In *anupaya*, there is no distinction between mind and matter, the individual and God. It is perfect attainment and not a state of incompleteness or striving.

Anupaya is sometimes called 'recognition', since it is based on a penetrating insight into the deepest truth. It is also called *sahaja samadhi* or the natural state, as though if we stopped being who we are not, we would naturally become who we really are. No amount of self-effort can arrive at this state. It is only through divine grace that the aspirant achieves it.

Utpaladeva says in one of his poems:

> It is not by virtue of meditation nor of recitation, but is without preliminary rules that Shiva manifests Himself uniquely thus (through grace and spontaneously) to that being full of love whose praises we sing.

That grace is free and picks whom it will and when it will. Since the Guru is the manifest agent of grace, this method (if it can be so-called) is often spoken of as *gururupaya*, 'the way of the Guru'. Through Guru's grace comes a *recognition* of our divinity and an awakening of real (as opposed to merely intellectual) inner experience.

In the three other *upayas*, the goal and the method are different. In *anupaya*, they are one and the same. The natural living of life in harmony with the Self becomes both the path and the destination. This state is extremely exalted, yet natural. *Anupaya* is not so much a 'high' state in the sense of an intoxication; it is rather a state that is profoundly balanced and integrated. It is human as well as divine. It is present and luminous. It is hinted at in this series of sutras in the *Shiva Sutras* (III. 25–29):

> The realised yogi becomes like Shiva.
> All his actions (however mundane) are worship of God.
> His words are like mantras.
> Knowledge of the Self is the gift that he disseminates (all round).
> He who has acquired mastery over the *shaktis* serves as a source of wisdom for others.

Thus the ordinary conversation of one established in *anupaya* resonates like mantra. It is full of truth and upliftment. Every action of such a one is worship because he is never separate from God. Then life is lived at ease, in perfect freedom, with unwavering knowledge of the truth. Living his ordinary life, he becomes a liberator for those who can understand the gift he offers. I will speak more about *anupaya* in a later chapter.

HIGHEST FIRST

I have described the *upayas* from the lowest to the highest, from the most physical to the most subtle. This is the order one would expect. Interestingly, the Trika discusses them in the reverse order. The highest means is given first. I am reminded of an incident that happened many years ago.

The teaching swamis around my Guru were skilled communicators. We used to say there were two types of swamis, the academic type and the theatrical type. Once one of the latter swamis proposed to teach the *upayas* the way I am doing here, from the lowest to the highest. He thought that this order would be more dramatic—he could guide his audience laboriously through the lower means, body and mind, and end with triumph and relief at the highest state. Everyone would be quite worked up and have an experience of the Self.

Baba didn't like this plan at all. He insisted the lecture follow the Trika's usual order from highest to lowest. He said there is a specific reason behind it. Perhaps this is the point: Shaivism tells us always to take the highest view possible. We hear of the highest, most direct means first. If we can't absorb that there are other means available. It is not that we spend years perfecting our *anavopaya* and then move up. We seek our toehold as near the summit as we can manage. We hear of the highest truth first. If we can grasp it, fine; if not, the next lower means is offered. Finally, we will rest in the yoga perfectly suited to our personality and level of development.

This is the compassion of Shaivism: it honours all beings with the understanding that since everyone is divine in his inner nature, no one is too dull to hear the highest truth first. That truth and its related techniques will resonate somewhere within the seeker even if he is not yet ready to understand or use them. There will be some benefit and the terrain will have become more familiar.

The higher means, being closer to God, as it were, contain more of His light and energy. Fundamentally, the whole philosophical system and practice of the Trika is an instrument for communicating divine grace in the form of illumination, peace and joy. The teachings are given in the knowledge that it is likely that the mind of the aspirant cannot yet grasp them. This is quite all right: the teachings are full of divine Consciousness and have the power to make themselves understood. They establish a beachhead within the Consciousness of the seeker. They are spiritual depth-charges, which stimulate the corresponding place of knowledge that already exists within each of us.

Chapter 10

Malas and Upayas:
Further Thoughts and Contemplations

Just as the surface of the firmament is not soiled by the clouds, smoke and dust, in the same way the supreme spirit is not affected by the modifications of maya.

Abhinavagupta, *Paramarthasara*, Verse 36

There is disease (limitation) in the form of the *malas* and medicine in the form of the *upayas*. You should not think that if you are a great yogi all you do is *shambhavopaya*, the highest *upaya*. Each of us has to work in each of the areas—the will, the heart, the mind and the body. Some believe that the *upayas* lead into each other but I think any well-rounded spiritual path works in all of them at once. Your practice will emphasise one more than another at particular times.

To summarise, *anava mala* affects the spirit and contracts the will. *Mayiya mala* affects the mind and creates duality. *Karma mala* affects the body and creates good and bad actions. We could even say that *anava mala* is our individuality, *mayiya mala* is our mind and *karma mala* is our body.

INQUIRY

When I realised that Baba's meditation instruction, 'Everything is *Chiti*', came from Shaivism, I read whatever was available on the subject. I became aware of Shaivism's main concepts: how pure Consciousness contracts to become us and expands again through spiritual practice. I contemplated, 'I am a contracted form of Shiva, afflicted with the three *malas* of will, knowledge and action'.

128

Trying to make my philosophical understandings practical, I reasoned that these contractions, if they are real, will show up in me, concretely. I observed myself in meditation. I found three major points of contraction within me, and they rang a bell in my mind. My hatha yoga teacher, Hari Dass Baba, had written of three *granthi,* or 'knots', which he described as obstacles to the free movement of the kundalini energy. There was the *Brahma granthi* located in the navel chakra; the *Vishnu granthi* located in the heart chakra; and the *Rudra granthi* located in the third eye.

My inspection convinced me that these three knots exactly paralleled the *malas.* I felt certain that the *karma mala* showed up in the navel, the *mayiya mala* in the third eye, and the core mala, the *anava mala,* resided in the heart. I could feel the contraction in those places and I had the desire to release them. Intuitively I knew that untying these knots or destroying these *malas* would not be easy, but I saw that at least I could visit them and examine them, and indeed I did so.

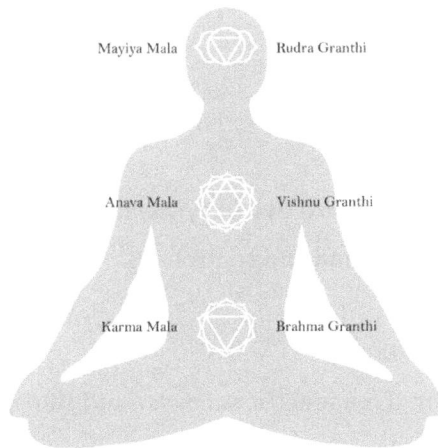

Contraction in the Chakras. *The malas correspond to the three knots in the navel, heart and third eye.*

I experienced the *malas* as contracted feeling and tension in those three centres. I also discovered, through inquiry, that subtle thoughts were intimately tied to the contractions, and that I could uncover those thoughts.

Abhinavagupta says:

> At a certain level of Consciousness, knowledge and action, although evident, are contracted. A blazing energy is (revealed within) the one who dedicates himself to removing the burden of this contraction.

This is perfect Self-inquiry. Contraction *(mala)* shows up directly in our body as tension. A yogi can approach the tension he experiences within himself directly through inquiry, and with sufficient skill and insight, unblock himself *(upaya)*. Since Shaivism asserts that 'everything is Consciousness', it follows that even our blocks are nothing but Consciousness. They are tense bundles of thoughts and feelings that can be unpacked by direct inquiry.

THE MALAS AS A-STATEMENTS

Although I didn't have a term for it then, I discovered that the *malas* could be expressed as A-Statements. An A-Statement refers to an *accurate* statement of present feeling, such as, 'I feel angry', 'I feel sad', 'I feel happy'. There will be a fuller discussion of A-Statements later in the book. My technique was to get in touch with the contracted feeling in meditation and 'ask it to speak' or inquire, 'what does it want to say?'

The contraction in the heart *(anava mala)* said things like:

- ◆ I feel sad.
- ◆ I am lonely.
- ◆ I feel separate.
- ◆ I feel hopeless.

The contraction in the third eye *(mayiya mala)* said things like:

- ◆ I need to understand and control this.
- ◆ There is chaos.
- ◆ I am confused.

The contraction in the navel *(karma mala)* said things like:

- ◆ There is a lot I want.
- ◆ I feel frustrated.
- ◆ I want my own way.

I discovered that I held these and similar statements within myself on an unconscious level. The task was to first make them conscious, then discover ways to let them go.

THE MALAS AND THE KANCHUKAS

Students often want to know where the *malas* are in relation to the *tattvas,* or the relationship between the *malas* and the *kanchukas*. The *malas* and the *kanchukas* have a similar, limiting and contracting function and are both part of the process of maya. But are they the same or two different things?

Shaivism talks about the movements of contraction and expansion in many ways from many points of view. These discussions have different origins, such as separate schools, scriptures or sages. Certainly, some of these insights are the result of direct perception in meditative states.

Even then, the same phenomenon might look different from each angle of approach. They work in the same direction and in that sense, they have the same general function. But sometimes, coming from different sources, they have no direct relationship to each other. It is probably wise not to force them to agree. Abhinavagupta gathered flowers from many meadows.

Yet, a way of relating the *kanchukas* and the *malas* is to consider that the *kanchukas*, taken together, constitute *anava mala*. They come into play and define the point where Shiva becomes the *purusha*. At the level of the causal body, the *purusha* does not yet have a body or mind. *Mayiya mala* manifests as the mind (*tattvas* 14 to 16) and is not different from the mind. Thus it enters the *tattva* map where the mind does. Similarly, *karma mala* manifests as the body (beginning at *tattva* 17) and is not different from the body. It enters the *tattva* map with and as the body.

Mayiya mala and *karma mala* can be considered outgrowths of *anava mala*. They come about as the mind and body are created. Shaivism says that a human being, a *sakala*, has all three *malas*, while other kinds of beings in subtle worlds have only one or two *malas*. None of this has much practical importance to the meditator. It is important, however, to have a general sense of the process of contraction.

Sri Nisargadatta gives a vivid image:

> The light of Consciousness passes through the film of memory and throws pictures on your brain. Because of the deficient and distorted state of your brain, what you perceive is distorted and coloured by feelings of like and dislike. Make your thinking orderly and free from emotional overtones, and you will see people and things as they are, with clarity and charity.

It is enough to understand that Shiva's powers, as they show up in us, have become limited. Now it becomes necessary to make the attempt to move back towards the light of Consciousness.

MEDITATION I: THE MALAS

By means of contemplation we can move the malas *from an idea to a bodily experience. Turn within and look carefully for areas of contraction and unpleasantness within your body. Carefully observe the navel, heart and third eye. Any unpleasant sensation, tension or contraction is the presence of* mala. *Don't try to get rid of it. Instead, spend some time investigating it. How big is the feeling? How strong is it? What emotion does it seem to be? Let the feeling 'speak' to you and see what it says.*

THE UPAYAS AS B- AND G-STATEMENTS

After exploring the A-Statements within me, I worked with another kind of statement that I later called the B-Statement. B-Statements are *beneficial* statements aimed at uplifting feeling, similar to an affirmation. B-Statements are broader than affirmations, however, because any statement that has the effect of uplifting feeling is considered a B-Statement.

Here are a few of them:

+ I am perfect.
+ I am perfectly content.
+ I have it all.
+ I have perfect understanding.
+ I can do anything.

These are B-Statements relevant to contraction of will, intellect and action. You say them to yourself inside your inner space: it is like trying them on. You see if they resonate, if they are congruent with the thought-feeling weather of your inner world. Some of them will be significant and provide an insight or shift of feeling. Some will point out a weakness, and some will have a healing effect. The Shaivite texts give characteristic B-Statements.

Here are three great ones:

+ I am Shiva.
+ I am universal Consciousness.
+ It is all the play of Consciousness.

>lifting B-Statements that come from the realm beyond maya, I
ements. They are a ladder thrown down to us from universal
sness. They are *Great* statements; scriptural statements; *God*

132

statements; *Guru* statements. G-Statements have a special power, a kind of charisma. They have intellectual content as well as dynamism. In Shaivite terms, they have *jnana* and *kriya*. When you get to the heart of the matter, all religions, all spiritual paths, are compendia of G-Statements. For a list of G-Statements see Appendix D.

Working with A-Statements, then B- and G-Statements, we directly apply the *upayas* to the *malas,* letting go of the contractions that limit us.

MALAS, UPAYAS AND SELF-INQUIRY

I call the method of Self-inquiry I am describing, the Shiva Process. In the Shiva Process we contemplate the feeling of contraction or expansion in four chakras within the body: the navel, the heart, the throat and the third eye. One reason why we use those four rather than the classical seven is because of the bodily location of the *malas. Karma mala* is associated with the navel chakra. A seeker will often experience frustrated doership and desire in that area. *Mayiya mala* is associated with the brow centre, the third eye. When we struggle for understanding we knit our brows. Finally, the *anava mala* shows up in the heart.

The throat centre is like a clearinghouse of communication. It often manifests blocked expression or blocked emotion, which usually comes up from the heart. While not the site of one of the primary knots, it is still critically important. When we encounter these blocks during Self-inquiry we make attempts to release them. This is direct application of *upaya*. Releasing the contraction in the heart, we work on the primary contraction of our ego nature, or *jivahood*.

MEDITATION II: THE KNOT IN THE HEART

Focus on the feeling in the heart. It is here that you can experience the anava mala, *where Shiva becomes you as an individual. Meditate on the feeling in the heart, trying to open it and release it into pure Consciousness, saying 'I am Shiva'. Become one with your true nature. Let your intuition guide you.*

SHAKTIPAT IN THE UPAYAS

Shaktipat, the awakening of kundalini Shakti by the grace-filled transmission of a true Guru, takes place differently in each *upaya*. My Guru used to speak of it most often from the level of *anavopaya*, which reflected his compassionate desire to awaken as many people as possible. He spoke about the Shakti being awakened at the base of the spine and moving up the *sushumna*, the subtle spine, and purifying the various chakras on its way to the abode of Shiva in the *sahasrara* or the thousand-petalled lotus in the crown of the head. Baba said innumerable experiences might occur on this journey—visions, lights, experiences of energy, bliss, divine love, physical movements and so on. And thousands of seekers received these experiences from him.

In 1975, when Baba instructed me to perform *shaktipat* awakening at Intensives, he gave me his wand of peacock feathers, which I still use, recited some mantras for my protection, and gave me certain instructions. He said, 'This is the true *diksha*'. He explained that *di* means giving, *ksha* means destroying. The Guru gives divine grace and simultaneously destroys ignorance.

Pratyabhijnahridayam Sutra 17 says:

By unfoldment of the centre, the bliss of Consciousness is attained.

'Unfoldment of the centre' refers to the process of *shaktipat* awakening. In *anavopaya* the centre refers to *sushumna*, as in Baba's model. But in *shaktopaya* the centre means *jnana* and *kriya*, and in *shambhavopaya* the centre is Consciousness Itself. In practical terms this means that a seeker whose *shaktipat* relates to *shaktopaya*, will discover that new understandings flood him and he is more skilful in his actions. A seeker whose *shaktipat* relates to *shambhavopaya* will have experiences of expanded awareness, some of them quite dramatic, and will find a general movement towards the widening of Consciousness. A seeker whose *shaktipat* is in *anupaya* will be instantly lifted into a new relationship with God or the Guru that is natural and permanent.

The *malas* and the *upayas* are important concepts in Kashmir Shaivism. We have traced the *movement down*, the contraction of Consciousness via the *malas*. Shiva shrinks himself to become *jiva*, a pale shadow of himself. At some stage in his worldly career, *jiva* discovers that he is not who he thinks he is. He stumbles across a path to higher Consciousness, yoga. In order to return to his former splendour, he adopts various yogic means, the *upayas*, and completes the journey of his soul and the extraordinary play of cosmic awareness.

The *upayas* can be classified by the yogi's understanding and his intentionality. If you feel your *sadhana*, for example, involves purification of the mind, then your yoga is *shaktopaya* and so on. The *upayas* are determined by the *object* of meditation. If the object of your meditation (the focus of your attention) is Consciousness Itself, you are in *shambhavopaya*. If the object of your meditation is the mind or thought, you are in *shaktopaya*. If the object of your meditation is something within the body or outside the body, you are in *anavopaya*.

SAMAVESHA

Finally, the *upayas* can be looked at as methods of *samavesha*. *Samavesha* is penetration by the Divine, or merger in the Divine. The individual soul obliterates himself in his Shiva nature. Sometimes the *upayas* are called forms of *samavesha*, as in *anava samavesha*, *shakta samavesha* and *shambhava samavesha*. The texts give 50 varieties of *samavesha*. In *shambhavopaya* the yogi achieves *samavesha* with Shiva by an act of will that plunges him directly into Consciousness. In *shaktopaya*, the yogi achieves *samavesha* with Shiva by appropriate mental activity. In *anavopaya*, the yogi attains *samavesha* with Shiva via actions or dualistic yogic practices. And in *anupaya*, the yogi understands that *samavesha* with Shiva is always the case.

The essence of *samavesha* is perfect merger. There must not be a layer of language or intellection between the individual and Shiva. This requires that thought-processes dissolve into inner feeling. The unified *feeling* of oneness is the true *samavesha*.

Jaideva Singh says:

> While Shakti, the Divine Creative Power, rejects [all the other senses], She retains *sparsha*, or touch. How is that Reality to be touched? Kshemaraja says: 'Tatsamvashat', i.e., by penetration [by *samavesha*], by diving mentally into its innermost depth. This is the mystic union.

The sense of sight, for example, casts pictures into the mind and is associated with the mind. It is not as close to the core of our being as touch or feeling. Hence sexuality is the most powerful of outer sensory experiences giving a taste of the Self. It is used everywhere by Abhinavagupta as a metaphor of divine *samavesha*. For example, there is this extraordinary passage (*Tantraloka*):

> Just as a female ass or mare [in orgasm], enters into the [delight of her own] Abode, the Temple of Bliss repeatedly expanding and contracting and is overjoyed in her own heart, so [the yogi] must establish himself in the Bhairava couple, expanding and contracting, full of all things, dissolved and created by them again and again.

Elsewhere, Abhinavagupta comments more soberly:

> The organs of sight, hearing, taste and smell are subtly present in earth and the other elements belonging to lower levels of reality, the highest among them being still within the sphere of maya, whereas touch resides at a higher level of energy as an indescribable, subtle sensation ceaselessly yearned for by the yogi.

There is a correspondence between touch, kundalini energy and *prana* (the breath). To experience true *samavesha* is to experience ecstasy or bliss *(ananda)*. While bliss is difficult to experience in ordinary life, the Shaivites insist that it underlies everything and is available in every moment. Thus, even in pain, even in adversity, the Shaivite will search for that *ananda* by means of *samavesha*. Bliss itself is the sign that *samavesha* has been achieved.

Kshemaraja conveys a portion of that bliss when he writes of the yogi's merger into I-Consciousness:

> When the yogi infuses everything with I-Consciousness, with the thought of I to begin with, relating everything, and finally with thought-free awareness embracing everything within himself, then he will experience the bliss of absorption into the state of the highest (divine) Experient which he will experience in his own consciousness by perfect meditation.

A SUMMARY OF MALAS AND UPAYAS

Karma mala says, 'I am the body'. This is counteracted by *anavopaya*, which says, 'I am free!' *Anavopaya* is the *sadhana* of the body.

Mayiya mala says, 'I am the mind'. This is countered by *shaktopaya*, which says, 'I am Shakti'. *Shaktopaya* is the *sadhana* of the mind.

Anava mala says, 'I am a person, a *jiva*'. This is countered by *shambhavopaya*, which says, 'I am Shiva'. *Shambhavopaya* is the *sadhana* of the Self.

THE UPAYAS AS PERSPECTIVES

As Lord Shiva looks out or down on the universe, He has two perspectives. The first is Absolute nondualism, pure oneness. In this mode, He is *Paramashiva*, the transcendental Absolute. He sees the one Conciousness as all part of Himself, saying, 'I am all this'. The second perspective (which is essentially not different from the first) includes the

Lord's experience of the creation. He sees it within Himself, not as separate. One could call this experience *anupaya* because multiplicity is perceived within the peace of unity.

As soon as the Lord sees the universe as separate, He becomes the *purusha*. Suddenly he is looking up at the universe from below and may take one of several perspectives:

+ I am the body. I create good and bad karma. My life is complex and difficult. *Anavopaya* must be practised.

+ I am the mind. My mind is separative and negative. *Shaktopaya* must be practised.

+ I am the *purusha*, a human individual. I feel alone, cut-off and weak. *Shambhavopaya* must be practised.

Thus all the *upayas* are methods of wholeness that depend on a individual's perspective. Does he identify with the mind, the body or the individuality? What illusion of himself does he hold?

A CAVEAT

My observation is that Westerners tend to look at the *upayas* and say, 'Shambhavopaya is the highest, therefore I'll do that'. This can be a superficial choice and harden the ego. The great saints that I have met, having completed their spiritual work, generally continue to engage in service to humanity, which is anything but a 'low *upaya*'. In fact, in the Tantric approach a strange phenomenon occurs in which the lowest becomes the highest. Just as the Guru's feet become the highest part of the Guru and not the lowest, so in realisation, the path of service becomes the highest.

Studying the *upayas* was for a long time the most interesting aspect of Shaivism for me. It is fascinating, and no doubt helps our understanding. But it is not of critical importance to classify your practice into which *upaya* you are following. It can even be an intellectual trap. A seeker doesn't approach the Truth saying, 'Let's see, my *sadhana* has focused on *anavopaya* too much recently. I'll have to adopt some *shaktopaya*'. That would be too mechanical. Instead, you should focus on the goal and adopt those means that naturally make sense to you.

The specific *upaya* is not important, it is the intentionality and the earnestness that is important. What is crucial is to do your *sadhana* in a way that is passionate and meaningful. When a yogic practice is not right for someone, the practice feels difficult, dry and fruitless. When it is right it feels easy, right and fulfilling. All of the means reach the same goal. All are, finally, methods of *samavesha*.

MEDITATION III: 'I AM PURE CONSCIOUSNESS'

Let's do an archetypal Shaivite meditation suggested in various texts. Contemplate, 'I am pure Consciousness'. If you can go directly into pure Consciousness then you are in shambhavopaya. *If you can't quite do that, but repeat to yourself the phrase, 'I am pure Consciousness', that is* shaktopaya. *Every time thoughts take you away from the contemplation, repeat the phrase to take you back. The difference here between* shaktopaya *and* shambhavopaya *is only academic. The important thing is to plunge deeply into Consciousness. Try to experience the feeling of pure Consciousness, of Shiva. Meditate for 10 minutes.*

MEDITATION IV: TOWARDS ONENESS

In this meditation, the seeker begins in separation from the Lord. He prays, worships and calls on Shiva. His attitude may be expressed as, 'I call on/invoke Shiva', 'Lord, please protect me', 'Lord, please give me what I want', 'Lord, you are so great!' All these are dualistic postures of prayer, imprecation and praise. The devotee is a separate body from the Lord. This is *anavopaya*.

After praying to and invoking the Lord in this way, the devotee is ready to begin the process of *samavesha*, or merging in Shiva. Now his statement is, 'I am Shiva'. There is no other, no separate Shiva. The process has become internal and is a battle within the mind of the devotee himself. His own mind tells him that he is not Shiva or strays away from the idea that he is Shiva. Doggedly, he churns the idea of his Shivaness over and over again until his mind is thick with that knowledge. This is *shaktopaya*.

Finally, the process becomes interior even to the mind. In *shambhavopaya*, Shiva *samavesha* is held by a steady flow of will, which is wordless and nondual. Each of these stages blends into the next one and together form an excellent meditation:

Anavopaya

Thinking of yourself as the devotee, separate from Shiva, talk to Him, pray to Him, implore Him, beseech Him, honour Him, question Him. Make known all your needs and wants. As you go deeper into this portion of the meditation, you should discover that there is an extensive conversation to be had with the Lord. Do this part as long as it is interesting and energised.

Shaktopaya

Now you are ready to begin to merge with Lord Shiva. You internalise Him. Saying, 'I am Shiva', feel yourself becoming one with Him. Just as Shiva is often depicted as sitting as a meditating yogi, now you are that meditating yogi. Let yourself vividly think about and feel the identification with Shiva. Shiva is first person to you now. Let this part of the contemplation seamlessly blend into . . .

Shambhavopaya

Now your mental contemplation in Step 2 bears fruit in Shiva-awareness, held wordlessly. Your awareness is held within in shambhavi mudra. *You don't lose touch with Self, even if you open your eyes. You are the creator, sustainer and destroyer of the universe. You are the awareness that holds all things. When you open your eyes, the universe comes into existence. When you close your eyes, it dissolves. Your existence as an individual being is one side of the coin of who you are, while Shiva is the other.*

Chapter 11

The Five Processes and the Yoga of Self-Inquiry: Burning It to Sameness

> Into the burning flame of His Consciousness he offers impurities in the form of the differentiation of internal and external conceptual constructs. His oblation to the fire is made without any effort.
>
> Abhinavagupta, *Paramarthasara*, Verse 76

W e have looked at the cosmic sweep of Shiva to *jiva* by contraction (the *malas*) and *jiva* back to Shiva by yoga *sadhana* (the *upayas*). Let us investigate the most interesting moment in the drama: where we are. In the midst of the *Pratyabhijnahridayam*, Shiva has fallen under the spell of maya and is deeply hidden by the cloak of the *malas*.

Kshemaraja asks a poignant question:

> Is there any mark appropriate to Shiva-state by which the Self even in the *samsarin* stage may be recognised as Shiva Himself appearing in that condition?

He is asking for any signs whereby you and I, as limited as we are, can know we are Shiva. And he answers, 'Yes, the five actions'. Everyone does the five actions or processes of Shiva. These five actions are *creation, sustenance, dissolution, concealment* and *grace*. Shiva does them, and when we see that we do them as well, we recognise our own Shiva nature.

THE FIVE PROCESSES

In Shiva's universe, the macrocosm, all things are subject to the first three processes of creation, sustenance and dissolution, or destruction. They are created, sustained for a while and then disappear. In the realm above maya there is nothing but grace, and in the realm of maya, concealment holds sway with grace or oneness sometimes flashing forth.

In the same way, these five processes take place in the microcosm, the small world of the individual. A thought comes into your mind, you *create* it. You *sustain* that thought in your awareness for a while. Then there is *dissolution*, when you let the thought go or it is replaced by the creation of another thought. And when you feel separate, that is *concealment*. When you have a sense of oneness, you are experiencing *grace*. We are constantly doing these five processes. Every human being performs these five actions as Shiva does.

The five processes fall into two groups. Creation, sustenance and dissolution are one group, parallel to the Hindu trinity of Brahma (creation), Vishnu (preservation) and Shiva (destruction). They tell the life story of everything, while the second group, concealment and grace, has to do with the spiritual condition of oneness or separation.

It could be said that concealment and grace belong to the inner world and relate to the condition of our soul. Concealment is the state of being afflicted by maya. Grace is oneness and salvation. Grace is the power in our life that gives wisdom and joy and all good things on every level. It is the most important of the five processes.

Baba writes, 'Grace is nothing but seeing objects as one with self-luminous *Chiti*, even though they may appear to be different'. Creation, sustenance and dissolution are always going on, but whether these go on against a feeling of alienation or oneness is crucial to a human being.

Why does Shiva practise concealment? I will tell you a story. I remember one question-answer session with Baba. This was a period in which I was grinding out my *sadhana*, 'frying', as we called it. And there was a question about getting old. Baba said, 'Well, it appears that I won't be reborn. But if I were to be reborn, it would be terrific. I would get a new body and do my *sadhana* with great zest!'

From his perspective he was saying that doing *sadhana* is a great thing. Full of bliss! From the point of view of liberation, your *sadhana* is ecstatic. So Shiva would think, 'That's fabulous—to be an individual and struggle back to Shiva nature. Wow, great idea!'

My thinking was, 'That's okay for you to think, Baba, but from my perspective of bondage, *sadhana* is no joy, thank you!' As an individual you feel, 'Oh my, I don't want to do this. This is too hard'. But it's the best thing you can do. All other games are lesser. This one is the Big Game—the game of bondage and liberation, separation and oneness. Everything in the human condition looks completely different if grace is in the ascendancy. From Shiva's perspective, concealment doesn't seem like the bad idea it does from ours.

Now we are ready for an even more simplified view of creation. This one again has three central players: Shiva, Shakti and *nara* (*jiva*, the individual). *Nara* is Shiva, but doesn't know it—yet.

Female movie stars sometimes complain there are few good roles for women, but in this universe, Shakti has the most interesting role. She has a double nature. She is *both* concealment and grace.

In the illustration below, the downward arm represents the movement of concealment, variously described as *mala*, *kanchuka*, contraction and separation. But Shakti has a complex, peculiar nature. She also stars as the upward pointing arm, where She manifests as grace, *sadhana*, techniques of yoga (*upaya*) and expansion. She is accompanied in both roles by an entourage of language deities: the fearsome *ghora* and *ghoratari* energies that create tearing thoughts and negativity when She is in concealment, and the uplifting *aghora* energies, which include G-Statements, mantra, prayer and affirmation once She is in Her gracious mode. Such a goddess, with Her double-bladed axe, is formidable indeed and must be worshipped and propitiated appropriately.

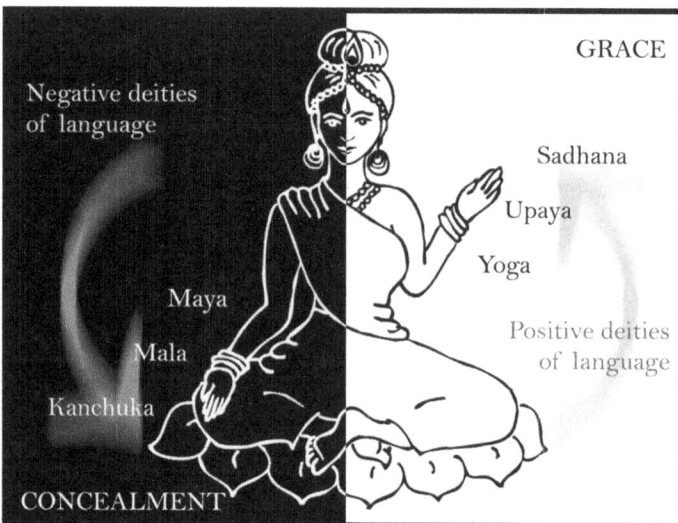

Shakti as Concealment and Grace. Formidable with Her double-bladed axe.

MEDITATION ON THE FIVE PROCESSES

Baba writes:

> The wise man contemplates the processes within himself and is soon intoxicated, identifying himself with Shiva. He sits calmly and watches the various thoughts arise in his mind. *Chiti* Herself becomes these thoughts. In the boundless expanse of Her blissful Consciousness, She creates and dissolves countless worlds. This is Her wonderful play.

Watch how thoughts come in, stay awhile, then disappear. The processes of creation, sustenance and dissolution are endless. The other two processes, concealment and grace, are the key, the secret. Watch how you constantly create separation and oneness. A thought comes in. It makes you feel sad or fearful. You experience concealment in the form of disharmony. Now you say the mantra, or have a pleasant thought, and you feel grace, oneness. In Shiva Process terms you are having downward and upward shifts. Keep watching these five processes. You can get to a place where, even when concealment occurs, it doesn't shake your sense of wholeness. Just like you, Lord Shiva does the five processes.

THE ESOTERIC FIVE PROCESSES AND SHAIVITE SELF-INQUIRY

Having described the five cosmic processes in *Pratyabhijnahridayam* Sutra 10, Kshemaraja discusses five esoteric processes in Sutra 11. While the five cosmic processes relate to the macrocosm, the five esoteric processes have to do with the way each of us experiences things that happen to us moment to moment. I regard this sutra to be the foundational text of Shaivite Self-inquiry—the Shiva Process. Let us look at Sutra 11:

> *Abhasana rakti vimarshana bijavasthapana vilapanatastani*
> As manifesting, relishing, experiencing as Self, settling of the seed, dissolution, these.

In the moment in which we experience anything, depending on our reaction, we create karma for ourselves and also happiness and unhappiness. It is well worth following Kshemaraja's argument carefully. Kshemaraja says:

> Whatever appears through the functioning of the Goddess of Sight and other perceptual functions is, so to speak, emanated, this is *abhasana* or manifesting.

If I look at this pen that I am holding, then I have *manifested* it. If I then turn my head and see a picture on the wall, now I have manifested that. (I have, at the same time, dissolved the pen, but we'll get to that later.) Or a thought comes into my mind: I have created that thought. That is *abhasana*, meaning creation, emanation or manifestation.

> An object being thus emanated, (that is brought forth into appearance), when (the Self) without shutting of the eye, relishes it for some time, it is maintained in experience till then by the Goddess of Maintenance. (This relishing of the experience for some time represents *sthiti*, or maintenance).

First you create it, and then you maintain it. Now I am 'relishing' my pen. It has a rich blue ink and copious flow so I can really relish it! First you create something, and then when it stays for a while it is sustained. Next is dissolution or withdrawal:

> It is withdrawn at the time of *vimarsha*, for which another word is sudden flash of delight, *chamatkara*. This knowledge of the object represents *samhara* (withdrawal).

When you enjoy the object, you have a flash of delight. The object is consumed in the delight. You destroy it, you take it back inside and uncreate it. Now it is a memory, it is no longer there. I have put my pen in my pocket so that I can no longer experience it in present time.

Jaideva Singh says:

> *Vimarshana* or *chamatkara* is the experience of 'Ahh, how wonderful!' It is like the delight of an artistic experience; hence it is called *chamatkara*, which means an intuitive flash of artistic experience.

Chamatkara refers to the delight we have in good food. By extension, it means *any* delight or agreeable experience. *Chamatkara* is the key to the aesthetic experience. It is withdrawal in the sense that we focus on the effect of an experience, while the experience itself is withdrawn.

Kshemaraja speaks of negative experiences also:

> However, if at the time of the reabsorption or withdrawal of the experience of manifoldness or differentiation, it—that is the object of experience—generates various *samskaras*, impressions of doubt, etc., inwardly, then it acquires the state of *samsara* in germ, which is bound to spring forth into existence again, and thus it superposes on the experient, the state of *vilaya*, concealment of the real nature of the Self.

Here is the basis of Shaivite Self-inquiry.

When you have a neutral experience, it happens and then it goes. It doesn't cause any waves or leave an impression. It simply withdraws and disappears. But another experience causes a wave, a negative vibration. There is an unpleasant impression left, which is stored within you. It could be doubt, fear, desire, anger or any negative colouring.

When you have an encounter with a person, if it is completely clean you walk away, no problem. But if there is a vibration of fear or hatred, then that goes into your unconscious and will come up again sometime. It is kept 'in germ, which is bound to spring forth into existence again'. It becomes a memory in seed form, which can become a tendency or repeating pattern of behaviour.

The brilliant English psychoanalyst and spiritual teacher, Maurice Nicholl, a disciple of Gurdjieff, understood this dynamic. He says:

> A negative impression will go to negative parts of centres. Impressions taken in of a person one freely dislikes will feed [the] negative emotional part. This then becomes stored with energy and will discharge itself on anyone from a trifling cause—i.e., one will become violent over nothing. We have to learn to take impressions in more consciously and not identify with negative impressions. Learn to be very careful in all this. People imagine that when no one is looking, they can indulge in as many negative thoughts as they like. In this way they increase negative emotions, which sooner or later will wish to rush forth and attack someone and hurt them. All negative emotions desire to hurt, and at the bottom of them are unlimited forms of violence.

Any situation in life that creates a negative vibration, an aftertaste, creates karma. Let us say you have a negative encounter with the grocer or someone, and then forget about it. The memory of that encounter is held inside. The emotional content comes up again. Something will trigger it later, perhaps by association of ideas. This creates a vicious cycle that tends to repeat.

Germ is a good word for it, because these latent emotions are like germs breeding. When we go through similar experiences they strengthen the tendency and increase our bondage. Every event that we assimilate with a negative emotion increases our karmic bank account.

While I was in Ganeshpuri with Baba I woke up to this mechanism. It fascinated me. It was the birth of a form of Self-inquiry that came alive in me. Self-inquiry involves looking at every event, every encounter, and asking, 'What is my present feeling?' 'What happened there?' 'How did that affect me?'

The question is, why do we become negative or toxic? From the Shaivite point of view we already are the Self, already positive. So it is our reaction, or, previous to that, our attitude, that makes us negative. The first task, then, is to know when we become toxic. Our next task is to get rid of the toxicity.

Some negative experiences at first don't seem negative. But they contain a hidden negative element, for example, a victory over another person. My tournament chess days come to mind. A win at chess implies a future loss. The ecstasy of victory is always accompanied by the agony of defeat for the opponent. At the same time, the fear of defeat colours the joy of victory. That kind of bliss is relative. It is the bliss of the ego and not the bliss of the Self. One part of Shiva is exultant, but another part of Shiva suffers.

In the same way, there are two kinds of humour. One is cruel and is at the expense of another. The other is uplifting and based on the human condition. The first creates karma, while the second produces a kind of spiritual experience. This was a painful lesson for me. I discovered that certain things I said, which I thought of as innocent, were actually hurtful. They held unconscious anger or judgment. Self-inquiry can distinguish these two kinds of humour and separate bliss of the ego from the bliss of the Self. Ego bliss always contains a painful or contracted element.

The 11th sutra of *Pratyabhijnahridayam* implies a microscopic, moment-by-moment analysis of our experience. Let us say you have an experience you would call enjoyable, but it is tinged with another element. You might detect a fear—a clinging, a yearning, or comparing the experience to a previous one, some little movement that contaminates it: perhaps a contraction, attachment or aversion. Or maybe a negative thought comes in, a doubt about the experience. Abhinavagupta says that, in general, Shiva has two ways of being: He hides or reveals Himself. Effective Self-inquiry can separate these two movements. Spiritually it is essential that you do. You will make extraordinary discoveries about what is really going on.

BURNING IT TO SAMENESS: HATHAPAKA AND ALAMGRASA

Kshemaraja continues:

> On the other hand, while it, i.e., the world, which has been reduced to a germinal form, is being held inwardly, and anything else that is experienced at that time, if it is burned to sameness with the fire of Consciousness by the process of *hathapaka* and by the device of

alamgrasa, then by bringing about perfection, the yogi enters the state of grace.

The yogi becomes aware that an impurity has entered him. Instead of letting that impurity affect him—his mood or behavior—he instead purifies it by yogic means. He burns it to sameness with Consciousness. He works with the feeling until whatever is painful or negative in it is processed. It is dissolved back into Consciousness until he is again at peace. Instead of using the feeling to attack or blame another, he dissolves it within himself by exposing it to the light of inquiry, and returns to peace. He might use mantra or any other yogic technique but in 'burning it to sameness', he eliminates the karmic element.

In Shiva Process we survey ourselves inwardly and discover places where we hold disharmony. Often we are not consciously aware of them. Our interactions or our attitude have created a tension in us that is visible when we look. It becomes clear that these unconsciously held tensions affect our life profoundly.

Gurdjieff discussed the same issues in terms of three forces. In his system, first force initiates a movement ('Let's do this'). It is met by second force, resistance ('I don't want to!'). It can be resolved by third force, which is grace, the resolving force ('I'll give you a dollar and an ice-cream').

The tension we feel is second force, blocked energy. This resistance is inherent in many, if not all, things in life. The yogic approach is not to push through second force, but to hold it within and work on it. 'Working on it' has a variety of meanings. Understanding is one of them. Once we understand something we can let it go or shift it. This is 'burning it to sameness'.

The text talks about two methods for bringing these 'germs' to oneness with Consciousness: *hathapaka* and *alamgrasa*. Here Abhinavagupta uses a gastric metaphor. In the stomach the digestive fire reduces all the heterogeneous foods to homogeneous sameness. In Consciousness, by the fire of yogic understanding, the yogi of the path of knowledge reduces the many to the one. *Hathapaka* and *alamgrasa* are not specific techniques but indicate a general approach. They imply any number of techniques.

Abhinavagupta says:

> All existing things hurled forcibly into the fire that rages in the stomach of one's own Consciousness, abandon all differentiation and feed the fire with the fuel of its own power. When the finite form

of all things is dissolved by this violent digestion, then the All, which feeds and sustains the divinities of Consciousness, becomes the ambrosia of immortality.

Hathapaka is a 'violent digestion' in which reality is devoured whole, in one gulp. *Alamgrasa* (*alam* = full, *grasa* = swallowing) is a complete and full swallowing of the world of differentiation until all separation and karmic residue have been consumed.

One myth tells us that Lord Shiva swallowed the poison that contaminated the ocean in order to save the world. His throat turned blue and He is called *Neelakantha*, (Blue-Throated One).

In our private universe we have to become Shiva. Fearlessly, we digest our moment-to-moment experience of life. We learn to live so cleanly that not a trace of emotional residue remains, no fear, desire, regret, nostalgia, rage or dissatisfaction.

Under normal circumstances, people will not do *hathapaka* when they swallow some poison. Usually, they will offload the feeling by dumping it on others, or escape it by diverting or drugging themselves.

The ashram of a *Siddha* is a different story. It traps seekers into *hathapaka*, offering no alternative. Of course, ashramites develop adaptive cunning and do what they can to escape, but ultimately the ashram places them face-to-face with their own experience.

One member of the ashram community, who is a schoolteacher, told me of a frustrating day at school where he was baited by some teenage boys. Instead of taking it inside, he erupted in rage at them. As a result, he felt humiliated and disempowered. Lashing out with anger seems strong but is actually weak. Another individual related an experience that took place at one of the many ashrams she has lived in. A work situation had gone sour and she felt misunderstood and manipulated. She took the feeling to her room and decided to hold it inside and try to break through. After a long and painful session filled with despairing prayer, the breakthrough happened and a light came in that dissolved her suffering. This is true *hathapaka*.

While ordinary people find themselves overwhelmed by negative situations and people, the sage can perform *hathapaka* and *alamgrasa*. He drinks the poison and has the inner skill to process all toxicity in the fire of his awareness.

Alamgrasa means full swallowing so that no seed, no germ of *samsara* remains. There will be no repetition because whatever has happened is gone. We will remember what happened, but it will have no control over us— whether consciously or unconsciously—because our relationship with it is emotionally clean.

Shiva Process work, like any disciplined Self-inquiry, is a form of *alamgrasa*. In every moment we drink the poison of the moment. We aspire to be like the swan in the *Vedas*, the *paramahamsa*, who separates the milk from the water and drinks only the milk; or the Vedic lotus that, growing out of the mud, nevertheless remains untouched by it. In practice we don't always achieve that. We want to drink the nectar of the Self but often end up with bitter draught.

When Self-inquiry is kindled in seekers they become intensely alive, intensely active. Their yogic awareness burns, assimilates, transforms and purifies. Individuals who have done Self-inquiry for a while become aware of every nuance of their reactions and feelings in every moment. This is not a form of narcissistic self-obsession, but a heightened awareness, like that of a woodsman who hears deeply into the sounds of the forest. Yogis of Self-inquiry are more aware of what is really happening than others. And they also have methods to deal with it—mantra, Self-remembering, *hathapaka* and *alamgrasa*.

When I watched my teacher meet people coming for his *darshan*, I saw someone who came fresh to every moment. The past was handled and let go, and he brought the full creative power of his love and Consciousness to every encounter.

In the martial arts you are trained to empty yourself so that you can meet whatever attack your opponent mounts, freshly and appropriately. You should not be encumbered by past memories or dysfunctional emotion. Each moment is a newly created universe, an arena of spontaneous action.

In the old EST training it was said you were not to be 'on it', that is, not to be positional. When you assume a position—intellectually or emotionally—you become hard and inflexible. You are tense and therefore beatable. But if you flow with situations and agree when you should agree, oppose when you should oppose, you minimise the negative. Even so, you are still going to get something on you. If you play in martial arts or if you live your life, you are going to get a few blows, aren't you? So you are going to have to do *alamgrasa*.

SHIVA VYAPTI: REALISATION IN SHAIVISM

One of Baba's favourite sutras was *Shiva Sutras* I.18:

Lokanandah samadhi sukham
The bliss of the world is the bliss of *samadhi*.

Sometimes Baba translated it as, 'The bliss of people is the bliss of *samadhi*'. The substance of what he meant was, if you know how to live normal life correctly you can experience bliss in that very life. Yogis go off to a cave, close their eyes, turn within and meditate, trying to attain that bliss. But you can experience that bliss in your life, and it is just like the bliss of the meditating yogi. That bliss is *jagadananda*, the bliss of the world. Shaivism says that it is not enough to go inside and experience bliss in your meditation; Shaivism calls that *atma vyapti*, merging in the Self. You have to go beyond that to what it calls *Shiva vyapti*, merging in Shiva as the world. *Shiva vyapti* is synonymous with *sahaja samadhi*, the natural state of liberation in life.

Baba would summarise his teaching by saying, 'Meditate on the Self, God dwells within you as you'. That was *atma vyapti*. He would also say, 'See God in each other'. That was a version of *Shiva vyapti*. To first honour your own Shiva nature and then to honour Shiva in others is the complete path.

Vijnanabhairava Dharana 77 says:

The same Self characterised by Consciousness is present in all the bodies; there is no difference in it anywhere. Therefore, a person realising that everything (in essence) is the same (Consciousness) is liberated.

In *Shiva vyapti* you take what you have attained inwardly, and bring it into your outer life. Some of us are better in life and some of us are better in meditation. Some of us find it easy to feel bliss in meditation but when we live our external life we get caught in anger and confusion. Others operate well in the world but cannot quiet their mind when they sit still. We have to be able to move in both the inner and the outer worlds to be complete.

Pratyabhijnahridayam Sutra 16 is about *Shiva vyapti*:

Chidananda labhe dehadishu chetyamaneshvapi chidaikatmya pratipatti dardhyam jivanmuktih
When the bliss of *Chit* is attained, the Consciousness of identity with *Chit* remains stable even while the body, etc., is being experienced. This state is *jivanmukti*, liberation even while one is alive.

A *Siddha*, a *jivanmukta* or liberated one, always moves towards the bliss of Consciousness. He makes that his first priority and it makes him a curious kind of person. I saw that in Baba. He was always centred in bliss and committed to bliss. He never lived for some lower end. Sometimes we sell out the bliss of Consciousness to some other thing; we don't prioritise our inner state above everything else. This happens when we want something so much that we go after it even at the cost of our inner bliss. Or the opposite might be true: we fear something so much that we avoid it at the expense of our inner bliss. In both cases we are selling out the bliss of Consciousness. Sutra 16 says, even while we are experiencing the body, even when we are in the waking state and moving about, we can remain in that space of natural *samadhi*.

Sutra 19 continues this theme:

> *Samadhi samskaravati vyutthane bhuyo bhuyash*
> *chidaikyamarshannityodita samadhi labhah*
> In *vyutthana*, which is full of the aftereffects of *samadhi*, there is the attainment of permanent *samadhi* by dwelling on one's identity with *Chit* (the universal, supreme Consciousness) over and over again.

Vyutthana means rising. Here you are rising up from meditation. You have had a deep meditation and the intoxication is still with you. In that intoxicated state you keep remembering the Self. The sutra tells us to remember the Self during ordinary life. In that way we stabilise in *sahaja samadhi*, the natural state of enlightenment.

In commenting on this sutra Kshemaraja says:

> A great yogi who has attained *samavesha* (that means one who has attained merger in the Self), is still full of the *samadhi* state. (Even when not meditating he is) still perceiving the entire mass of entities to be dissolving in the *Chit* sky, like a bit of cloud in autumn, reeling joyfully, owing to the persistent aftereffect of the savour of *samadhi*, like one intoxicated, resorting to introversion again and again and meditating on his identity with Consciousness.

Here the yogi gets up and, still feeling the aftereffects of profound meditation, reels around like a drunk, feeling the ecstasy, the intoxication of oneness. In conventional yoga the aspirant often sees the senses as a great enemy, their pull taking him away from the Self. But in this state, the great yogi uses the senses for communion with the world, which is nothing but divinity.

The *Saubhagyahridaya* makes this point with an extraordinary image:

> Shiva, seated in the heart, enjoys the marvellous things offered by the Goddess who comes and goes from the heart to the tips of the sense organs; the universe trembles in its turn with this same Consciousness: it is no longer anything but bliss, that of the Self.

Spanda Karikas Sutra II.5 describes the same *sahaja* state in a different way:

> He who has this realisation (that is identity of the Self with the whole universe) being constantly united with the divine, views the entire world as the play (of the Self, identical with Shiva) and is liberated while alive. There is no doubt about this.

All this is Shiva. All this is Shiva. That is the contemplation, again and again and again: 'I am Shiva; all this is my play; this is the play of my own awareness'.

Spanda Karikas Sutra II.7 continues:

> This alone is the acquisition of ambrosia leading to immortality; this alone is the realisation of Self; this alone is the initiation of liberation leading to identity with Shiva.

If comedians like to leave us laughing, and tragedians like to leave us reflecting deeply, yogis like to leave us soaring in Consciousness. The last aphorism in the *Shiva Sutras* (Sutra III.45) says:

> *Bhuyah syat pratimilanam*
> The yogi will again be united with his true Self; that is he will be reabsorbed in Shiva.

The *Pratyabhijnahridayam* Sutra 20 ends:

> *Tada prakashananda sara maha mantra viryatmaka purnahanta veshat sada sarva sarga samhara kari nija samvid deyata chakreshvarata praptirbhavatiti shivam*
> Then, as a result of entering into the perfect I, the perfect I-Awareness or Self, which is in essence light and bliss and of the nature of the power of the great mantra, there accrues the attainment of lordship over one's group of deities of Consciousness that brings about all emanation and reabsorption in the universe. All this is of the nature of Shiva.

That means that you gain control over your mind, your emotions and even your senses. Instead of leading you towards separation, they obey you and bring you to oneness. Your mind doesn't have tearing thoughts, but uplifting thoughts; it doesn't have attacking thoughts, but loving thoughts. That is gaining lordship over your Shakti, your own being, and all its faculties and powers. Wisdom and the Self are firmly in charge. You are not at the effect of your bad tendencies.

Spanda Karikas IV.1–2 says:

> I pay homage to that wonderful speech of my Guru which is like a boat for crossing the fathomless ocean of doubt and is full of words, which yield wonderful meaning. I offer my reverential prayer to *spanda*, in the form of *paravak*, the divine I-Consciousness which acts like a boat in crossing the fathomless ocean of doubt regarding my essential nature.

> The attainment of this treasure of knowledge, difficult of attainment and on its being well-preserved in the cave of the heart, it would always be for the good of all.

This knowledge is for the good of all and nourishing for the spirit. These texts and all the great Gurus point us to a place within, a capacity within, of divine Consciousness. Once we discover that place our joy is increased, our peace is increased and our wisdom is increased. Not only can we meditate deeply, but even our outer life takes on the characteristics of meditation. And we live it with joy, passion, love and scintillating intelligence.

MEDITATION ON THE ESOTERIC FIVE PROCESSES: DAILY REVIEW

Think about everything that happened to you today. Think about every encounter with people and if it is relevant, think about any strong thoughts or feelings you experienced. Sort your experiences according to how vivid they were, becoming aware of the three or four most dramatic events of the day, whether positive or negative.

Now take the most negative and dissonant event and examine the impression that was left with you when the experience was over. Name the emotion. See if you can burn it to oneness with Consciousness via gradual or sudden means. Persistent effort may be needed in some cases, while some may be solved by a quick insight.

This is a meditation that is profitable to do every night as a review of the day. It yields great insight.

Chapter 12

The Divine Narrator

> The Lord, one might say, is peaceful when the group of the *tattvas* are peaceful, excited when they are excited, and dazed when they are dazed. But from the transcendental point of view, He is not thus.
>
> Abhinavagupta, *Paramarthasara*, Verse 38

T he great sage Shankaracharya says:

> To taste within his own heart and in the external world, the endless bliss of the Self, such is the reward obtained by the yogi who has reached perfection and liberation in this life.

We are in bondage, not to our government or political system, but in bondage to certain limiting tendencies in our own mind, within our own spirit. Freud would call this our unconscious: tendencies of ignorance and blindness that have been passed on to us by our culture, our parents, trauma in youth, past lives—however you want to frame it. These limiting tendencies, which are subtle and hidden, imprison us. Yoga says that we can overcome them. Why overcome them? Because they cause us frustration, irritation and enervation. We realise only the smallest part of our potential if we don't overcome these limiting and binding factors.

Can we overcome these tendencies? Psychoanalysis says we can—up to a point. Yoga goes further. It says yes, indeed we can. Our true nature is free, superb, marvelous, full of joy. This very bondage keeps us from the experience of joy and luminosity.

When we go to sleep at night, when we attain deep sleep, we experience peace. Of course nobody says, 'I'm blissful', during sleep, but later we say, 'I was blissful'. So we are able to attain that within ourselves. Then we go out into the world and many things annoy us—so many irritating people, so many unfair things. Shankara says we can attain that peace not only within ourselves but also in the outer world. This is the reward of liberation, the glory of being a yogi.

The great Tukaram Maharaj sang:

> I've built my home in the realm beyond illusion. I live there eternally in that formless state. Liberated from the snare of this world, I have attained unbreakable union. My ego is vanquished forever. O Tuka, I have merged into perfection everlasting.

While most of us live separately in the realm of illusion, a great being, a *Siddha*, lives in the witness state beyond ego identification.

The Kashmiri sage Kshemaraja makes it practical. He says, 'Constant absence of depression, even while he remains in the body, is the glory of the great yogi'. Forget about the ideas of liberation or enlightenment. 'Absence of depression' is a great attainment and also very contemporary.

A narrative from Vedanta tells the story of liberation from wrong understanding. It is the story of a lion cub that strayed from his family and got lost in the woods. He was adopted by donkeys.

In those days the washermen used their donkeys to carry the washing. The older donkeys taught the lion cub how to do that and how to bray. The lion cub made a horrible donkey. His donkey family thought there was something essentially wrong with him. He needed some balancing, some therapy, because he couldn't bray well. He wasn't good at doing any of the donkey things. He felt that too, and had tearing thoughts: 'I'm a bad donkey. I'm a loser'. He took all the courses and workshops and tried earnestly to improve himself, but nothing worked.

Then one day a great lion came upon the scene. He saw all those donkeys in a row, carrying the wash, and there was the lion cub carrying the wash, too. And he was offended. He thought, 'What is he doing there?' and roared.

They all ran away, except the lion cub who was too naive. When he saw the lion he said, 'Don't eat me! Don't eat me!'

But the great lion said, 'No, no, no, come here with me', and took him to the river. He said, 'Look at our reflections in the river, what do you see?' The donkey-lion said, 'Oh, we look alike! Are you a donkey?'

And the lion said, 'No, you fool, you are a lion!'

The lion, of course, represents our true Self and the donkey represents our ego self. We play games, we worry, we bend ourselves to please other people. We don't have to do any of that: always we have that great glory within us. So the young lion awoke, began to roar and learned about his own true nature.

This is our story: we are lions that have become donkeys. The story of our soul's progress in this world is the story of a descent into something lower, something less than what we actually are; a loss of our glory.

In the Wordsworth poem, 'The Ode to Immortality', the child comes trailing clouds of glory from heaven and, as he becomes socialised, he loses it. We love young children because they have a divine quality, a memory of that oneness and ecstasy. As they get older, it falls away and they become neurotic like everybody else.

This is our story: we have come from something noble and become something contracted. This is no mystery to us. In our life-script, we are on the page where we've become contracted. But the rest of the story is the important part: we reclaim it. A great lion comes and tells us, 'You know, you're not that', and then we start to roar. That's the rest of the story. That's called yoga, awakening, spirituality. And we've come because we've had a taste of that, a knowledge of that, an intuition of that, and we want the rest of the story.

Cinderella is a similar story. Cinderella also was uncomfortable in her world, and she knew she belonged somewhere else. She felt like a donkey in that world, then awakened to another world. There are many such stories, cultural myths about people who don't know who they are and then awaken.

Baba told of a time during his *sadhana* when he was going through a phase of intense anger. He went to his Guru, Bhagawan Nityananda, and said, 'I'm experiencing a lot of anger'.

Nityananda replied, 'That's not you, that's not you at all'.

When I heard that story, those words resonated—'That's not you at all'. In fact, Baba had a lot of anger. Even after he became a world Guru he was legendary for his anger. It scared us half to death. So what was Bhagawan Nityananda saying about Baba's anger? He was saying your anger is not your essential truth. The part of you that gets jealous, the part of you that gets scared, the part of you that gets angry and won't forgive, the part of you that feels far from God, that has doubt, is not you at all. That is just your persona, a mask. The real you is the one who trusts, the one who loves, the one who is open. That is the real you. That is the story of human birth, and the sages are the only ones who tell us that story.

Any good narrative needs a villain for dramatic tension. When I grew up in Brooklyn we all followed baseball. We loved the Dodgers and hated the Yankees. But the Yankees won every year. It must have been boring for those Yankee fans with their suburban ranch-style houses and station wagons. The Dodger fans had bathtubs in their kitchens (It's a New York thing, you had to be there). Anyway, we loved to hate the Yankees. They were our villain, the obstacle that made things interesting.

In Shaivism, the villain, the dramatic element, is ignorance—maya. It is the power of maya that differentiates and creates limitation. Because of maya, individual souls are deprived of their power. Their sovereign freedom is hidden by their own maya. Our own maya, delusion, inhibits us, as in the saying, 'You are your own worst enemy'. We often see this when athletes defeat themselves psychologically. They lose when they could or should easily have won.

We do that, too. When an individual is strongly affected by this impurity, he feels he is lost and worth nothing as a human being. He feels as though he is a helpless victim of circumstances. In reality, he himself has created the circumstances as a consequence of his past actions. It is an ironic situation. At first it doesn't seem possible, it seems as if the world is simply stacked against you. But after you have been meditating awhile you see deeper. You see that you create circumstances somehow unconsciously, out of your own karma. You foul your own straw, then you want to run away from your own creation, which is only your own reflection.

Jiddu Krishnamurti says, 'The very activity of the mind is a barrier to its own understanding'. Our own mind, with its attitudes, its judgments, its endless chatter, creates the block. We meditate to become still and go *deeper* than the mind. If we detach from the mind we can reach the wellspring of wisdom and clarity that exists within us. Our minds are useful but not always reliable. So it's good to become quiet and drop back from the mind in meditation, to become the witness of the mind. Then we get in touch with the lion in us. Then intuitions flow from that deeper place and new understandings emerge.

THE DOCTRINE OF RECOGNITION

In my past I was a literary person. I taught literature and was a literary scholar. In my studies of Shaivism, I became aware that one of the main texts we look at, the *Pratyabhijnahridayam* is actually a literary narrative. It's an exciting story.

Pratyabhijnahridayam means, the *Heart of the Doctrine of Recognition*. It is Kshemaraja's short summary of the philosophy of Self-recognition in Kashmir Shaivism. What is recognition? It is looking in the mirror and seeing that you are a lion (if you are a lion). It is to remember again who you really are: 'That's not who you are, this is who you are'.

The school of Self-Recognition says that the Self is always present, even now, but we don't recognise it. When we do recognise who we really are, everything is transformed. The *Pratyabhijnahridyam* indicates that when the seeker knows the Self directly, he stands face-to-face with himself. Ultimately it tells us that no new 'Self' has to be discovered, sought or created. Our familiar old Self is the very one we seek—we have simply been guilty of wrongly identifying it with the body and the ego rather than Shiva.

Utpaladeva, the originator of Self-recognition, says:

> Because of ignorance, the 'I' in the limited subject has never before been looked upon as the Lord. This teaching, through bringing the powers to light, prompts people to do so.

Kshemaraja's first two sutras in *Pratyabhijnahridayam* say:

> Supremely independent, universal Consciousness is the cause of the universe.

> Of its own free will, this universal Consciousness unfolds the universe on its own screen.

The basic stuff of the universe is universal Consciousness. The physicists would say it is universal energy, but Shaivism says that not only is this energy energetic, but it is also conscious. It is aware; it is not material.

You know by direct experience that you have Consciousness. It sits firmly on your neck. You've got a miraculous capacity to see, to understand, to think and to contemplate. Western science seems to assume that Consciousness evolved from matter. Shaivism says that Consciousness is primary and prior to all matter. Everything in the universe is part of universal Consciousness; there is nothing apart from it.

THE NARRATOR

Now let me ask you this: who is speaking in this text? Who says that universal Consciousness created the universe out of its own free will and on its own screen? Who is talking here? The *narrator* is speaking. In a novel, there is a voice, a sometimes invisible character, that tells the story. Certain novels are narrated in the first person— 'I did this and I did that'. That kind of narrator doesn't know everything that is going on. He is a character in the novel. Sometimes the reader knows more than that narrator. Other novels are told from the point of view of the omniscient narrator, who is privy to the secret thoughts of all the characters. He says, 'And then Emma thought this', and 'Mr Darcy felt—', and so on. That narrator is not a character in the novel. He is the author. Actually, the omniscient narrator is really God.

In the *Pratyabhijnahridayam* the narrator is Shiva. He tells us what happens and despite all danger he always knows that everything is okay. The *Pratyabhijnahridayam* has another character, the protagonist. *He* doesn't know that everything is okay. Like any character in a novel, he goes through a period of suffering and loss.

The scholar Kamalakar Mishra says, 'When a brilliant light passes through a curtain it becomes dim. The more transparent the curtain, the brighter the light becomes. When impurity is removed, the more the light of the Self shines, the greater is Self-realisation'. It is a nice metaphor. Light is within us and our personality, our mind, is like a curtain that obscures it. As we grow in Self-knowledge, it gets more gauzelike, more transparent, and the light comes through. Whenever I have met a great soul, what is remarkable is the light, the aliveness, the luminosity that comes from him or her. And we, too, have that same light, though it may be hidden. Even in our present state we always have some amount of Self-realisation, for Consciousness is working in and through us.

This is what the narrator of the *Pratyabhijnahridayam* says. He is not the kind of narrator that says, 'Oh, things are getting really bad for the hero: he's neurotic, penniless and miserable and living in a dive off 42nd Street'. Our narrator keeps saying, 'Even then the light shines in him'. You know, a good editor might have helped him because he destroys the tension! He keeps telling you that everything is fundamentally perfect. 'It's okay even then . . . even then it's okay, even then there's light'. But this is not a novel, and the narrative has a different purpose.

In life, we may sometimes lose faith. A best-selling book is titled, *Why Do Bad Things Happen to Good People?* In *Paradise Lost*, John Milton attempted to 'justify the ways of God to man'. You could point to many horrible events in the world, but the narrator always sees things from inside the divine perspective. That same narrator operates in us and explains our life the way the narrator of the sutras does. But events and our emotional reactions to them often drown him out. He is the Witness, the Voice of the Self. He makes G-Statements. He gives understandings from the divine, holistic perspective.

Let us look at Shiva's story in the *Pratyabhijnahridayam*. The text describes a war between opposite movements. Essentially it is a struggle between wisdom (or expansion) and ignorance (or contraction) that shows up clearly in the vocabulary of the sutras.

KEY WORDS IN THE PRATYABHIJNAHRIDAYAM

In the right column are the negative words used in the 20 sutras. Read down that column. Kshemaraja doesn't use the word evil the way some of the other religious narrations do. He uses the word 'contracted', which is one of the worst words in this system.

The negative words refer generally to contraction, limitation and ignorance. A person so afflicted becomes a 'transmigratory being'. That is somebody who gets reborn endlessly because he is still on the wheel of desire. What did Bob Dylan say? 'What is the price you have to pay to keep from going through all these things twice?'

'Deluded by one's own powers' is a great phrase. I love that. We delude ourselves with our own thoughts and feelings. There is no external enemy. Now look at the 'positive' column. The phrase, 'as Shiva does', is the narrator saying, 'you do it just like Shiva does'. The individual human being is just like Shiva in some way, is just like that divine being. Then Consciousness turns in, 'inward movement', acquires Consciousness, 'inherent power of *Chiti*', and 'bliss'. Finally our hero attains *samadhi* and Self-realisation and mastery, 'perfect I-Consciousness'.

The text offers more positive terms than negative ones. That is because its task is grace-bestowal. It is heavily weighted towards the highest truth. Here in this set of terms is the dramatic conflict and resolution of the narrative.

POSITIVE / GOOD (EXPANDED)	SUTRA	NEGATIVE / EVIL (CONTRACTION)
supremely independent	Sutra 1	
free will unfolds	Sutra 2	
	Sutra 4	contracted
	Sutra 5	descending contraction
	Sutra 6	maya
	Sutra 9	limitation of Shakti *mala*-covered
as Shiva does	Sutra 10	
	Sutra 12	transmigratory being deluded by own powers ignorance
full knowledge inward movement rising to universal Consciousness	Sutra 13	
fire of *Chiti* burns the fuel of the known	Sutra 14	descends covered by maya
acquiring inherent power of *Chiti* assimilates the universe	Sutra 15	
bliss of *Chit* attained identity with *Chit* liberation	Sutra 16	
unfoldment of the centre	Sutra 17	
samadhi attain permanent awareness dwelling on identity with universal Consciousness	Sutra 19	
enter perfect I-Consciousness light and bliss power of the great mantra attainment of lordship over one's group of deities of Consciousness all this is Shiva	Sutra 20	

Key Words in the Pratyabhijnahridayam

THE PLOT OF THE PRATYABHIJNAHRIDAYAM

Let's follow the *Pratyabhijnahridayam* narrative. (For the text of the *Pratyabhijnahridayam,* see Appendix B.) The first two sutras describe the divine cosmology of Consciousness. The third sutra is fairly neutral. It says that the universe is one and now has become many, but our hero is still comfortable. The fourth sutra says that the individual in whom Consciousness is contracted, still has the universe as his body in a contracted form. The narrator tells us that things are not yet too bad. Even though we are contracted, we are a lot like Shiva.

But with the fifth sutra it gets bad. Suffering begins. *Chiti* Itself, Consciousness Itself, descending from its stage of perfect expansion, becomes *chitta* (the mind) through the process of contraction. Now our hero has his first really bad day. Universal Consciousness becomes *chitta,* your mind. This is a significant statement. Universal Consciousness, which creates and underlies the whole universe, has become your little mind. The ocean has withdrawn and left a puddle on the beach. But it is the same water. Your mind, your awareness, is exactly like universal Consciousness. There is not one bit of difference between them, except that it's a smaller, more limited thing. There is something else here: the hint that by examining awareness you can know the highest truth. You can know Shiva by examining your own awareness. This is perhaps what the Bible meant when it says that we are created in His own image. If you want to know what divine awareness is like, just look at the limited form of it inside yourself.

Immediately after this strong statement about contraction, the narrator makes the point that even in this contracted state of the world there are still hints of grace, hints of expansion. In Sutra 8 he says the positions of all the different philosophies are only various roles of Consciousness of Self. So all systems of thought, all doctrines, all religions—each of them has a bit of truth. It is not that one is true and the others are false. Everything is Consciousness, everyone's world view makes sense. Every understanding makes sense to the person who holds it. Yes, there is delusion, but there is also logic in it.

The ninth sutra is the lowest point, where our hero bottoms out. It is the darkest hour. The narrator says:

> In consequence of its limitation of Shakti, Reality, which is all Consciousness, becomes the *mala*-covered transmigrating individual soul.

This is a shattering, accurate analysis of suffering. It is limitation of energy. Do you know the feeling that happens when you lose energy, like air going out of a balloon? Have you ever had a project that you have had huge enthusiasm for and then discovered that it couldn't happen? Or your husband or wife said, 'No, no, no. That's silly!' Or you had your own negative thought, 'Oh, it's probably no good'. That is loss of Shakti, loss of energy. It is a downward shift. The narrator tells us that the hero, the Lord, has become small and pitiful—his expansive energy has contracted. This is the low point of the drama. We are just about midway through the sutras, we're at the ninth sutra, and now the hero is without any Shakti. He has to claw his way back.

But wait! Here again in the next sutra (Sutra 10) is the divine compassionate voice of the narrator telling us things are still okay.

> But even then the individual soul performs the fivefold act as Shiva does.

I have described the fivefold act in the last chapter. What is happening in this dramatic moment here between Sutras 9 and 10? The hero is thinking, 'I'm miserable, I've lost everything'.

But the narrator turns to us, the audience, and confides in an aside, 'He thinks it's bad, but look, even now he is still a lot like Shiva. He is still doing Shiva-like things. He's thinking, he's acting, he's feeling; he does the fivefold act; he's doing all those things that Shiva does'. The narrator tells us, 'See, even there, there is hope'.

After this message of hope from a higher perspective, Sutra 12 vividly returns to the hero's state of contraction:

> To be a transmigratory being means being deluded by one's own powers because of (one's own ignorance).

The hero is deluded and his delusion is not the result of external forces, but rather his *own* powers. His mind, his emotions, his intuition, which should all lead him to the light, have betrayed him and misled him.

THE TURN

After rock bottom comes the turn. In the 13th sutra, well past the midpoint, the voyage of the hero starts to turn around.

The narrator says:

> Acquiring full knowledge, *chitta* itself by inward movement becomes *Chiti* by rising to the status of universal Consciousness.

A fantastic turn of events, a powerful upward shift. Earlier, we learned that *Chiti*, universal Consciousness, by turning outward becomes the individual mind. The mind gets caught in the outer world of senses and, comparing himself to other people, becomes limited. Now, at this stage of the hero's process he turns within and meditates; he leaves the outer, goes inside and expands back to That. He's had a good meditation, he's found his true nature, he turns within and experiences the Self as universal Consciousness. Like the fairy tale, this is a hero who is of noble birth but who thought he was a commoner. He is a lion who thought he was a donkey.

Sutras 5 and 13 make a wonderful pair. They encompass everything in Shaivism. In Sutra 5, universal Consciousness contracts and becomes the mind. In Sutra 13, the mind, by an inward movement in meditation, becomes again universal Consciousness.

Let's do a small experiment. Often when you meditate, you might start repeating your mantra or visualise something and the mind creates all kinds of thoughts that distract you. Right now, notice what happens the very first moment you turn within. Let's verify what Sutra 13 claims. See if there's an expansion. Observe exactly what happens and notice, if there is a movement, where it takes place—is it in your head, your chest, your navel area? What is the nature of the movement? Try it several times. Open your eyes, look around. Close your eyes again. Is there an inner shift of any kind? A change in feeling? Any kind of change? This is inner research. Is Kshemaraja right? Do you feel that movement in the first moment of turning inward?

The narrator says in Sutra 14, a charming sutra:

> The fire of *Chiti*, even when it descends to the lower stage, though covered by maya, partly burns the fuel of the known.

Even when things are at their worst, signs of divinity are there. Even when an individual thinks he's a commoner, he still has nobility of spirit. He lives on the streets of New York as a homeless person, still, he performs a kindness to another homeless person: he shows his inherent nobility.

Then comes the triumphant upward sweep in Sutras 15 to 17. They say:

> By acquiring the inherent power of Consciousness, he assimilates the universe to himself.

> When the bliss of Consciousness is attained, he becomes one with Consciousness and attains liberation, even while alive.

And by the unfoldment of his centre, he attains the bliss of Consciousness.

By nurturing his higher nature, not his lower nature, by meditating daily, by doing practices, by working with his mind to move it in positive rather than negative directions, he attains his natural birthright, his Shiva nature.

The 18th sutra is a key one:

Herein are a variety of means for unfolding the centre and knowing the Self . . .

It says, 'Here's how you do it'. Until then, it's a fairytale. First our hero gets contracted and then he gets expanded. But somebody might say, 'Okay, Shiva, Mr Smart Guy Narrator, how do you do it? You've been in jail, then you're free, there must be a way'. So if you've been in prison, there must be a practical means of escape. The 18th sutra says, 'Have a buddy send in a cake with a file in it'. It says, 'Have someone come in and give you a disguise and you can leave. Have a confederate sitting under the wall in a getaway car!' It gives techniques of meditation. It is full of methods of *sadhana*, which I will further discuss in the next chapter.

In the post-*samadhi* state called *vyutthana*, which is full of the aftereffects of *samadhi*, there is the attainment of permanent awareness of the Self by dwelling on one's identity with the universal Consciousness over and over again. (Sutra 19)

The 19th sutra says now that you are free, you might have a transitional period where you are a bit wobbly, like our hero. It says that you should keep dwelling on your true identity again and again. Keep thinking, 'I am Shiva, I am Shiva', until you feel really established in it. At first our hero says, 'I am a lion, I am a lion', but sometimes the thought comes up, 'I am a donkey'. If something goes wrong he immediately thinks, 'I am a donkey'.

Likewise, even after you have practised for some time, your donkey consciousness can come up. 'Oh, I'm a donkey, I'm quitting, I'm leaving, I'm a donkey. I can't live in this lion world'. It does come up, so you have to keep remembering, 'I am a lion, I am a lion', for as long as the donkey tendency is there.

Someone once complained to a sage about how long the path was—it seemed to have no end. The sage said, 'It's not the path that is long but your ignorance is long!' He could also have said that the path is exactly as long as your ignorance.

Shiva Sutras 1.17 says:

vitarka atmajnanam
Conviction is knowledge of the Self.

To gain that conviction we must continually bathe our minds in higher wisdom.

THE GOAL

And in the last sutra in the *Pratyabhijnahridayam,* the 20th, the narrator describes the hero-as-realised-being:

> As a result of entering into the perfect I-Consciousness, which is in essence light and bliss and of the nature of the power of the great mantra, there accrues the attainment of lordship over one's group of deities of Consciousness. All this is of the nature of Shiva.

I will discuss the esoteric statement, 'the attainment of lordship over one's group of deities' in the chapter, Shakti Chakra. It means you have full control over all aspects of your mind. You don't allow your mind to work against you, to attack you, to put you down. You don't let your mind defeat you with tearing thoughts in whatever enterprises you undertake. You have control over it. You make it work for you, not against you. Then you have great power and effectiveness.

I often refer to tearing thoughts. These are thoughts that attack us, like 'I am weak. I am worthless. I am no good. That other person is better than I am'. Tearing thoughts are an extraordinary psychological phenomenon. When cells take the wrong path and start to attack the organ they live in, we call it cancer. Tearing thoughts are a kind of autoimmune failure of the mental body. The mind, which should be used for our benefit—solving problems, understanding issues, writing poetry—instead turns against us with devastating effect. Enemies are insignificant when our own minds tear into us.

If there is a single phenomenon that epitomises being deluded by your own energies, it is tearing thoughts. A tearing thought is a terrorist who has already penetrated your deepest defence system and lives in your hometown with vile intentions. If you could stop this one tendency you would be entirely transformed. When we have a failure in life, it is not so much the defeat that brings us down, but what we take it to mean about ourselves. We say, 'Oh I lost that game, therefore I'm worthless'. We have a tantrum, we take to our bed, we make everyone suffer for miles around. The one who suffers most is us. If we didn't have tearing thoughts, we would simply say, 'Now what can I learn from that? That's good, I'll do that next time'. And we move on cleanly and clearly.

If you are successful in some aspect of your life and if you examine your inner process, you will discover that you are not afflicted by tearing thoughts in that area. We defeat ourselves by getting caught in the pernicious downward spiral of tearing thoughts. Overcoming tearing thoughts is true lordship over our deities of Consciousness. How to do it? Through yogic practices and by constantly contemplating your Shiva nature.

So that is the story of the Hero of Recognition. In some sense, the hero has merged spiritually with the narrator. It is a pity that the narrator doesn't say at this point, 'And folks, that little boy was me!' But I'm sure when they make the movie, Hollywood will improve the ending.

Abhinavagupta tells the same story in a different way. He says:

> The consciousness of an individual is limited to the mind, intellect and ego. These function in thought-forms under the power of maya, whose main characteristic is the making of differentiation. Still it is also inspired by divine Shakti. If the limited ego of the individual adopts a pure thought like the following: 'I am present everywhere, everything is in me', then by constant persevering determination, his thought-dominated maya will end in the thought-free, intuitive state.

G-statements like, 'I am present everywhere', 'Everything is in me', are statements that come from a higher source and reconnect us to our true nature. We have to salt our awareness with these statements or we will sink into the mundane and limited. They help us overcome the tendency towards negativity that depletes us of our Shakti, our spiritual energy.

Do that contemplation with intent. Be like the narrator and find supporting evidence for it. The Voice of Tearing Thoughts is an alternative narrator—the Narrator from the Dark Side. He always seeks evidence that you are a fool, evidence that you are incompetent, evidence that you are a loser. And he calls attention to it at every opportunity. 'There, see, you are a loser!' But that is not the narrator of this text. This narrator says, 'You're a winner, you're great, you're noble, you're sublime', and finds that evidence. So we have to have the right narration, the right voice-over as the accompaniment to our life. This is the right one: 'I am the Self, I am Consciousness, I am present everywhere. Everything is in me'.

MEDITATION ON YOUR SHIVA NATURE

Each of us is the hero of Pratyabhijnahridayam. *We have recognised our Shiva nature. If you have a feel for it, meditate with Abhinavagupta's statement, 'I am present everywhere, everything is in me'. This takes subtle intellect. I perceive the whole world via my awareness, therefore my awareness is everywhere. As the hero, you have investigated yourself and you have recognised your Shiva nature. Go deep within, with the understanding, 'I am Shiva'. Meditate for 10 minutes.*

Chapter 13

Methods of Meditation I: Pratyabhijnahridayam Sutra 18

> Thus awakened by the power of mystic insight, he sacrifices all dualistic thoughts in the luminous flame of the Self, and becomes identical to that light.
>
> Abhinavagupta, *Paramarthasara*, Verse 68

When we say universal Consciousness it is a phrase that is almost too big and too spacious. I like to think from the inside out, which is also the way Shaivism works, from your consciousness to God. Start small, look at yourself. Don't speculate about God, know yourself. Don't think about universal Consciousness, look at your own consciousness.

Abhinavagupta says:

> Consciousness is the perfect medium of reflection. The light of Shiva's Consciousness is like an infinite perfectly polished mirror in which everything in the universe, every thought, feeling, moment and person is reflected.

Your consciousness is a perfect medium of reflection. The light of *your* consciousness is like a perfectly polished mirror in which everything is reflected. If I say, 'think of an orange', immediately, as in a perfectly polished mirror, your mind can think of an orange. There is a story that Baba used to tell about the Guru who told his disciple, when you meditate, don't think of a monkey. Of course, when he sat to meditate all he could think of was a monkey. Baba said you should not meditate like that. Consciousness just grabs and reflects these things. Take a moment and think about the wonder of your own awareness, how it reflects things, sees things, understands, remembers, broods, feels. It does so many functions, it is so plastic—and extraordinary.

Abhinavagupta says:

> In the same way as the mirror underlies everything in the reflection, so God as Consciousness, pervades everything reflected in it.

When you look in a mirror you see many images, but when you analyse it, you know that the mirror underlies it all. In the same way our awareness underlies everything we experience. On the macro level—on the level of the universe—universal Consciousness underlies everything.

Abhinava continues:

> The only difference being that there is no outer object reflected in Consciousness, the original object is also a reflection.

This is a mind bender! There must always be an object that the mirror reflects. But Consciousness has no object outside of itself. Consciousness simply takes that shape. Your mind doesn't have to see an automobile to think of an automobile. Maybe at some point it saw an automobile. But your own awareness can take the shape of an automobile. Your mind can also invent something you never saw. This is one mystery of awareness.

The practice of yoga is to learn the rules of our own awareness from inside it. How do I work? Why am I happy? Why am I sad? Why do I get angry? Why do I get depressed? How can I be in a good space most of the time? How can I avoid bad spaces? These are important questions that we don't often ask. Instead, we ask questions like, 'How can I get ahead?' 'How can I make a lot of money?' 'How can I meet Mr Right?' 'How can I have a successful career?' Those questions are important. I am not the kind of yogi who disparages such questions, but there are questions to ask first, like, 'How does my own consciousness work?' 'How do my emotions work?' 'How does my mind work?' These are primary. When we can answer them it becomes easier to find Mr Right, and the right career and the right car.

Richard Wilbur, a modern poet, was a hero of mine in the 1960s. He says:

> Mind in its purest play is like some bat
> That beats about in caverns all alone,
> Contriving by a kind of senseless wit
> Not to conclude against a wall of stone.

It has no need to falter or explore;
Darkly it knows what obstacles are there,
And so may wave and flitter, dip and soar
In perfect courses through the blackest air.

And has this simile a like perfection?
The mind is like a bat. Precisely. Save
That in the very happiest intellection
A graceful error may correct the cave.

The mind is like a bat in the dark, wandering around. It could always beat itself against the wall of the cave. You know, 'blind as a bat'. The mind is like that. When the mind goes negative it turns against us. It goes around in its own world, sometimes avoiding the sides of the cave and sometimes smashing against them.

Wilbur says, '. . . in the very happiest intellection, A graceful error may correct the cave', which is a way of talking about grace. The mind is usually caught within its own limits, but sometimes experiences an expansion or intuition of something higher.

The *Pratyabhijnahridayam* talks about the drama of Consciousness: the great Lord Shiva undergoes an experience of contraction and suffering, then rediscovers Himself and moves back to His rightful nature. Shaivism says we are that very One, lost in the middle of that narrative. We are right now in the part of the drama where we suddenly awaken to the problem.

The lives of great saints are archetypal because you can see the whole drama of everyone in them. The Buddha, for example, had a privileged upbringing. He was a prince and lived mechanically for awhile with everything anyone could want. Then an awakening occurred. He became aware of aspects of life his father had kept from him. No matter what he did, how rich, successful or powerful he was, he would not be able to overcome the suffering inherent in the fabric of life: old age, disease and death. He awoke to his real situation. With resolve to understand his true nature, he began his search.

In that moment the journey takes a turn. Like the Buddha, we run on our programming, we are on automatic pilot. Then, something awakens us to the idea that there is more to life than we have been told. We want it and seek it. It is mysterious and elusive. Then somehow, through some grace, we discover that there is a path and we start to explore it. The pattern is archetypal, but each individual story is unique. Then the soul is on its journey back.

In the *Pratyabhijnahridayam*, Sutra 18 is unique. It is the sutra of transformation: it offers concrete practices and meditation techniques.

Here at the ashram, we have a traditional evening chant, the *Arati*. At the end of the chant, the custom is to bow to the altar where we have the pictures of the Gurus of our tradition. Bowing is strange to Westerners, but in India, people love to bow not only to the Guru or a *sadhu* or sage, they also bow to their mother and father. It is a cultural symbol of respect. Around Baba people used to say it is good for the ego, it puts the head below the heart. They tried to find an acceptable explanation.

I noticed one person was not bowing after *Arati*. She told me it was hard for her to bow. I said, 'It's easy. Put your feet about shoulder-width apart. Get your weight forward and then move down to your knees, pretending there is a contact lens on the floor'. She was making it too important.

She went away and later came back, 'I can't bow to myself and I can't bow to God', she said. 'I have a block there. But I can bow to the path.'

I agreed it was a good solution. I also bow to the path of yoga. The path of yoga is such saving wisdom, so uplifting that I bow to it everyday. Bowing is not important, but a person should be free enough to bow or not to bow when it's appropriate.

In Ganeshpuri, we used to bow to Baba when we saw him for the first time each day. Once someone told him she didn't always feel devotion for him, she didn't feel like bowing. And he told her, it doesn't matter. Just do it. Don't worry about it. He was saying, be simple, don't break your brain over something like that. Don't wait till you have the correct emotion. Just do it and forget about it. Or don't do it. He was practical that way.

Anyway, the 18th sutra represents the path and I bow to that path. This is practice. The great Zen master Dogen says:

> Although the Buddha nature is amply present in every person, unless one practises it is not manifested. Unless there is realisation it is not attained.

The Buddha nature is the Self. We do have to practise. Even though the Self is present, we have to overcome our bad tendencies—the negative habits of mind—to establish ourselves there.

VIKALPA-KSHAYA: THE DISSOLUTION OF THOUGHT-FORMS

In Sutra 18, Kshemaraja begins by describing an easy means to unfold awareness. Using this means an aspirant 'can shatter all the fetters of rigorous disciplines like *pranayama*', and other difficult yoga practices.

Kshemaraja writes:

> The aspirant should keep his mind focused on pure awareness, restraining the differentiating thought-forms that take him away from his real nature. By not thinking of anything at all, by seizing the thought-free state, he will become used to regarding his awareness *(Chit)* as the real knower and not his body/mind. In a short time he will attain absorption in deep meditation.

This is *vikalpa-kshaya*, the dissolution of thought-forms. The point is to keep the mind still, to focus on awareness itself, not the individual thoughts. The mind continually creates thought-forms, *vikalpas*. Kshemaraja says to focus on the *avikalpa* state, the state without *vikalpas*.

Pure awareness can be found in the space between two thoughts and also the space between two breaths. It is also the background of the mind that is *prior* to the mind. It is the witness of the mind or the container of the mind.

Maheshwarananda says:

> The intermediary state suspended between the object left and that which one hasn't yet attained there, O Mother! is that which (the yogis) consider to be Your nondual reality.

The space between two thoughts is a pause so the slate can be clean and another thought can come. You have to clean the whiteboard before you write your next thing. That little space between two thoughts is pure awareness.

It is a fallacy to think that you have to strangle the mind to get to this state. Simply look at the part of your mind that is peaceful and thought-free. Even though part of the mind is producing thoughts, focus on the part of the mind that is thought-free. Ignore the thoughts. My Guru once told me that thoughts were not the problem. I should focus on the Self and pay less attention to the thoughts.

Kshemaraja uses the word *hridaya*, which means 'heart'. Jaideva Singh explains:

> *Hridaya* here does not mean the physical heart, but the deepest Consciousness. It has been called *hridaya*, or heart, because it is the centre

of reality. It is the light of Consciousness in which the entire universe is rooted. In the individual, it is the spiritual centre.

Kshemaraja quotes *Ishvara-Pratyabhijna*:

> By giving up *vikalpa* and by one-pointedness of mind, one gradually reaches the stage of mastery.

The *Spanda Karikas* say that when there is no *kshoba*, mental agitation, then occurs the highest state. Notice it does not say no *mentation*, it says no *mental agitation*. It is natural for the mind to produce images. When there is no negative thrust to the process, the state of the Self is attained. Thought-forms do not obstruct the Self when there is peace with no agitation.

Kshemaraja quotes *Jnanagarbha*:

> When, O Mother, men renounce all mental activities and are poised in a pure state, then by Thy grace is that Supreme State realised at once, which rains down the nectar of undiminished and unparalleled happiness.

The 'nectar of undiminished and unparalleled happiness'. Not bad. This technique and similar ones, are *shambhavopaya*, the meditation of Shiva. Shiva is thought-free awareness, *prakasha*, or supreme light. When a yogi meditates on that awareness and makes that awareness his method, he is practising *shambhavopaya*. It is the highest means, since it transcends thought. This *shambhavopaya* method is popular in Zen and is called Dzogchen in Tibetan Yoga. It is direct but relatively difficult, so Kshemaraja descends a notch or two and offers other methods.

He says:

> If many means are described someone may enter (the state of *samavesha*, or divine Consciousness) through any one of them.

The sages are compassionate. They offer many paths, many ways, a menu of possibilities. You also should be very agile in your spiritual practice. Don't worry about what is not working for you on a particular day, look for what is working for you. Go with what works. There is always a way, by skilful means, to focus the mind—or almost always.

MEDITATION I: VIKALPA-KSHAYA

Let's investigate for a moment. Close your eyes and go inside. Where do you locate the very core of your being, your centre? There is no right answer. Just look for it. Where in the body is it? While you are there, what's it like? You might find it in the third eye or the heart, or the top of the head, the energy centre called the sahasrara. *What is it like? A solid mass? A vibrant mass? Don't follow your thoughts. Stay with your awareness. Looking in, what is the shape of your inner being? Who are you in yourself, without reference to your body? Now look at your mind as though from a distance, as though it were someone else's mind. Now open your eyes. That is* vikalpa-kshaya.

SANKOCHA OF SHAKTI

Kshemaraja's next two techniques are in the method of *shaktopaya*, the way of Shakti. *Shaktopaya* techniques work within the mind, in the realm of language. In Kashmir Shaivism the letters of the alphabet are considered creative *shaktis*. Shiva is the pure light of awareness *(prakasha)* and Shakti is Self-reflexive intelligence or languaging *(vimarsha)*. In both *sankocha* (contraction) and *vikasa* (unfoldment) of Shakti, the meditator works with his energy to attain the Self.

Kshemaraja writes:

> The *sankocha* of Shakti means turning in towards the Self, by (withdrawing the Consciousness), which is spreading externally through the gates of the senses (towards the objects).

In this technique we pull back our awareness and don't let it go outside. Kshemaraja quotes the *Katha Upanishad*:

> The Self-Existent One pierced the openings (of the senses) outward.
> Hence one looks outward, not within one's Self.
> Some wise man, wishing to taste immortality
> With reverted eyes (i.e., looking within)
> Beholds the immanent Self.

God could not experience the physical world because He had no senses. He had to assume a body equipped with senses in order to experience the world. He is looking through *your* senses at the world.

This meditation is reminiscent of one taught by the great sage, Patanjali, in his *Yoga Sutras. Yogas-chitta-vritti-nirodhah:* Yoga (meditation) is to still the thought-waves of the mind.

Patanjali's method might be summarised as:

♦ It is the nature of the mind to pursue objects.

♦ The mind reflects the form of its objects.

- Yoga begins with withdrawing the outgoing tendencies of the mind.

- When the mind is tranquil and without object, then it is empty of form.

- The empty mind reflects the form of Consciousness.

This is a form of *sankocha* of Shakti. While Patanjali Yoga often is seen as the antithesis of the Shaivite approach in its wilfulness and rigor, Kshemaraja has no compunction to adopt it here. In general, the Shaivite authors were extremely practical and tolerant. They respected the methods developed by all traditions of yogis, even their ostensible opponents. The *Vijnanabhairava*, for example, mixes techniques that are clearly Shaivite, 'Everything is Shiva', with others that are redolent of Buddhism, 'Meditate on the Void'. A true Shaivite embraces all because Shaivism includes all.

MEDITATION II: SANKOCHA OF SHAKTI

Let's do the sankocha *of Shakti, the contraction of Shakti. Our senses spread outward. This is our predicament: the world is fascinating. We are always looking out. What can we get? What can we attain? Who is our enemy? We look for positives and negatives out there. For a minute, entertain the notion that you are God looking out at the world. The Self-Existent One is seeing with your eyes. The Self-Existent One is pleased that you have given Him the opportunity to see this beautiful world that He has created. You are Shiva. See the world clearly, O Shiva. Don't let the foolishness of your individual mind obstruct it.*

Kshemaraja compares the sankocha *of Shakti to a tortoise withdrawing its legs. Pulling back Shakti in this manner allows us to rest in the ever-present, or the Self. We are going to bring the Shakti back like a tortoise. For one minute bring all your attention into one big contracted ball inside yourself. Pull it back from the senses. Make a little ball inside yourself. This is* sankocha *of Shakti.*

VIKASA OF SHAKTI

Vikasa of Shakti is expansion. The senses are open to the outer world, but the attention is directed inward to the Self.

Kshemaraja quotes *Kakyastotra*:

Intentionally throwing all the senses simultaneously and on all sides into their respective objects and remaining (unmoved) within like a gold pillar, you (O Shiva) alone appear as the foundation of the universe.

This is *bhairavi mudra*, also called *shambhavi mudra*. *Bhairavi* and *shambhavi* both refer to Shiva. *Mudra* is from *mud* (joy) and *ra* (to give). It is a posture or disposition of the mind or physical body that gives inner joy. *Bhairavi mudra* is a posture of Self-awareness. When we are involved in the world we give ourselves away, we get absorbed in other people, in things and externals. We lose sight of the Self.

Baba always associated *shambhavi mudra* with his Guru, Bhagawan Nityananda, who was totally absorbed in the experience of Shiva. In the pictures of Nityananda you can see that he is always focused inside. Baba was wonder-struck by the intensity of his inwardness. It is hard to imagine Bhagawan getting terribly fascinated by any external thing. 'Look Bhagawan! Look at this!' Yawn. He was so focused on his inner being. Although I did hear a story—one of the few personal stories I ever heard about Bhagawan Nityananda—that he was lying about one day, muttering to himself. His devotees wondered what he was saying. The Russians had just launched Sputnik, their first space satellite—in 1957. Somebody told Bhagawan about it and he was repeating, 'Sputnik, Sputnik, Sputnik'. So perhaps he kept abreast of the news. And of course, he loved coffee. He drank his coffee in the morning, and he said, 'Sputnik', and THAT'S IT! The rest of it was *bhairavi mudra*.

MEDITATION III: VIKASA OF SHAKTI

Bhagawan Nityananda certainly didn't care what other people thought of him. Imagine if you completely didn't care what other people thought of you. That is a big one.

Let's try an exercise on vikasa of Shakti, bhairavi mudra. *Close your eyes, go inside and feel the Self, the 'I am' within. Be aware of your inner world. Do you have a feeling of yourself in that inner space? Say, 'I feel my Self'. Be aware of yourself, be within like a gold pillar. Slowly open your eyes and look at the outer world while still being in touch with the feeling of yourself, not losing it. Remain within like a gold pillar. When you open your eyes don't look at other people, but look up on the wall somewhere. Feel yourself even while the eyes are open. See if you can retain the feeling of the awareness of Self or if you lose it.*

When you use an idea such as, 'I am Shiva and I sit like a gold pillar', it puts you in that state and continues to play there in subtle form. Still, it feels thought-free and very focused and very vibrant. It isn't difficult to get into that state, but it is difficult to stay in it. Notice what pulls you out—an attachment, memory, fear, desire, the pull of the world, tearing thoughts. Plunge in again and again. Eventually, it becomes your home rather than a place to visit.

KRAMA MUDRA

In the 19th sutra, a related technique is indicated: *krama mudra*. The Krama School is one of the main schools of Kashmir Shaivism and the word *krama* means 'succession'. We have already seen how *atma vyapti*, Self-realisation, and *Shiva vyapti*, realisation of Shiva in the world, are both necessary. In *krama mudra*, the mind swings from the inner to the outer world and back again. In doing this, the two worlds are married in Consciousness. Outer objects are filled with energy of the Self, while the inner world is seen to include everything.

Abhinavagupta says:

> The aspirant should practise the meditation over and over again with the *japa* of his senses both in an extroverted way in which he regards objective manifestation *(srishti)* as Shiva and in an introverted way in which he regards the withdrawal of manifestation *(samhara)* also as Shiva. This is the ever-present *hridaya japa*.

Japa usually refers to the repetition of a mantra. It comes from a root which means 'to utter in a low voice or whisper'. Abhinavagupta uses it here metaphorically since the *krama mudra*, like mantra repetition, is a succession of acts that take place in time. Here the acts are not verbal ones, but a series of reversals of the direction of awareness.

I have found the *krama mudra* contemplation to be one of the most effective methods of bringing the inner and the outer together and of bridging the gulf between matter and Consciousness.

MEDITATION IV: KRAMA MUDRA

Sit comfortably, close your eyes and be aware of your inner world. After a few seconds, open your eyes and be aware of the outer world. Keep moving back and forth in this way for a few minutes. Don't try to do anything. Just be aware of the flavour of the inner world and the flavour of the outer world. Carefully notice the similarities and differences.

After doing this for some time, you will notice that both the inner and the outer contain the vibration of the Self, in which case you need do nothing more. Or, you will notice that the inner is superior to the outer in the experience of the Self. In this case make the attempt to maintain the taste of the Self, even when you open your eyes. You can see how this exercise is related to the bhairavi mudra, *but the heart of it is in simply successively tasting the inner and the outer. Just by doing that, without manipulating anything, much is gained.*

VAHA-CHEDA

The 18th sutra suggests a few more meditation practices. *Vaha-cheda*, the cutting of the *vahas (prana)*, is an *anavopaya* technique based on bodily awareness. Here one focuses on the heart and quietly says, *K* without any vowel. It is like a clicking in the heart. If you do it right, it has a marvellous effect, clearing the heart of pain and tension. I have used that when something has entered my heart-space that I want to clean.

ADYANTA-KOTI NIBHALANA: HAMSA TECHNIQUE

The *hamsa* mantra technique was a great favourite of Baba Muktananda's. The meditation here is to focus on *dvadashanta*, the space between two breaths. If you measure 12 finger-widths down from your nose, you reach the region of the heart. That is the inner *dvadashanta*, where the in-breath ends. Similarly, if you measure your breath as it comes out your nostrils, you will find it goes out approximately 12 finger-widths again. The space outside where it ends, is outer *dvadashanta*.

In doing the practice, let the breathing be natural. Focus on one of these two spaces. We tend to stay in the outer one for a longer time. Baba taught it by telling us to hear the inbreath as the sound *ham*, meaning, 'I Am', and pronounced, *hum*, and the outbreath as the sound *sah*, meaning, 'That'. Thus, breathing in refers to the inner world, and breathing out refers to the outer world. This technique is more a state of Consciousness than an utterance. The mantra is not really pronounced, but knowledge power, the power of language, is joined to the breath.

Kshemaraja tells us:

> The first point is the heart. The last point is the measure of the 12 (a measure of 12 fingers). *Nibhalana* means exercise or practice by fixing the mind at the time of the rising of *prana* and its coming to an end.

Kshemaraja quotes the Agamic text, *Vijnanabhairava*, Dharana 28:

> If one fixes one's mind at *dvadashanta* again and again howsoever and wheresoever, the fluctuation of his mind will diminish and in a few days, he will acquire an extraordinary status.

The *Vijnanabhairava* gives four different versions of this meditation in its first four *dharanas* or techniques. They are:

Dharana 1: Focus on the two *dvadashantas*, the place where the breath pauses, both inside and outside. Focus on the throb of Shakti at those points and remain mindful of it even during the breathing process.

Dharana 2: Focus on the pause between breaths.

Dharana 3: Focus on the *sushumna*, the middle channel of the spine, not on the breaths. This leads to the thought-free state.

Dharana 4: Retain the breath both inwardly and outwardly, then *apana* and *prana*, the inbreath and the outbreath, become one.

Notice the subtle differences. Combining your awareness with the breath yields powerful results. Everyone's experience will be unique. Try them all and find what is most comfortable for you.

By contemplating *dvadashanta* you are moving from awareness of thought to awareness of the space behind thought, the thought-free state: Consciousness. One pathway is the space between two breaths, which is analogous to the space between two thoughts. The more you come back to pure awareness, the stronger your mind gets and the deeper meditation goes.

Swami Lakshmanjoo placed a lot of importance on the space between two breaths. He said that real meditation involved 'unbroken, continuously refreshed' focus on that space. If that focus is maintained properly a strong experience of inner energy results. The juncture points where one manifestation is withdrawn and another has not yet come into being are places where the Self, the substratum of all manifestation, stands revealed. I am speaking not only of the space between two breaths, but also the space between two thoughts, the moment between sleep and waking, the junction point between night and day. Lakshmanjoo said that meditation is particularly effective at dawn and sundown. Those transitional times are considered holy in India and are greeted with worship and the waving of lights to the image of the deity. As we have seen the *sushumna* is also called *madhya*, the 'centre'. When one focuses on the space between two breaths one enters the 'third breath', which is the *sushumna*.

MEDITATION V: THE SPACE BETWEEN THE BREATHS

Let yourself focus on the space between the breaths, whether it is on the inbreath or the outbreath. Try it for a moment. Breathe in and out and see if you can focus on that space. You may see it, you may feel it. Take a few minutes. What is that space like? It is still. When you focus on the stillness, the stillness will get unstill; thoughts will come in. But when you breathe again, you get back to it. Inside or outside—it is the same point.

Now sit in an alert way but not rigid; you don't have to look like a statue of the Buddha, but comfortably alert. Watch the breath come in and go out; come in and go out. Concentrate on the dvadashanta; *the space between the breaths.*

THE BREATH OF THE THREE RIVERS

I will mention another breath meditation which is not discussed in the 18th sutra, but is related to the *hamsa* meditation and is powerful. I call it 'the breath of the three rivers'. In India, there is a Kumbha Mela, or great spiritual gathering, every year. Millions of pilgrims, sages and yogis participate. It is held at a number of sites, one of which is the city of Allahabad. The site is said to be the confluence of three rivers: the Ganga (Ganges), the Yamuna and the Saraswati, and therefore, very auspicious.

The problem for the skeptical observer, however, is that only two rivers, the Ganges and the Yamuna, appear to meet there. He is assured that the third river, the Saraswati, is certainly there, though invisible. Some say it was once an actual river that dried up, others say that it is an underground river, still others say that it is a mystical and subtle river.

The breath is the meeting of these three rivers. The inbreath and the outbreath are the Ganges and the Yamuna. If you focus on the movement of the breath within the body, ignoring the breath entering and leaving the body, but just observing the movements that occur within the body, a 'third breath' will emerge, in the form of an upward flowing energy. This is the mysterious Saraswati, which is also the *sushumna* or the kundalini energy.

Abhinavagupta speaks of the same meditation using a fiery rather than a watery metaphor: sun, moon and fire. He relates it to a triad that is everywhere in his writings: the knower, the known and knowledge. The known (outer objects) is related to the moon, because outer objects shine by reflected light. The means of knowing (the mind and senses) relates to the sun because it is by the light of these that the outer objects are known. The essence of the sun, that which makes it brilliant, is fire itself, and in this symbolism, fire refers to the light of Consciousness, which empowers the mind and senses. Through the interaction between sun and moon, fire is revealed.

Shiva Sutras III.44 says:

> *The prana shakti* flows in the left *(ida)*, right *(pingala)* and the central *(sushumna) nadis*. By constant awareness it abides in the *sushumna*, the centre, which is supreme Consciousness.

The *nadis* are the subtle nerves and *ida* and *pingala* are associated with the left and right nostrils. The *prana* or life-force generates our external life and our psychological life. Both *ida* and *pingala* rise and subside in the space of Consciousness, the *sushumna*, which can also be accessed by focusing on the space between two breaths.

The technique I am describing here is different from the focus on the space between two breaths. Rather, keep the attention on the inbreath and the outbreath and be alert for the third breath, which is *sushumna*, the manifestation of the Self. That third breath will arise by itself spontaneously.

Through the inner contemplation of the inbreath and the outbreath, the third breath, kundalini Shakti, is revealed. The third breath does not go in and out of the body, but rises up the *sushumna*. It is the hidden river known only to yogis. Fittingly, in 1971, as the bus I was in, filled with pilgrims, paused to admire the confluence of the Ganges and Yamuna at Allahabad, suddenly Neem Karoli Baba appeared on the other side of the bus. I felt that mystically the third river had revealed itself in his person.

MEDITATION VI: THE BREATH OF THE THREE RIVERS

Try this: sit quietly and watch the breath. Let breathing be natural. Now, forget about the air going out and the air coming in. For you now, that doesn't exist. As you breathe you will watch the energy move up and down within your body. Again, this breath does not move in and out, it moves up and down. Your prana is charging your body with energy. You will know that you have attained the 'third breath' when you feel an unmistakable and powerful energy vibrating within and moving upwards. This practice awakens or activates the kundalini.

You can direct either your outbreath or your inbreath or both to a certain chakra or physical organ or region. This meditation is energising and healing. It strengthens the life-force within the body and can cure disease. It is the best health technique I know.

Chapter 14

Shaiva Tantra: The Yoga of the Upward Shift

Taking firm hold of That, the *spanda* principle, the awakened yogi remains firm with the resolution 'I will surely carry out whatever it will tell me'.

Spanda Karikas, I.23

I n the last chapter, we looked at some of the techniques in Sutra 18 of *Pratyabhijnahridayam*, techniques such as meditation on thought-free awareness and the *hamsa* mantra. After discussing all of these, the sutra ends with 'etc.'. This is significant. Kshemaraja says, 'The word *adi* (etcetera), refers to the practice of *unmesha* condition'. *Unmesha* refers to the expansive upward shift of feeling that one experiences when the Self is contacted. Kshemaraja explains that the movement of the universe has two aspects, the arc of descent, *nimesha*, in which Shiva becomes a person, and the arc of ascent, *unmesha*, in which a person becomes Shiva. In *nimesha*, Consciousness becomes matter and in *unmesha*, matter returns to Consciousness.

In Chapter 11, I spoke about the five cosmic processes, which were fairly complex. In fact, those five processes can be reduced to these two movements of contraction and grace, multiplicity and oneness. Looking carefully within, a meditator will discover that his own mind contains both of these movements in the form of the downward shift and the upward shift.

UPWARD SHIFT YOGA

Following the upward shift is a perfect yogic practice. It is the practice of Shaivism in the world. You have undoubtedly felt an upward shift, a sudden feeling of vibrancy, many times in your life. When you see a good movie you might feel uplifted. Or when someone says something kind, or when you accomplish something. You've also experienced the downward shift, the contraction.

Spanda Karikas I.21 says:

> Therefore, one should be always on the alert for the discernment of the *spanda* principle. Such a person attains his essential state (as *spanda*) even in the waking condition in short time.

The *spanda principle* is the same as *unmesha*, the upward shift of feeling. Unfortunately, the mind wants to look for negativity, how you've been mistreated, how things are unjust, how that person is a sinner—downward shifts. Baba used to say, 'A crow, even in heaven, would eat shit!' The mind is like that crow; even in the most favourable circumstances, the mind loves to dwell on negativity. You have to train the mind to eat good thoughts. This is the practice of looking for what is expansive and uplifting.

In this vein, Kshemaraja quotes several *dharanas* from the *Vijnanabhairava*:

> When one experiences the expansion of joy of savour arising from the pleasure of eating and drinking, one should meditate on the perfect condition of this joy, then there will be supreme delight. (Dharana 49)

> When the yogi mentally becomes one with the incomparable joy of song and other objects, then of such a yogi, there is, because of the expansion of his mind, identity with that (i.e., with the incomparable joy) because he becomes one with it. (Dharana 50)

Swami Lakshmanjoo calls such moments *kama-kala*. He explains that *kama-kala* refers to the bringing together of two things. *Kama* means desire, the force that brings the two things together. In this context it is the conjunction of the tongue with delicious food or of the ear with beautiful music. Any of the senses might come into play. Although *kama-kala* usually refers to the sexual act, Lakshmanjoo says it actually refers to any such conjunction. In the most general way, it is the conjunction of subject and object. We've already seen how the force of maya separates the 'I' from the world. When this split is healed by an inner act of contemplation, there is a definite upward shift or vibration of Shakti.

Lakshmanjoo says, 'Everywhere in these unifications, in these conjunctions, he experiences the state of kundalini'. Interestingly, the Hasidic masters use the same word, *unification*, in discussing their method of uniting the world to the Divine.

Lakshmanjoo quotes the *Vatulanatha Sutra*, in which we hear that the 'great festival of unification' *(mahamelapa)* is the meeting of the *Siddhas* and the yoginis, in a rite of sexual tantra. He comments:

> The truth is that all contacts are sexual, it refers to all sensual contacts. In this way, hearing is a sexual contact. Seeing is a sexual contact. Smelling is a sexual contact. Touching is a sexual contact. Tasting is a sexual contact. So in this verse, the word *Siddha* refers to I-Consciousness and the word yogini refers to whatever objectivity united with it.

Lakshmanjoo calls this unification *charya-krama*. Here, he uses the term 'sexual' at the highest level of its reach, where it merges in spirituality. He makes the point that only highly qualified aspirants can actually practise *charya-krama* without danger of a fall. Sexual tantra is often used as an excuse for sexual indulgence. That is not to say that it is always thus. I have known several great masters who seemed to have practised it in the divine way.

The ancient and mysterious symbol, the *shivalingam*, sacred to Shaivism, is an eternal embodiment of *charya-krama*. The *shivalingam* is clearly and graphically the representation of a phallus, the *lingam*, inserted in a vagina, the *yoni*. One wishes that Dr Freud had studied this symbol, for in it he would have discovered a raising up of sexuality to the Divine, instead of a reduction of everything to physical sexuality. The *lingam* represents the cosmic marriage of opposites, male and female, yin and yang, matter and Consciousness. It stands for the unity-in-diversity that is the nature of Consciousness.

Abhinavagupta tells us that the *lingam* represents knowledge power *(jnana shakti)*, while the *yoni* represents action power *(kriya shakti)*. Remember that *anava mala*, the primal limiting condition that turns Shiva into an individual, has two forms: *knowledge without action,* and *action without knowledge*. When Shiva becomes contracted He suffers His catastrophe in these two ways: He retains understanding, but is impotent *to do*. Or, He is full of relatively effective doership but has little wisdom.

Joining his knowing and doing, as in the symbolism of the *shivalingam*, the aspirant heals his problem and experiences an increase in spiritual energy. In the Gurdjieff system a third force is necessary to emerge from two primary forces that block each other. A single object or idea is something set in form (first force). It is cut off from the whole and therefore is static. The energy in it is relatively restricted and blocked by the simple fact that it has definite form, just as a single thought cuts itself off from the ocean of Consciousness. A second object or thought needs to be introduced to challenge the original and test its boundaries by inviting it to change shape and dissolve in Consciousness. This second force sets up a tension that is resolved by the form of grace (third force) that comes to hand, in which energy is freed and upliftment ensues.

Enjoying sexual love, food or beautiful music, a yogi knows that the upliftment he derives is nothing but the Self. The ordinary experiences of life can become a vehicle of spirituality, if our awareness is tuned in the right way. A true Shaivite is not opposed to, or afraid of pleasure, rather he regards pleasure as an experience of the Self. All the things that give us pleasure turn us to the Self. But instead of saying, 'that was a great song', we should say, 'that puts me in touch with the Self'.

I don't mean that you should actually say that, because people will think that you are a yoga lunatic. But even while celebrating a song, or a singer, a part of you should know that your experience is in you, your response is from your inner being. If you didn't have that as a potential within yourself, no singer, however great, could elicit it.

Even the experience you have of love for another person is a trigger of your own love. Instead of saying, 'Darling, I love you!' you should say, 'Darling, you make me feel my own love!' It's terribly unromantic, isn't it? Be warned that if you speak to your beloved that way she will say, 'You cad! Mr Darcy, I'll never marry you!' So keep this knowledge inside yourself.

Kshemaraja again quotes the *Vijnanabhairava* (Dharana 51):

> Wherever the *manas*, the individual mind, finds satisfaction, let it be concentrated on that. In every such case the true nature of the highest bliss will shine forth.

What a fantastic statement; what self-acceptance and appreciation of the divine nature of the world! Whatever you love, whomever you love, let the mind focus on that. Then shift from the object to the feeling that the object awakens and meditate on that. That will lead you to the Self.

Finally, Kshemaraja says, 'Or any other meditation on the Self, full of bliss, may be inferred'. Here is where you should be creative in meditation. Whatever gives you bliss, whatever opens you to bliss, meditate on that. Let your intuition work. The yoga of Kashmir Shaivism is intensely practical. It is anything but moralistic. It tells us to make use of our natural (healthy) proclivities and turn them to the Divine.

DOUBT AND CONVICTION

Living the Shaivite life implies constant attention to energy. When we move in the right direction, energy increases and expands. When we go in the wrong direction, we become depleted. All the negative *matrikas* and negative emotions deplete us. Abhinavagupta says that it is not thought that is the real problem, but doubt. Doubt creates a block in Consciousness. The mind says, maybe this, maybe that; maybe yes, maybe no. This creates a tension and freezes a person at the place of doubt. He no longer flows in Consciousness. In fact, Consciousness is hidden by uncertainty. He cannot move until the doubt is overcome or turned away.

I have already quoted *Shiva Sutras* I.17, which says:

Vitarka atmajnanam
The knowledge of the Self is conviction.

Only certainty leads to knowledge of the Self, and certainty only comes from higher things, not from the world of opinion. The Shiva yogi lives his life with courage and passion. If you are in the woods with two paths leading away from a clearing, like the hero in the famous poem by Robert Frost, if you are full of doubt and do not act, then you never leave the clearing. A Shaivite knows that all roads lead to Shiva, and Shiva has infinite faces. He knows that it is far better to take either path and walk it. If it is the wrong path, he will learn it quickly enough. In the highest sense there can be no wrong choice since there is nowhere to wander away from Shiva.

I often use the metaphor of the 'doorway': this path is a doorway to Consciousness; this practice is a doorway to Shiva; this attitude is a doorway to the Absolute; the Guru is the doorway to God. I realised that I unconsciously held this metaphoric vision of life. Shiva is close at hand just behind the veil, just behind the door. So the Shaivite, in his life as in his yoga, should act courageously, knowing that everything that he needs will come. At the same time, he must be sensitive and aware and accept the feedback that comes from the world, which is nothing but *Chiti*. *Do the yoga that you understand at the level that you understand it and do it with full conviction.*

MEDITATION ON THE BLISS OF THE WORLD

The comprehensive Shaivite meditation is to find the bliss of the world. The world is complex and hidden in it are kernels of light, of divinity. We can be like the crow and ignore what is joyous and find the negative. Or we can be like the swan. In India the swan symbolises discrimination. It is said that if you were to throw milk into a pond, the swan could find the milk and leave the water. It has the ability to extract what is truly valuable.

When I became a swami I received *paramahamsa sanyassa*. A *paramahamsa* is the supreme swan: a sage is expected to have highly developed discrimination. A true *paramahamsa* should be able to separate the wheat from the chaff. He can find the bliss that is hidden in the world.

Now, let's do the meditation of a paramahamsa. *Look within and separate the wheat from the chaff. Find the bliss hidden inside. Or alternatively, think of any person or experience that gives you a feeling of love or joy. Gradually move away from that person or activity and focus fully on the experience of love or joy. See if you can expand that experience. Immerse yourself in it. Let's meditate for 10 minutes.*

Chapter 15

Methods of Meditation II: The Vijnanabhairava

This divine work is incomparably great. It is the wisdom of Bhairava, the wisdom of His own Self. It partakes of the true nature of the Supreme Principle.

Baba Muktananda, *Secret of the Siddhas*

I n the last two chapters, I have drawn on one of my favourite texts, the seventh-century Tantric work, *Vijnanabhairava*. In this chapter, I will cite what I call 'essential *dharanas*', *dharanas* that embody the essence of the Shaivite approach and to which I return again and again. The *Vijnanabhairava* predates the *Shiva Sutras*, and was an important source on which the Trika sages drew. It contains the quintessence of the *Rudrayamala Tantra* and is a compilation of 112 *dharanas*, or meditations, with many more implied.

I think of the *Vijnanabhairava* as a living mystical entity or realm in which all possible meditations dwell. It manifests as an extremely wise, tolerant and humorous Shaivite sage, drunk with the omnipresence of Shiva.

I learned from the *Vijnanabhairava* to use spiritual ideas as methods of meditation. You can ride a spiritual idea to the Self, or at least as far as it will take you. My studies of the *Vijnanabhairava* were the source of the concept of the G-Statement.

A *dharana* does not have to be a long meditation, it can simply be a quick movement towards the Self. When we use a spiritual idea as a *dharana*, we are using it yogically and not intellectually, for vertical rather than horizontal reference.

A small pedantic point: I give the *dharana* number following Jaideva Singh, not the verse number, which most scholarly works follow. Singh's *Vijnanabhairava* is the only text the majority of my readers will encounter, and I think it is good to think of these exercises as *dharanas* rather than verses.

ESSENTIAL G-STATEMENTS: DHARANAS 40, 42 AND 81

Dharana 40:

> When an aspirant contemplates with mind unwavering and free from all alternatives his whole body or the entire universe simultaneously as of the nature of Consciousness, he experiences supreme awakening.

Dharana 42:

> The yogi should contemplate the entire universe or his own body simultaneously in its totality as filled with his (essential, spiritual) bliss. Then through his own ambrosia-like bliss, he will become identified with the supreme bliss.

In Dharana 40 the meditator contemplates, 'All this is Consciousness', with his eyes open. Or, turning within and observing his subjective experience with eyes closed, he again says, 'All this is Consciousness'. He should be able to see directly that his whole experience is held in his own awareness. This single *dharana* contains the quintessential secret of Shaivism.

Dharana 42 completes the understanding of Dharana 40. Here the meditator examines his feeling and says to himself, 'All this is bliss', whether inside or outside. The difference between 40 and 42 is that in 42 the attention is on feeling and in 40 the experience is more intellectual. Taken together, these two *dharanas* constitute the union of thought and feeling.

While it is easy to intellectualise that everything is Consciousness, it is more difficult to experience everything as bliss. In the second *dharana* the meditator should become aware of his feeling experience and try to experience the present feeling as a permutation of bliss, or find the bliss at the core of, or behind, the present experience. Practising these two *dharanas* gives the highest rewards.

This set of two *dharanas* is completed by Dharana 81:

> After rejecting attachment to one's body, one should, with firm mind

and with a vision, which has no consideration for anything else, contemplate thus, 'I am everywhere'. He will then enjoy (supernal) happiness.

The meditator uses the G-Statement, *sarvam idam aham*, 'All this is myself' or 'I am everywhere'. This approaches the same goal as the previous two *dharanas* from a different angle. Clearly, as my body, I cannot be everywhere. When I say 'All this is myself', *this* refers to everything I see or sense. Only as Consciousness can I be everywhere.

HANDLING DESIRE—THREE STRATEGIES: DHARANAS 73, 74 AND 75

This set of three *dharanas* on desire is useful for *sadhana* and illustrates the *Vijnanabhairava's* universal and eclectic approach.

Dharana 73:

> Having observed a desire that has sprung up, the aspirant should put an end to it immediately. It will be absorbed in that very place from which it arose.

Here, a desire, having arisen, is renounced by the aspirant. This is the *yogic approach* of cutting off unwanted *vikalpas*. It is effective if you have a strong mind or a weak desire.

Dharana 74:

> When desire or knowledge (or activity) has not arisen in me, then what am I in that condition? In verity, I am (in that condition) that Reality Itself (i.e., Consciousness-bliss). (Therefore the aspirant should always contemplate 'I am Consciousness-bliss'.) Thus, he will be absorbed in that Reality and will become identified with it.

Here, the meditator observes his condition before desire, knowledge or activity has arisen. He identifies with the transcendental and not the personal reality. This is the *Vedantic approach*.

Dharana 75:

> When a desire or knowledge (or activity) appears, the aspirant should, with the mind withdrawn from all objects (of desire, knowledge, etc.) fix his mind on it (desire, knowledge, etc.) as the very Self, then he will have the realisation of the essential Reality.

Here is the *Shaivite* or *Tantric approach*. Instead of getting rid of the desire (as in 73) or focussing on the reality prior to desire (74), he focuses on the desire itself, seeing it as the Self, as *Chiti*. He turns his mind away from the thing that is desired to focus on the feeling of desire itself. Through contemplative awareness he will experience that desire as a wave or pulsation of Consciousness.

In comparison, in the yogic approach, the desire is seen as a problem to be chopped off. In the Vedantic approach it is seen as an illusory superimposition on the underlying reality. In the Shaivite approach, the desire is fully entertained and honoured as *Chiti* Itself. While I am clearly enchanted by the Shaivite approach, all three of these weapons should be in the arsenal of a great meditator.

SHIVA IS EVERYWHERE: DHARANA 91

Dharana 91:

> Wherever the mind goes whether towards the exterior or towards the interior, everywhere there is the state of Shiva. Since Shiva is omnipresent, where can the mind go (to avoid Him)?

No *dharana* is more useful to the meditator than this one. When confronted by a restless mind, negative thoughts or impenetrable blocks, reflecting that even these things are nothing but Shiva, is the most effective method.

THE ESSENCE OF TANTRA: DHARANA 93

One of the characteristics of the Tantric approach, which Shaivism exemplifies, is a predilection for honouring the natural unfoldment of life: playing life 'as it lies'. While a Tantric will certainly make effort to attain high states of Consciousness, he will also search for these extraordinary states within the ordinary context of living. Last chapter I talked about this Shaiva Tantra—how a Shaivite yogi will use the natural pleasures of music, food and sexuality as doorways to divinity.

In Dharana 93, the yogi finds the experience of higher Consciousness in certain unexpected moments of life:

> At the commencement and end of sneeze, in terror, in sorrow, in the condition of a deep sigh or on the occasion of flight from the battlefield, during (keen) curiosity, at the commencement or end of hunger, the state is like that of Brahma [the Absolute].

It is not likely that our self-observation is so powerful that we take a snapshot of ourselves during a sneeze. But think about it for a moment. When I sneeze my mind completely stops and a white light explodes in my brain. I suspect something similar happens to you. In each of these unexpected and oddly chosen moments, a certain psychological state arises in a person. It is 'like Brahma'. During keen curiosity the mind is still and open. Attention is fully focused on the issue at hand. Someone wrote that the attitude in meditation should be like the expectant hush of an audience as the curtain rises on a play.

These ordinary/extraordinary mind moments are called 'fleeting *samadhis*' in the South Indian text *Tripura Rahasya*. The author of *Spanda Karikas* must have strongly related to this *dharana* because he writes (I.22):

> In that state is the *spanda* principle firmly established to which a person is reduced when he is greatly exasperated or overjoyed, or is in impasse reflecting what to do, or is running for life.

An accomplished meditator learns to distance himself from states like anger. Even when anger arises he notices that a part of himself has become the witness of the anger and minutely observes the entire phenomenon of anger within himself. At a certain stage, an aspirant will relish (but not provoke) such emotional events as an opportunity for self-study.

I especially like the image evoked by this verse. Here the meditator is at an impasse, perhaps paralysed between two alternatives. Suddenly he shifts his attention from the choice he finds difficult to make, to the state of Consciousness in which he finds himself. He discovers that that state is full of *spanda*.

I had just such a moment in the late sixties. I opened a door in New York and a gun was thrust in my face. In that moment I went into a heightened state that turned out to be life-transforming.

Just as the *turiya* state stands behind the states of waking, dream and deep sleep, barely hidden and always bursting forth, so too Shiva humorously manifests Himself in a cosmic dance of hide and seek. With a nod and wink He shows Himself to us in a sneeze and sigh and when we are running for our lives.

ONE WORD G-STATEMENTS: DHARANA 107

Dharana 107 says:

> 'Eternal, omnipresent, without depending on any support, all-pervasive, lord of all that is' – meditating every instant on these words in conformity with their sense, one attains his object [has fulfilment].

We have seen in the chapters on the *tattvas*, how the *kanchukas*, or cloaks, limit the eternality and all-pervasiveness of Shiva and bind the individual in time, space and causality. This *dharana* counteracts the effects of the *kanchukas* by using, as G-Statements, the very qualities of Shiva that have become contracted. Thus the meditator contemplates omnipresence, eternality, any of the attributes of Shiva that appeal to him. As Jaideva Singh says:

> By constantly pondering over the implication of these words, the mind of the aspirant becomes chockfull of the essential reality of Shiva.

By meditating on the attributes of Shiva, the aspirant attains Shiva *samavesha*. He becomes Shiva.

EQUANIMITY: DHARANAS 100 AND 101

My Guru sometimes amused me by the way he handled questions about negative emotions. A person would ask him, 'Baba, how can I give up anger?'

Baba would say, 'Give up anger!'

Another would say, 'Baba, I am full of jealousy'.

He would answer, 'Jealousy is not good'.

Once I heard a friend of mine tell him, 'Baba, I am full of ego'. And he said, 'Ego has no place here'.

The *Vijnanabhairava* offers a similar set of instructions:

- ♦ The aspirant should have the same attitude towards friend and foe.

- ♦ He should remain the same both in honour and dishonour.

- ♦ He should maintain neither aversion nor attachment.

Here are the full *dharanas*:

Dharana 100:

> Because of the conviction that everything is full of *Brahman* (who is also the essential Self of all), the aspirant has the same attitude towards friend and foe, remains the same both in honour and dishonour, and thus because of this conviction (the conviction of the presence of *Brahman* everywhere), he is perpetually happy.

Dharana 101:

> The aspirant should neither maintain the attitude of aversion nor of attachment towards anyone. Since he is freed of both aversion and attachment, there develops *Bhramabhava* or the nature of the divine Consciousness (which is also the nature of the essential Self) in his heart.

Both of these *dharanas* give moral instruction. They tell us how to live spiritually in the world. In Dharana 100, the G-Statements of Shaivism support our equality consciousness. Having become convinced by our study of Shaivism, that everything is Consciousness, and having also experienced that in states of meditation, we use that idea as a platform for applying it in our life. Gurdjieff called this 'thinking from the work'. That is, making use of spiritual ideas operationally rather than reducing everything to a series of personal reactions.

Dharana 101 comes from a different point of view. Here, the avoidance of aversion and attachment is used as a yogic method. If one strives not to be attached and not to hate, one eventually grows in divine awareness.

In a way, these *dharanas* are like Baba telling us to 'give up anger'. Remarkably, these 'instructions' often had a transforming effect when they came from Baba's lips, doubtless because of the Shakti that he carried. The same is true here. Teachings from the heart of Shiva bring with them the grace to apply them.

The essential message of the wisdom of Bhairava is that Shiva is very, very close indeed. Every student of Shaivism should become friendly with its spirit.

Chapter 16

Turiya: The Fourth State

> The waking state is *vishva*, the totality which is limitless because of its diversity. The dream state is *tejas*, the splendour resulting from the majesty of light. The deep sleep state is *prajna*, wisdom, because it is a mass of Consciousness. Transcending these, there is the fourth state.
>
> Abhinavagupta, *Paramarthasara*, Verse 35

L et us think for a moment about the difference between living in a universe in which *matter* is the basic stuff or a universe in which divine *Consciousness* is the basic stuff. What is the difference? Let us decide which of those two we have. On the face of it, it could be either.

Matter is certainly more fixed than Consciousness. Matter is stuck in form. Things are slow to change. They are dull and inert. They are unintelligent. They don't have purpose or meaning. Only intelligence, Consciousness, has purpose. The person who shapes matter has purpose. But matter itself is just like clay, it is passive. 'Matter' is etymologically related to 'matrix', and both suggest the mother's womb. On the other hand, Consciousness is full of purpose, full of will, thought, feeling, intelligence and imagination. And, if that is the basic stuff of the universe, then there is purpose and meaning in the universe.

Now how can you argue one way or the other? The Western scientific view (at least at this stage of Western science) says matter is the source of the universe.

On the other hand, the Shaivite masters argue that everything I know, that I see, that I sense, is experienced through my own awareness. Everything that *you* know in your life you also experience only through your awareness. Everything that we know and experience is held in our awareness. In personal experience, awareness holds everything.

It is possible to imagine a condition not held in awareness, but it is awareness imagining that condition. You cannot get away from awareness. But it is still a big step away from thinking of it as conscious energy.

Shaivism says that awareness is not something that evolved. No, the *basic stuff* of this reality is aliveness, is awareness. When you dream at night, the whole world that is created in your dream is made solely out of your own awareness. Shaivism makes the extraordinary leap that this world of the waking state is also made from that same divine awareness.

Further, Shaivism describes the process by which awareness steps down, becoming more inert or dull, as it devolves into the universe, into matter. As it moves towards matter it gets more and more dense, it vibrates less intelligently, less quickly and finally becomes inert. But, even in its most inert phase, it has Consciousness as its centre. Shaivism talks about this process of contraction, how we got into this predicament of bondage, and it also talks about the path back to our real nature.

The Shaivite texts say that a human being is divine awareness or Shiva contracted, and has all the properties and abilities of Shiva. Shiva is exactly the way that we are: Shiva is a feeling, thinking, creating entity, only with no limitation. When we practise with intense conviction we actually merge in Shiva.

The *Vijnanabhairava* Dharana 85 tells us to contemplate in this way:

> *Sarvajnah sarvakarta cha vyapakah parameshvarah*
> *Sa evaham shaivadharma iti dardhyac chivo bhavet*
> I possess the attributes of Shiva. I am omniscient, all-powerful and all-pervading; I am the Supreme Lord and none other.

Despite our inherent divinity, sometimes, maybe most of the time, maybe all of the time, we *feel* limited in various ways. Limitation is reflected in the way we use language. When language moves towards limitation and separation, it creates hatred, suffering and weakness. When language moves towards expansion it creates upliftment, divinity and love.

In your awareness, when you have tearing thoughts, when your mind is filled with negative self-talk, your whole being shrinks. You become disempowered. If you are an athlete, you make a bad shot. If you are looking for a job, you will give a bad interview. When your mind is filled with buoyant thoughts, uplifting thoughts, positive thoughts, you will be good at whatever you are doing. You will get the job, you will be successful. So in our interior world language can move in these two directions. It can move upwards towards expansion and joy, or it can move downwards towards suffering. Shaivism teaches us how to move language towards expanded awareness.

THE STATES OF CONSCIOUSNESS

Consciousness may be one thing, but it is also a vast ocean that contains many things. In the first place, there are the three states which we go through constantly: waking, dream and deep sleep. To be accurate you could say that Consciousness in the waking state goes through many states as well. You go through anger, you go through fear and you go through joy, through boredom, to name a few. Gurdjieff would say that they represent different 'I-s'. In each, you are a different person. The world looks completely different. When you are in a state of paranoia, the world looks absolutely different from when you are in a state of great joy and confidence. Your world is different, you are different, people relate to you differently, and things happen differently for you. There are many different states of Consciousness.

Let's talk about the three states—waking, dreaming and deep sleep. *Shiva Sutras* I.7 says:

> *Jagrat svapna sushupta bhede turya bhoga sambhavah*
> The bliss of turiya or the fourth state of Consciousness arises even during the different states of waking, dream and deep sleep.

The sutra says that there are three states—waking, dreaming and deep sleep—and there is a fourth state, beyond those three. This fourth state is a state that people who are not practising some kind of inner discipline, some form of meditation, don't know about. Actually, Shaivism says that they do know about it, but they don't know that they know about it. This fourth state is called the *turiya* state, which means 'the fourth state'. It is a state of higher Consciousness.

When you go so deep in meditation that you go into the stillness and connect with the Self, you are in *turiya*. It can be called 'yogic trance', or *samadhi*. But this sutra is saying something different. Here, *turiya* is not a fourth state separate from the other three, but actually it is the substratum of the other three. A person who practises Self-remembering or mantra brings an element of *turiya* into his waking state. The waking state of a sage is permeated by *turiya*. The unusual state of 'lucid dreaming' in which the dreamer is aware of himself as the dreamer also partakes of more of *turiya* than an ordinary dream.

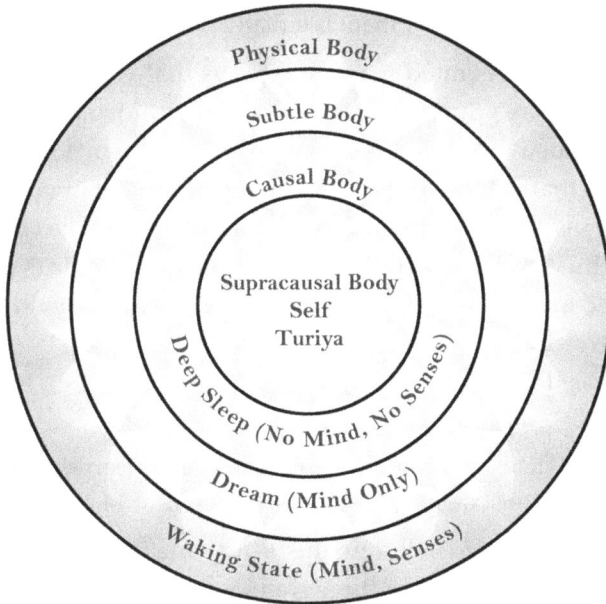

Mandala of the Four States of Consciousness. The four states correspond to the four bodies.

I'll give you a parallel: in the Shiva Process we sometimes talk about the great areas of life. There is career, which includes money, work and creativity. Then we have health and body. We have relationships, which include family and marriage and children and friends and colleagues. Finally, the fourth area is yoga or spirituality.

Do you see the parallel to *turiya?* Spirituality actually pervades the other three states like *turiya* pervades waking, dreaming and deep sleep. You need to use your yoga, your spiritual intelligence, in all the other areas of life. If you use yoga in your relationships then your relationships will work better. If you use yoga in your career then your career will work better. Spirituality is the substratum.

Baba discussed this aphorism in *Siddha Meditation:*

> Most people think that a *jnani* or a saint is someone who lives in
> silence in a cave, his eyes closed, his breath and other functions
> suspended for long periods, lost in *samadhi*—the highest trance. But
> to a real *jnani*, such a yogi is only a child. Having come to know the
> true nature of reality through his Guru's grace, a *jnani* has ceased to
> differentiate the waking, dream, deep sleep and *turiya* states from one
> another. To him each of them is equally full of the same supreme bliss.

Shaivism is an integrated teaching: it says that you can practise yoga
and meditation in your life. Other Indian philosophies emphasise
withdrawal and have a little life-negative spin on them. On the contrary,
Shaivism says that you can only really do it in the midst of your actual life.
By skilful means and by right understanding you can make your life work
for you in such a way that it becomes revelatory of the Divine in every moment.
Indeed, to find the Divine in the midst of the ordinary is *turiya* in the Shaivite
sense of the word.

Shiva Sutras III.20 says:

> *Trishu chaturtham tailavad asechyam*
> The three states of waking, dream, and deep sleep should be poured
> into the fourth state like the uninterrupted flow of oil.

The yogi should try to maintain the *turiya* state of Consciousness in the
background while in the other three states so that he will not get trapped
again in the illusions of the lower states. This is interesting language isn't
it? You should 'pour these three states' into the *samadhi* state. *Samadhi* means
immersion, so we are talking about giving the three states *samadhi* in the
fourth state. We need to recognise some experience of the 'fourth state'
before this instruction can make any sense. How can we do this? Let's stop
for a contemplation.

MEDITATION I: THE FOURTH STATE

*Close your eyes, take a deep breath then exhale slowly and fully. For a moment
you won't see anything or think anything, but you will still be conscious. That
'background' Consciousness is a glimmer of the fourth state. It is the underlying
foundational Consciousness that becomes overlaid with the awareness of specific
things, feelings and thoughts in the waking and dreaming states. It becomes
overlaid with the awareness of nothing in deep sleep.*

LIVING IN AWARENESS

An oil-soaked rag is permeated by the oil; it has the properties of both the rag and of oil. When the three states are offered into the fourth, they become like the rag soaked in oil. Let's talk about the waking state, because we are in the waking state. We can pour this waking state into the *turiya* state. We can discover the transcendental state that is with us in this moment and in every moment. That is yoga.

Let us talk about the dream state, too. We dream. Things seem real and important. Then we wake up. The things of the dream disappear. Usually, they are so ephemeral we don't even remember them. When we dream, the physical world disappears. In deep sleep, both the dream world and the physical world, and even our self-awareness disappear. But when we wake up to *turiya*, the three states are seen as equally real and equally insubstantial. They are seen against the backdrop of the detached witness.

Baba writes:

> In *turiya* one drinks the highest bliss but a real *jnani* or yogi drinks the ecstasy of *samadhi*—the bliss of manifestation—even in the waking state, seeing the entire waking world as an expansion of Consciousness.

It is relatively easy to experience the peace and joy of *turiya* while meditating, but the accomplished yogi has developed a faculty, as it were, that connects him to the Self, even in the waking state. When he meditates, he gets to 'indulge' in *turiya*. He doesn't have to think about or do anything else. An inner channel has been opened; he hears an inner frequency that others do not. There is nothing mysterious about how this has happened: such a yogi has made effort and directed his attention to the subtle dimension of life. He remembers the Self under all conditions. Through yogic practice, he develops the *habit* of *turiya*.

Imagine living your life in complete bliss. This is the possibility the great sages have shown us. This is the path they have blazed. Firm in their understanding, they flow with whatever arises. They may experience sorrow or other things, but they always remain in touch with that *turiya* state. None of the negative states will last very long.

Baba writes:

> The bliss which is the same and unchanging in all the states is the bliss of *turiya*. To an actor all the scenes in a play are equally his creation and his joyful sport. Whether they provoke tears or laughter they mean the same to him.

WONDER RASA: THE ATTITUDE OF WONDER

An actor doesn't care whether he is playing Hamlet or Mr Bean. He is enjoying the craft of acting. He doesn't get attached: 'Oh God, I killed Polonius again!' The bliss of *turiya* is accompanied by an almost childlike sense of wonder.

Shiva Sutras I.12 says:

> *Vismayo yogabhumikah*
> The different states attained in the course of yogic practice are filled with wonder.

You know, it is not very sophisticated to be full of wonder, but it is very attractive. In the movie *Big*, a boy becomes a grown man overnight, but he is still a 13-year-old emotionally. He gets a job in a toy company and has the enthusiasm of a boy for toys. To see an adult with the wonder *rasa* of a 13-year-old is highly amusing. His fellow workers think he's a bit strange but his enthusiasm makes him successful. Every little thing delights and fascinates him.

Abhinavagupta says, 'The complete absence of wonder is in effect a complete absence of life'. Conversely, aesthetic receptivity—and Abhinavagupta is very interested in aesthetics—is allied to the capacity to be open to God. A sage says, 'A person who appreciates works of art has a heart'. He has a receptive heart, a capacity for wonder.

Abhinavagupta says:

> Aesthetic receptivity is to be immersed in an intense state of wonder consisting of the arousal of vitality. Only he whose heart is fed by this infinite and nourishing vitality, only he who is dedicated to the constant practice of taking delight in this form of pleasure, only he and none other is preeminently endowed with the ability to feel wonder.

The great yogi enlivens himself. He gets rid of deadness. A lot of our deadness is false sophistication. We think it is sophisticated to be bored, to be filled with existential ennui. Perhaps that is what the Swedish filmmaker, Bergman, taught us, but much of our deadness is despairing thoughts, tension and anxiety. And so the yogi enlivens himself, he works on his awareness to find the liveliness, the life that is behind everything. This is how we find *turiya*, the fourth state. The fourth state is enthusiasm itself, it is bliss itself, it is joy itself. And that is potential within us.

The Shaivite scholar Mark Dyczkowski writes:

> In order to heighten the awareness of his own nature, which the power

of maya has obscured, he must try and fix his attention on the instant in which he feels this wonder welling up inside him in moments of intense joy, confusion, anger or fear. By attending to the sudden emergence of the *spanda*—the vibration of the transcendental fourth state of Consciousness—at these times, and establishing himself in a state of introverted absorption, he should, as Kshemaraja puts it, 'Vitalise the living Self by that very life itself'.

That is what the yogi has to do: he has to find signs of life in himself. The doctor looks and says, 'Ah, there are vital functions': some of us live as though we are dead, even though our pulse is beating. We are just living out our days, waiting to be thrown into the coffin. It is not enough that the pulse is beating: the heart should be stirred, the mind should be alive, we should be open.

Every one of us has that capacity. Every one of us also has dead areas. We have dead areas where we are attached, where we are worried, where we are afraid. We have dead areas where we are stuck in superficial thinking, or conventional thought, or where we don't want to face the truth. But if we probe deeply, if we look deeply with great sincerity and passion we can discover this aliveness, this wonder. What we have to do is find the fourth state behind the other three states. How can we do that right now? Yes, look! Always the answer is to become present and look within.

THE PLAY OF CHITI

When I got to Baba's ashram he didn't talk about Shaivism that much, yet there was one theme that kept emerging in his question-and-answer sessions. It *always* grabbed me. Later I learnt that this was a theme from Shaivism. It is when he talked about the 'play of *Chiti*', the 'play of Consciousness'.

At one session he said:

> During meditation all kinds of thoughts arise from within, all sorts of things happen, and you should not worry about them. As many thoughts as there are objects in the universe can arise in your mind, because the universe is nothing but the mind of God. One poet saint said that all dualities such as joy and sorrow, happiness and misery, honour and insult, good and bad, virtue and vice, high and low are nothing but shadows of the mind. They are nothing but creations of the mind. Some of them may be good and others may be bad. You should not attach any importance to them.

Maya, the cosmic illusion, is not somewhere *out there*. It is *in here*—in our mind, in our attitude, in the way we evaluate things that happen.

Baba said:

> Let these various thoughts arise within you as they may, the more you try to catch your mind the more it will escape your grasp and become scattered. Therefore give up that futile attempt, become calm and meditate on God.

> Do not impose any conditions on meditation such as that your mind must be in a particular mood because your mind will never obey. Understand that the mind is nothing but Consciousness.

Perhaps you are not certain that the whole universe is Consciousness, but you will admit for sure that your mind is Consciousness. Then make use of these principles within your own mind.

Sutras 5 and 13 in the *Pratyabhijnahridayam* shed enormous light on the mind. Essentially they say that when *Chiti*, universal Consciousness, contracts and looks outward through the senses, it becomes the mind. Then again, when the mind withdraws from the outer world and turns within it expands and becomes universal Consciousness again.

Baba said:

> This is the truth of the mind, regardless of what you may think about it. The mind is nothing but a different name for the Goddess *Chiti*. Goddess *Chiti* Herself becomes the mind, and if you understand this truth, that would be the highest meditation. With this understanding you would be able to purify your mind immediately, and you would not have to use any other technique for calming your mind, because your mind would become calm by itself. Even in the midst of different thoughts, whether good or bad, you should feel the same satisfaction, the same happiness that you feel while having visions of gods or goddesses, or visions of the blue light, or the Blue Lord. Then you will see how quickly you can progress in meditation. Because you reject bad thoughts and accept good thoughts and because you are presently expelling some of your mental impressions, you are not able to meditate successfully.

So don't fight bad thoughts, don't go after good thoughts, see it all as the play of Consciousness. Whatever thoughts come and go in your mind, it is the play of Consciousness. This is a higher *upaya*, a higher means. It is certainly okay to fight bad thoughts. That is a valid and venerable method. But this is a higher *upaya*, a more sophisticated means.

A sage said:

> The mind is the cosmic power of Shiva, the cosmic Shakti of Shiva who dances in ecstasy. The mind should be worshipped, it should not be subdued.

Think of your mind as the cosmic power, like the dancing Shiva. He dances the universe into creation; he creates, sustains and destroys. He dances into every form. Think of your own mind as the dancing power of Shiva. Look how creative your mind is. It can come up with so many esoteric tearing thoughts. It moves easily from putting you down to putting your friends down, to putting the government down, to putting your husband or wife down, and back to putting yourself down. So it dances and sports—so much imagination. It even makes up things; it finds bad things where there aren't any. It is wonderful. 'The mind should be worshipped, it should not be subdued.'

All the different thoughts, good or bad, are permutations of the one Consciousness. Watch the play happen with reverence and compassion. Behind the play there is bliss, there is illumination. Moods come and go. If you are sad now, it will pass. Say the mantra intensely. Cling to the knowledge that 'all is *Chiti*'.

MEDITATION II: THE DANCE OF THE MIND

Let's meditate in this Shaivite manner. Watch the mind, the mind is the Shakti of Shiva. Truly, you are Shiva; the mind is your Shakti. The mind dances your whole universe into creation. According to your mind every choice in your life is made. It creates your whole life; it is an instrument of great power. As we have seen many times it is a double-edged sword. The mind is something that can cut through ignorance to the truth and it can also cut off your own head. So let it dance. Worship its dance, don't try to channel its dance into certain grooves. Let it dance its own dance and watch it from a distance. Everything is the play of Chiti, *the dance of Consciousness. Meditate for 10 minutes.*

Chapter 17

The Rasas: Abhinavagupta, Art and Spirituality

> Shiva Himself becomes the stage, the actor and the costumes. He holds
> His sport for His own sake, and for His own delight.
>
> Baba Muktananda, *Siddha Meditation*

The Indian yogi, philosopher and sage, Shankaracharya, was partly
responsible for the otherworldly tone of Indian spirituality. He
summed up his teaching in a short statement:

> *Brahman satyam jaganmithya jivo brahmaiva naparah*
> Brahman, the Self, or the Absolute, is real—the world is unreal. The
> individual soul is nothing but Brahman.

To Shankara this world is an illusion, and only the inner Self, the highest
truth, has reality. Nothing in this material world can attain the Self or the
ultimate. In other words, we are doomed to a hopeless quest in this world
of despair and lack. And the path that he gave, the method of Advaita
Vedanta, is a method of negation. It is *neti, neti*, which means, 'not this, not
this'. Whatever you see, it is 'not that'. You meditate; a thought comes up,
'not that'. A feeling comes up, 'not that'. You want a house, 'not that'. You
want a relationship, 'not that'. It is all negation. After this profound process
of negating and denying, you strip away all that is false. In the end you are
left with only the Self, the Absolute, Brahman. That alone is real.

As you might think, art would not do well in such a world. It would not
be perceived as having much value. Even the Buddha was fairly negative
about art.

He says:

> Like a wailing, singing is regarded in the discipline of the Noble
> Ones. Like madness is dancing, and childishness is laughter showing
> the teeth.

This uneasy relationship between art and religion wasn't confined to
the East. It also happened in the West. Often religion looks at art as suspect,
self-indulgent, possibly sensual, trivial and often shocking. The English
humorist A. P. Herbert said:

> As my poor father used to say
> In 1863,
> Once people start on all this art
> Good-bye moralitee!

This understanding is widely held in religious circles. In the middle
ages in the West, a concept arose called *dulce et utile*, which means the
sweet and the useful. Churchmen believed that art's rightful place was to
serve the dogma of religion or the *thought* of religion. Art should serve the
church and create an attractive packaging of religious ideas. The largely
illiterate masses could view paintings and appreciate and understand
religious things. Here art is seen as a confection, sweetly dressing up
religious truths.

Later, with the Renaissance, art went in a different direction and became
worldlier. It gave up serving religion and investigated humanity. A new
understanding of the place and function of art emerged, along with
staggering technical breakthroughs.

In 1818 the French philosopher Victor Cousin said:

> We must have religion for religion's sake, morality for morality's sake,
> and art for art's sake. The beautiful cannot be the way to what is useful,
> or to what is good, or to what is holy. It leads only to itself.

Here again are the beautiful and the useful, *dulce et utile*. This concept
of art for art's sake is still familiar today—art, not in service of the church
or God, with no justification outside of just being beautiful. My Uncle
Michael loved to quote a poem by Emerson, which some early teacher of his
told him was the most perfect poem in all literature.

Emerson said:

> If eyes were made for seeing,
> Then beauty is its own excuse for being:

The American poet Walt Whitman said, 'The priest departs; the divine literatus comes'. In the 19th century art had become a substitute religion: God is dead, art lives. The real priest is the inspired artist. This is the religion of art. And, when art becomes a replacement for God, you also have a swelling of the artistic ego.

Sigmund Freud characteristically remarked:

> The artist is a neurotic . . . he is doing what he does for honour, power, riches, fame and the love of women.

Freud's rather cynical vision is a relief—the artist was getting rather inflated.

Still, in the 19th century, many artists like Whitman and Emerson looked for the spiritual in a nondogmatic way. The early 20th-century German artist, Max Beckman, was influenced by Vedanta. He says:

> What I want to show in my work is the idea that hides itself behind so-called reality. I am seeking the bridge that leads from the visible to the invisible . . . One of my problems is to find the Self, which has only one form and is immortal . . . Art is creative for the sake of realisation, not for amusement. It is the quest of our Self that drives us along the eternal journey we must all make.

As before, art is not trivial, not just for fun or beauty. Art is for something higher. This time, for spiritual realisation. Beckman wants to penetrate the illusion of the world and see beyond it to the spirit.

Many artists have seen art as a means of personal and social transformation. Die Brucke was a group of 20th-century young German Expressionists who saw art as a means of taking man to a higher plane. Their art was so strong and disturbing that art critics and historians used the phrase 'the shock of the new' to describe it. In that moment of shock from the visual impact of the art, the artists hoped to create a gap or opening in the consciousness of the viewer through which the artists' perspective or vision could slip.

The 20th-century artist Piet Mondrian was a Theosophist, strongly influenced by Eastern ideas. To him, his abstract forms represented higher truth. My father, who was a modern artist, detested Abstract Expressionism in general, and Mondrian most of all. He believed passionately, as I heard innumerable times as I grew up, that the figure in art should not be lost. There should be the figure but also abstraction. He wanted a mix, the physical and the spiritual you might say. He hated the aesthetic that Mondrian represented and he hated spirituality that denies the world. He would have loved the understanding of Abhinavagupta.

Abhinavagupta stands out ever among the great sages of Kashmir Shaivism. He had done intense *sadhana,* or spiritual practice. He had attained Self-realisation—he was a *Siddha*. In addition, he was more than a great yogi. Many great yogis rarely or never speak. They may live in caves in the Himalayas and have few disciples. Abhinavagupta had an encyclopaedic mind. The only one like him might be the 20th-century sage Sri Aurobindo. Once he attained enlightenment, Aurobindo started writing and created a library full of books. Abhinavagupta wrote texts in Sanskrit on the Tantras and yogic philosophy and practices. Then, late in his career, he turned his mind to aesthetics. He represents a rare conjunction of art and spirituality. If you study aesthetics in university you might come across the aesthetic theorist Abhinavagupta in your anthology as I did as an undergraduate. You wouldn't know that he was also a great yogi.

As the pre-eminent spokesman for Kashmir Shaivism, Abhinavagupta's view opposes Shankara's Vedanta. Where Shankara's Vedanta says that this world is a trap and an illusion, Shaivism says it is the embodiment of the Divine. Shankara talked about maya, the cosmic illusion, portrayed as a deceptive female deity. Abhinavagupta spoke of the Goddess Shakti, or spiritual energy, portrayed as the divine Mother who redeems the material world. Imagine two groups of people talking about the same person. One group doesn't like him and speaks badly about him, presenting the negative view. That is like the Vedantins. The other group likes him and they say wonderful things. That is like the Shaivites.

The truth is, both points of view are valid. It all depends on your angle of vision. In our analogy there is a huge difference in these two points of view, but in a yogic sense, both views lead to the same goal.

Shaivism talks about Shiva's five cosmic processes, which incorporate all of life. The first three are creation, sustenance and destruction. Everything in form goes through these three changes. They can be seen as the ultimate calamity—old age, disease and death—or the modality by means of which new life forms. In the image of the *nataraj,* the fourth process, concealment, is represented by an infant being ground under Shiva's foot.

Shiva Nataraj. *The characteristic figure of the* nataraj, *the dancing Shiva, is a powerful symbol of the Shaivite vision.*

Do not get sentimental about that baby—he represents maya or ignorance. It is the demon child of Shiva and Shakti. Finally, the fifth process is also the most uplifting—grace. While delusion creates separation and casts us down, grace is the principle that creates unity or oneness and uplifts all souls. The Shaivite point of view includes everything, the whole tapestry of life: the good, the bad, life and death, all of it. It is life-positive, life-affirming.

A Tantric text says:

> His body is the universe. His speech pervades the worlds. His ornaments are the moon and stars. The purest one, Shiva, He the first dancer, to Him I bow.

Shiva dances the universe into creation. In Kashmir Shaivism, the aphorism *Nartaka atma* (*Shiva Sutras* III.9) means, the Self is the dancer or the Self is the actor. Against the background of Brahminical orthodoxy, it is audacious to use this metaphor from the world of art.

In Shaivism, the world is not seen as an obstruction but as a *theophany*, a manifestation of God, that actually discloses God to us if we can but see Him. In such a world, art has a distinguished place. In the world of Abhinavagupta, art is important. How important? Kashmir Shaivism says that the highest experience you can have in life is the experience of the Divine. This is the *summum bonum*, the highest or chief good. It is the experience of a yogi or a mystic who realises the truth within himself as Brahman or the Self.

Abhinavagupta lists two worldly experiences that are closest to that one. One of them is sex and the other is the aesthetic, the experience of all forms of art. These two experiences in our mundane life are the closest to the yogi's experience of the Absolute. Further, says Abhinava, each of these experiences, handled rightly, can take us to the Absolute. So a new point of view has emerged *vis-a-vis* art. It should not just be entertainment, nor should it merely serve religious dogma: *it should give an experience.*

Aren't we close here to our contemporary point of view? We expect art to give us something, some emotion, some feeling, some experience. That is why the temper of Shaivism is modern, and why it can speak to us in our time. Abhinavagupta says that art nourishes the highest aspect of the audience, the *sensitivity* of the audience, revealing the experience of the Self by (his words) a 'sudden flash of the scintillating light of Consciousness'. We might not call it that, but surely we have all had uplifting experiences in a movie, a play, from music, or a painting or reading.

Abhinavagupta is talking about the experience of *pratyabhijna*, Self-recognition. The Self-Recognition School says that the yogic wisdom and experience you get through meditation is nothing new. It is already within you and nothing has to be added. That is why we have an affinity for great works of art and that is why the experience of the Self is possible for everyone. What we need to do is re-cognise, to know again, that which we have somehow forgotten. In the genuine aesthetic experience a great work of art triggers the experience that is always potentially within us.

Abhinavagupta worked with an interesting aesthetic concept called *rasa*. He didn't invent this idea, but he developed it in the direction of spirituality. *Rasa* is a metaphor from cooking, and also from Ayurveda, traditional Indian medicine. *Rasa* is the delicious juice from a vegetable. It is the essence and best part of a thing—tasty and nourishing. By extension it means a sense of aliveness and richness. In art it is that *je ne sais quoi* that makes something scintillating and deeply engaging. It is emotional and uplifting.

If you go to an Indian restaurant and order a meal, you may get a stainless steel tray with a portion of rice in the middle, surrounded by several small cups filled with different dishes. Called a *thali*, it looks like a painter's palette. The Indian meal is nonlinear, something I had to get used to when I first lived in India, because we eat in a linear manner in the West. We begin with soup and finish with dessert—or cheese or fruit, depending on the country. In India, the dessert, the sweet—everything—is offered from the beginning. Ayurvedic medicine talks about six *rasas*, or six tastes: sweet, salt, sour, bitter, pungent and astringent. Each *rasa* affects the body differently. A good Indian meal contains all the *rasas*. It makes me wonder whether nonlinear eating comes from nonlinear thinking, or if nonlinear eating causes nonlinear thinking.

In any event, art has different aesthetic flavours. It is like a *thali*. You don't end with the sweet. The sweet is part if it. You move to the sweet periodically in the midst of your meal. In art these *rasas* are not different foods, but emotional colourings. The true palette of an artist then, is the emotions he works with. He combines them in different ways to create different dishes, different genres and different effects on the audience. Some artists, like Shakespeare, work with a full palette of emotional *rasas*. Others work within a narrow range. Think of Picasso and Cezanne. Both are undeniably great artists, but Picasso experimented endlessly, while Cezanne restricted himself to a more narrow area of investigation.

According to Abhinavagupta, the artist or the poet fills with *rasa*, fills with emotion. He is then said to have 'vision'. But it is not enough to have an inner feeling, an aesthetic *rasa*. You also have to express it. You must have craft and be able to put it into a work of art. Then, as Abhinavagupta says, the feeling is like 'a liquid that overflows a vase'. It spills over and transfers to the audience. The artist fills the world with his original feeling.

From Abhinavagupta's point of view you judge a work of art by whether it is *nirasa* (without *rasa)* or *rasavant* (with *rasa)*. Once I had a discussion with Baba about writing and he said, 'You have to put *rasa* in it'. Art that does not have it, that is merely intellectual, dry or technical, won't give the aesthetic experience. It has to have some energy, some life, some sweetness. All these conditions produce the experience of *chamatkara*, which is pronounced *cha-mat-ka-ra*, similar to the sound of smacking your lips in satisfaction upon eating a delicious dish. This is the aesthetic experience. It is interesting to me that the underlying metaphor is from food.

For Abhinava, the aesthetic experience also has the feeling of *wonder*, the sense of something great and ennobling. There is an opening out of the Self and a sense of awe. The mundane is transcended and a higher life is glimpsed.

THE RASAS

The number of *rasas* varies according to different authors—one, eight or nine, 10 or 12, or an infinite number of emotional colourings. Abhinavagupta talks about a palette of nine *rasas*, eight ordinary ones and one transcendental. Originally these *rasas* were applied to poetry and drama, but later they were applied to painting and all the arts.

Here is the menu of *rasas* that Abhinavagupta gives:

- Erotic *(sringara)* — Love
- Comic *(hasya)* — Laughter
- Pathetic *(karuna)* — Sorrow
- Furious *(raudra)* — Anger
- Heroic *(vira)* — Noble enthusiasm
- Terrible *(bhayanaka)* — Fear
- Odious *(bibhatsa)* — Disgust
- Marvellous *(adbhuta)* — Wonder
- Tranquil *(shanta)* — Serenity

To think of the emotions as a palette or *thali* full of different flavours is a significantly Shaivite approach. While many yogic disciplines narrow the range of acceptable emotions, the vision of an artist is different. He is more interested in richness and life than in purity. He has a tolerance of negative emotions.

In normal terms, the opposite of a yogi is a *bhogi,* a pleasure seeker. It is Shaivism's claim that it offers both yoga and *bhoga*, both spiritual freedom and enjoyment of the world. No wonder then, that the great Shaivite master Abhinavagupta is also the principle articulator of the *rasa* theory of art. It is a truly Shaivite approach to accept all emotions, both negative and positive, as part of the fabric of life and to enjoy their interplay, not seeking to eliminate any of them, while remaining anchored in higher Consciousness. If the yogi is Shiva seeking purity and control, the artist is Shakti, tolerant as a mother, cherishing even the apparently negative aspects of life.

DISGUST

In working in the area of the Shiva Process, I developed a theory which named three principle negative emotions: anger, fear and sorrow. All other negative emotions seemed reducible to these. In re-examining the list of *rasas*, however, I noticed that a fourth negative emotion, disgust, is listed. Superficially, one would not put disgust on the same level of importance as the other three, but on deeper reflection, it is as weighty. Perhaps it is more visible from the perspective of India, where in its higher octaves it is a yogic emotion, fuelling the asceticism that led to the renunciation of Shankara and the world weariness of the Buddha.

We don't have a comparable ascetic tradition in the West. Underlying all negative emotions is the familiar duality of *raga* and *dvesha*—attachment and aversion. We go towards some objects and recoil from others. The four negative emotions spring from this duality: anger and sadness from *raga* (attachment) and fear and disgust from *dvesha* (aversion). The Shaivite yogi may begin like the yogi or Vedantin, with a disgust for the world and worldliness, but he doesn't end there. Once his heart is uplifted by Shiva's grace, he can find no world to reject, but only Shiva everywhere.

A whole chapter could be devoted to any one of the *rasas* of course. The erotic *rasa*—there's *Romeo and Juliet*, D. H. Lawrence's novels, lots of films, and the more spiritual eros of the Krishna *lila*. Hollywood's favourite form combines the erotic *rasa* with the comic *rasa*, what we call romantic comedy, which is *laulya* in Sanskrit. *Laulya* means all of Meg Ryan's movies and most of Rock Hudson's and Cary Grant's. Then you have the pathetic *rasa*. The emotion behind the pathetic is sorrow, or sadness. Different periods, different cultures find they have a taste for sadness. The 19th century, for example, was much more tolerant of this emotion and you can see it in the writing and the romantic music, much more so than in the classical period which preceded it. In our day, the blues, of course has sadness by definition, but it is often redeemed by self-ironic humour.

It would be interesting to sit down with a list of your favourite films and see which *rasa* or *rasas* they most embodied. There are plenty of examples of the terrible and the odious, but it has been said that this is not the age of the heroic. In earlier times, with simpler faith, the heroic mode was popular, as in the Greek epics. But even if our time is more suitable to the antihero than the hero, we still have our share of heroes like Indiana Jones and Luke Skywalker. Similarly, I think the marvellous is making a return to aesthetic favour in our time. As spirituality grows, people have less mundane tastes and want to feel wonder. There are many more movies and TV shows with a supernatural element these days than a few years ago. The last *rasa*, which Abhinavagupta handles in a particular way, is transcendental and has a special place. It is *shanta rasa,* the peaceful, and I will speak of it in a moment.

There is another thing that Abhinavagupta discusses that is worth noting. He says that things that you might hate in life, you like in art. That is possible because of what we would call aesthetic distance. He calls it generalisation. You move from the specific, what I want and what I don't want, to a general situation, and then, because of detachment, you can experience the aesthetic pleasure in it.

SHANTA RASA

Shanta rasa is Abhinavagupta's specific contribution. He believes that this *rasa* underlies all the others as the most basic and independent. When you experience any *rasa* at its highest level it turns into *shanta rasa*, the feeling of serenity. It is as though the different emotions are waves on the ocean and the ocean itself is peace. All the different *rasas*, then, are permutations of the one underlying *rasa*, *shanta*.

A Shaivite author wrote:

> At the moment of shock, when we experience the terrible *rasa* or the odious *rasa* or the moment of joy in musical elevation, the mind becomes still. Then the light of our true nature, the Self, flashes forth and illumines our consciousness with its brilliance.

According to Abhinavagupta, *shanta rasa* arouses a mental condition that brings transcendental bliss. He says that *shanta rasa* cannot be presented directly. You have to sneak up on it through laughter, heroism, fear or other intense emotion. He adds, the only way it can be presented directly is to portray a great yogi at the point of realisation. Aristotle seems to approach *shanta rasa* from a different perspective. A work of art elicits strong emotions in the audience, such as pity or fear, evoking empathy. When these emotions are cathartically purged, what is left might be *shanta rasa*. In Buddhist art, the portrayals of the Buddha are suffused with *shanta rasa*, a sense of transcendental peace, as are the Hindu depictions of Lord Shiva in meditation.

One movie is brought to mind that strikes me as a yogic parable—*The Truman Show*. It seems to me reminiscent of the life of the Buddha, though told in a curious way. Truman's entire life is a television show. Unknown to him, the community where he lives is actually a giant stage set and all the people in his life—including his wife and co-workers—are actors. People in the outside world avidly follow Truman's every move, and everything is under the control of a Svengali-like director, of whom Truman is unaware. Truman's controlled environment is like the Buddha's. Both were shielded from the truth since birth. As cracks in the edifice of untruth start to appear they begin to wake up. They look around and inquire, 'What's going on?' In a great leap both leave their lives and, risking everything, go through a doorway into the unknown.

Of course, while the Buddha went through the door that led to enlightenment, Truman went through the door that led to the backlot of a movie studio. Both stories are parables of our soul's journey of awakening. We discover that things are completely different from the way we thought, and we wake up to a new reality. But we can only follow Truman to the point where he makes that heroic choice. That is his enlightenment. It's hard to imagine a sequel. We don't really want to know what happens after that. Similarly, in romantic comedy the couple finally gets together: you don't want to know about what happens next—the mortgage, the kids, the therapist and the health insurance. That would be situation comedy, a different genre, a different *rasa*. You draw the curtain there.

Maybe that's why Abhinavagupta says that *shanta rasa* can only be portrayed under certain conditions. If the audience meets those conditions then it can attain the ultimate. Abhinava says:

> The sensuous enjoyment of a work of art leads to the grasp or realisation of the Absolute if the necessary subjective conditions are present in the experiencer.

What are these conditions? We began with the *artist* overflowing with emotion. He puts that emotion into his *work*. Now we come to the third part of this triad: *the audience* or the observer, the receptacle of that same emotion.

THE AUDIENCE

The audience must have the quality of sensitivity and openness. The word in Sanskrit is *sahridaya*. *Hridaya* is heart. *Sahridaya* means same-hearted, or possessed of heart, or having the consent of the heart. We are not talking about an audience that is cultivated or educated, but an audience that is open.

A cultivated audience may not be open. Knowledge, taste, or even cultivation can get in the way of being the perfect audience. The perfect audience simply opens. Abhinavagupta says that the open audience is 'ready for tasting', and has an elevated capacity for wonder. The important aspect is wonder, the *Ahhh* experience. To allow yourself to experience wonder you have to be simple. You have to allow yourself to be childlike, and often we are too sophisticated. We look at things without allowing ourselves the experience of wonder.

Abhinavagupta says:

> Complete absence of wonder is an absence of life. Aesthetic receptivity —being endowed with heart—is to be immersed in an intense state of wonder that enlivens the body.

How far is that from modern cynicism? It is also far from modern 'cool'. If you're too cool you can't allow wonder. When I was a teenager I used to go to cafes in Greenwich Village, in New York. It was the days of hip and cool, when they would read poetry and coolly snap their fingers. You would not say, 'Ah that's great!'

Abhinavagupta says:

> Indeed, when he hears sweet songs,
> When he is no longer content with staying in the middle,
> and being indifferent, when a tense vibration starts in his heart,
> Then it is called the power of bliss and this man becomes
> the 'same-hearted' one (sahridaya).

This vibration in the heart is the aesthetic response. The heart of the artist opens, the audience opens, and both relish the experience, the *chamatkara*, the deliciousness. Then in that very moment, the same-hearted audience becomes one with the artist and becomes as great. Abhinavagupta says that they become one in this experience, in this spirit.

It reminds me of a second encounter between Lord Krishna and Arjuna that followed their discussion recounted in the *Bhagavad Gita*. In the *Gita* they were on the battlefield when Arjuna expressed his doubts and worries about the coming battle. Krishna told him, 'Be a warrior Arjuna, it's your duty to fight'. Then Krishna gave an exquisite teaching in 18 chapters about yoga and meditation, the path, the Self and related matters.

Years later, after the war was over, Krishna and Arjuna were together again. Arjuna said, 'Lord, do you remember on the battlefield at Kurukshetra, we were about to fight the war and I was in despair?'

Krishna said he remembered.

Arjuna said, 'You told me great things then about meditation and yoga. I was very inspired, very uplifted, but now I can't remember any of it. Could you tell it to me again?'

And Krishna said, 'Well, Arjuna, what happened then, the conditions were perfect, you were wide open and you drew the teaching out. Now, I can't remember the teaching myself, either'.

Just as Guru and disciple have to connect in openness and love, so there has to be the right interplay between the open audience and the artist for there to be that transmission.

Krishna said, 'I will try. I will tell it to you as best I can'.

He gave another rendition, but there was a lot less energy in it. Maybe we could call it the 'B' version of the *Bhagavad Gita*.

Abhinavagupta says that it is not easy to find or become the sensitive audience:

> Our normal condition is an opaque heart devoid of wonder. [We live] in a thick layer of mental stupor.

Gurdjieff said that ordinary man is a machine, he is mechanical and soulless. Worry, fear, desire, greed, lack of attention, attachment to petty things put him into a stupor and give him an opaque heart.

Abhinavagupta says that the audience can work on itself like a yogi would to become the perfect audience. He lists several obstacles to overcome. One obstacle is that the audience might lack imagination. It might be too gross for the subtle things portrayed on the stage. Abhinavagupta asks, what can an audience do about that? Well, it can go out and live life with more sympathy. It can broaden itself through life experience. That, of course, would not be much help for *tonight's* performance, but it might help later. Another obstacle to our being the perfect audience is that we identify with the story. You have just broken up with your husband, and the story is about a divorce, so you are upset by the content of the story and that prevents you from opening to the aesthetic experience. Yet another obstacle is that we are lost in our private world. We are so caught up in our own thoughts, feelings and emotional drama that the artist can't reach us. We are not available. The antidote that Abhinavagupta proposes is for the artist to dress up his creation with strong stimulants. Perhaps that is why rock and roll is a suitable art form for our age.

When, however, the sensitive spectator transcends these obstacles and becomes the ideal aesthete, the ninth-century Shaivite sage, Bhattanayaka, says:

> The spectator, absorbed in the tasting of this *rasa*, turning inward, feels pleasure through the whole performance. Sunk into his own being, he

forgets everything (pertaining to practical life). There is manifested in him that flow of inborn pleasure, from which the yogis draw their satisfaction.

Here the theatre-goer has the same experience as the meditating yogi. But Abhinava's goal is to take us beyond even that—to make our whole life a work of art. In *Tantraloka*, his supreme work on yoga, he says:

> The wise one, in order to worship properly, should offer back into the highest abode that *rasa* which flows and trickles from the multitude of existing things. In the divine abode of the body, I adore you, O Shiva, together with the Goddess, day and night. I adore you with the priceless goblet of the Heart which is full of the ambrosia of bliss. This world, full of various tastes and flavours, is cast into the Heart. I squeeze it. The supreme nectar of Consciousness, which removes birth, old age and death, flows gushing from it. Opening the mouth wide I devour it, the supreme oblation, like clarified butter, and in this way, O Supreme Goddess, I gladden and satisfy you day and night.

By devotion, by meditation, by self-mastery, we banish all fear, worry, depression and self-concern and experience an endless flow of *rasa* even while living our ordinary life. We become the ideal artist and audience of our own life. Having eliminated all obstacles, and all grossness from our souls we become truly *sahridaya*, 'possessed of heart'. Like the hero of a Keats poem, we live every moment in touch with ecstasy and the subtle dimension of life. In essence we live in the constant experience of the Self. This is the crown of Abhinavagupta's vision.

MEDITATION ON THE RASA OF THE DIVINE

Let's meditate in the spirit of rasa. *Become* sahridaya; *let your heart be open and sensitive. Within you, the Supreme Artist, the Lord of the Self, creates works of beauty, love and joy. The Self may appear in any form. It may come as anger. It may come as sadness. All of these are permutations of the one universal emotion. Whatever arises within you is a* rasa *of the Divine. Meditate for 10 minutes.*

Chapter 18

Language Mysticism in Shaivism I: Matrika

The alphabet itself has immense importance; it is God's creative power, his Shakti, which has taken the form of the letters of the alphabet.

Baba Muktananda, *I Am That*

A Shaivite sage says:

This world does not appear to thy devotees in the same way that it appears to others.

A person imbued with *Shiva drishti*, the *rasa* of Shiva, sees a different universe. His whole world is transformed: it is no longer a material place of loss and scarcity, where everything is running out and running down. Divine Consciousness ever refreshes itself, it is ever abundant. This is the vision of mysticism: the signs of the Divine, the footprints of God, are everywhere.

The *Spanda Karikas* say:

When there is *unmesha* or revelation of the essential nature of the Divine, there is the *pralaya* or disappearance of the world. When there is *nimesha* or concealment of the essential nature of the Divine, there is *udaya* or appearance of the world.

You can go in two directions only. If you see with the vision of Consciousness, the vision of ignorance will disappear. But if you see with the material eye, the vision of God will disappear. This has a practical application. If you look at your life and you see problem areas, you are probably looking at that area in a material way, from the point of view of lack, of matter, of give and take, and ego. If you transform your vision, you will experience an upliftment, an upwelling of energy. Then you are seeing with Shiva's eye.

LANGUAGE, BONDAGE AND LIBERATION

Fundamental to this shift in vision, and to the way we experience things in general, is language. In fact, the entire drama of bondage and liberation is linguistic. Language is the defining and characteristic activity of a human being. It is inherent in human beings because Consciousness is the essential nature of a person. The linguist Noam Chomsky acknowledges this when he says that human beings are born with an innate language capacity. He says that we have 'mental organs' that are parallel to our physical ones.

Chomsky says:

> Certain schools of linguistics believe that the human mind at birth contains the structure of thought—even moral thought—through which it perceives the world.

Since a person's essential nature is oneness, language is natural and inherent to him because it is an essential expression of Consciousness.

The way we use language, both inwardly and outwardly, affects our state. In our inner world language, thoughts seem to 'just happen' to us. In fact we can—and should—gain understanding and control there. Unless we do, we remain at the effect of forces of neurosis and contraction established by our past. We did not examine and understand in the past, hence we suffer now. If we begin to understand now, we spare ourselves future suffering.

We have the wrong way of thinking and speaking about things. There are actual energies that create negativity and separation in us. In *Spanda Karikas* it is said that particular linguistic forces are always intent on concealing a person's true nature and involving him in delusion. If you look carefully at your own mind, you will see tendencies that pull you in the wrong direction. They are strong. They are like deities, little monster deities in you, that make you feel bad about yourself. They show up in your self-talk, your interior monologue.

Spanda Karikas I.20 says:

> They push down people of unawakened mind into the terrible ocean of worldly existence which is hard to cross.

'They' refers to the negative deities of speech, which create negative thought patterns. They must be overcome by practice.

Shiva Sutras III.19 similarly says:

> The yogi should beware of the different ruling *shaktis*, *Maheshwari* and others, who are inherent in the different groups of letters such as *ka*-group because even though he has some attainment, through ignorance he may still be deceived by these *shaktis*.

Thus language that moves us in the wrong direction is the primary delusional force.

Kshemaraja, in a memorable passage, says:

> Because he does not rest in his real nature even for a moment, being exploited by the group of powers, therefore he is called a bound soul. He is deprived of his glory by the goddesses Brahmi and others presiding over the groups of letters. As such, he is tormented by gross and subtle words which penetrate within all kinds of definite and indefinite ideas, and he feels, 'I am limited. I am imperfect; I may do something; this I take, this I reject, etc', and he is thus led to joy or sorrow. Being exploited by the group of *shaktis*, he is called *pashu*, or bound soul.

Clearly, language plays a central role in the Shaivite universe. As we have seen, Shaivism describes 36 levels, or *tattvas*, of Consciousness, from pure Consciousness at the top. The lowest level of manifestation is the material world, yet Shaivism tells us that even the material world is *Chiti*, Consciousness. The material vibration may be dense and slow, but it is simply the low end of a continuum.

Similarly, language extends from the highest, most perfect language, down to the most gross language. Gross language is the kind of language that creates hatred and separation. At a much higher level is a beautiful love song, at another high level is, for example, Shakespeare's writing. And, at a higher level even than that, higher than the poetry of a great writer, is scripture. Sacred writings come not from the human mind (and these are scriptures of all the traditions) but from the Divine—whether they are channelled and brought in via a sage or found under a rock. (We regularly look under every rock in the ashram!) These sacred writings come from a higher source, beyond the mind.

When I studied literature, one piece of poetry that fascinated me was 'Kubla Khan' by Coleridge:

> In Xanadu did Kubla Khan
> A stately pleasure dome decree
> Where Alph, the sacred river, ran

Through caverns measureless to man
Down to a sunless sea . . .

It was magic—it seemed channelled from a world of pure poetry. Coleridge himself did not know where it came from, since he received it in a dream. Perhaps opium was partly responsible, but whatever the source, I felt it allowed me a glimpse of a higher level of discourse.

My father was an artist. Not long before he died at the age of 94, he had a dream vision. In it he visited a realm of art of a kind he had never experienced on earth. It was a purely abstract art and it amazed and inspired him. This was remarkable because all my life I had heard him rant against pure abstraction. But now he felt that he had experienced a higher world of art with possibilities he had never conceived.

FOUR LEVELS OF SPEECH

Shaivism delineates four levels of speech, beginning with the spoken word and progressively becoming more subtle, more interior and more conscious. Gross speech is called *vaikari*. One level more subtle and interior is thought. Thought is language that remains in one's inner world. This level is called *madhyama* (middling). One level more subtle still is *pashyanti*.

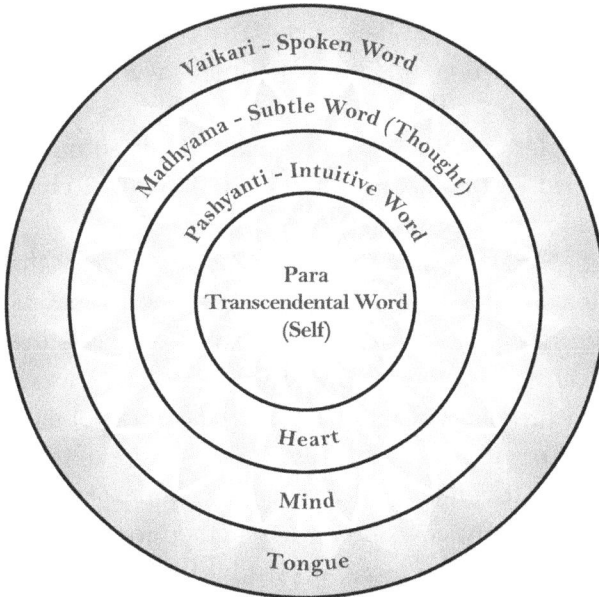

Mandala of the Four Levels of Speech. Speech exists on four levels, gross and subtle.

This is inner speech before language is formed. It is the pure impulse of intuition. Here we receive meanings all at once in one gulp.

In *pashyanti* Mozart received whole symphonies, which he later wrote down note by note. Here scientists grasp solutions to their problems holistically, later to be expressed laboriously in equations and formulae. This is the level of direct *knowing*. The spoken word is like the leaves of a tree, it is the visible manifestation of something deeper and more central. Whatever is spoken or argued has its deep roots in Consciousness.

Abhinavagupta says:

> Discursive, dualistic thought certainly is discourse, but in its deeper nature, it is awareness *(vimarsha)*.

Music provides a good illustration of deeper levels of speech. My boyhood music teacher used to tell me at every lesson, 'Music is a universal language that comes from the heart'. Abhinavagupta would have agreed with her. He said that a sweet melody is a gross form of *pashyanti* because it is speech without letters and words. Music lovers often have the experience of being taken to a deep, preverbal level of meaningfulness by music.

In a most practical way, we can see the interplay of these levels of speech in normal conversation. Often a conversation is, in reality, two conversations going on simultaneously. The conversation at the spoken level of speech *(vaikari)* is different from the conversation at the level of thought *(madhyama)*. We might be saying polite things on the surface, but harbouring murderous thoughts underneath. While both parties might be observing the rules of politeness, they are both likely to be aware of the different situation deeper down.

The ancient Sanskrit grammarians had posited these three levels of speech. Abhinavagupta added a fourth: *para* or transcendental speech. It is also called *paravani* or *paravak*, supreme speech. This is the level of the pure Self, the *aham vimarsha* or pure divine Consciousness. This level is prior to specific meanings or intuitions. But that does not mean it is a void or a blank. Far from it. It is meaning itself. The nature of Consciousness is meaning-in-itself. It contains all languaging within itself in seed form. Language is a relatively slow and partial method for conveying meaning. Shiva is the arena of total meaning, all possible thoughts and feelings, ideas and expressions, held at once, simultaneously and eternally.

At this level of language is the creating word of the Gospel of John ('In the beginning was the Word . . .'), and it is at this level of speech that divine creativity takes place, 'Let there be light'. Such speech is inherently effective: '. . . and there was light'. In the same way, the words of realised beings are powerful, just as the mantra they give is powerful. I was always respectful of anything Baba told me, even if it made me uncomfortable. I held his utterances to be powerful words of truth.

The four levels of speech correspond to the four bodies described by the yogic scriptures. The spoken word is the speech of the physical body, thought is the speech of the subtle body, intuitive knowing is the speech of the causal body and pure Consciousness is the speech of the Self.

MEDITATION I: THE LEVELS OF SPEECH

We will use the levels of speech as a contemplation to reach pure awareness (paravani). *Go inside and listen to your mind speaking. This is the* madhyama *level of speech. Now see if you can get in touch with the* pashyanti *level. You might state a subject like, 'basketball' or 'ballet' or 'poetry' or 'stock market'. Then hold the whole subject in your mind without thinking particular thoughts about it. That is* pashyanti. *Let that subject go, let it merge in meaning-in-itself that underlies it. Now you are at the* para *level. This is awareness in itself: it has the capacity to think of anything, but it is not yet thinking of anything specifically. Feel into the* para *level. It is luminous and full of energy.*

MATRIKA

Shiva Sutras I.4 says:

Jnanadhishthanam matrika
The source of limited knowledge is *matrika*.

Matrika means the 'unknown mother' and it refers to subtle inner speech. It is the inner matrix of our minds. *Matrika* provides the linguistic filter through which we view the world. It is 'unknown' or 'misunderstood' because it operates largely in our unconscious, having a decisive effect on our lives without our being aware of it.

Swami Muktananda writes:

When *Parashakti*, who is also called *Chiti Bhagavati,* the universal Consciousness, limits Herself, she manifests in the form of *matrika,* the group of letters, or sound-syllables. *Matrika* is the cause of one's pain and pleasure. All the thoughts and feelings which arise in the mind—happiness and unhappiness, desire, agitation, love, expectation and jealousy—are the work of *matrika*.

Matrika refers to the letters of the alphabet. The Shaivite sages created a language mysticism reminiscent of the Kabbalistic tradition of the medieval Jewish sages. The Sanskrit alphabet has 50 letters. The 16 vowels represent Shiva, the 34 consonants represent Shakti. Each of the consonants represents a *tattva*, or level of manifestation, below the level of Shiva-Shakti. Because this manifest universe is a reflection of Shiva, the consonants are arranged backwards as in a reflection: the first consonant, *ka*, representing the last *tattva*, earth.

Viewed this way, the universe is the verbal play of the Lord. It is divine language made manifest and given body. Think of all the vowel sounds run together like an *Om. Aeiooouuuaaaeeeiii.* Vowels, Shiva, give a transcendent sound but no meaning. Only when the consonants enter the picture to chop off the eternal vowel sound, do meaning and concrete entities enter the picture. *Chap, lap, cap, man, land* . . . Because consonants make use of and shape the eternal vowel sound, some of them can be and are voiceless. But vowels *are always voiced.* Thus Shakti is necessary for the manifestation of the universe; and all manifestation is a creation within Shiva.

The vowels are the male power. They are called *bija* or 'seed' or 'semen', and are associated with Shiva. The consonants are feminine, are called matrix, or *yoni* (womb) and are associated with Shakti. The *yoni*-consonants give form while the vowels provide dynamism.

There was a medieval Jewish sage named Abraham Abulafia who developed language mysticism in a most unusual and extraordinary way. He felt that since the creation took place through words ('And God said . . .'), the letters of the Hebrew alphabet were therefore the most basic building blocks of creation. He thought, therefore, that if an individual meditated by manipulating the letters of the alphabet in certain ways, he could get in touch with the same forces that created the universe.

His method is complex but basically something like this: the meditator selects a text from the Bible or a holy name of God and then permutates and cycles the letters in every possible way. Taking the letters of the mantra *Om Namah Shivaya*, for example, a Kabbalist might say to himself such things as *Havasaya Shavanomaya Asahama Vasavisayav* and so on. Continuing this way, his consciousness ascends and he feels that he is staring directly into the matrix or source of the universe.

When I encountered Abhinavagupta's astonishing work, *Paratrishika Vivarana*, I saw that he was, in some respects, a kindred spirit to Abulafia. That work is packed with a detailed language mysticism. It gives a picture of living in a universe generated by Shiva's speech, which is the *logos*, the divine creating word. It is not my purpose in this book to plunge into that particular ocean of *matrika*, however, I will give one more example to give a flavour of Abhinavagupta's language mysticism.

Abhinavagupta, for example, takes the word *Aham*, 'I am'. It consists of three letters: 'a', 'ha' and 'm'. He tells us that 'a' denotes Shiva (the first letter of the alphabet contains and implies all the others), 'ha' denotes Shakti, and 'm' denotes *nara*, that is, all individual souls and objects. *Aham* is therefore known as the *shrishti bija*, the seed mantra of creation. The universe is created from Shiva (*a*), via Shakti (*ha*) up to the objective world (*m*).

Now Abhinavagupta tells us that *Ma-ha-a*, which means 'the great' reverses the process implied by *Aham*. *Ma-ha-a* is known as the *samhara bija*, the seed mantra of the process of withdrawal. Here the universe withdraws itself from the objective world (*ma*), via Shakti (*ha*), to reside in Shiva (*a*). Notice that both processes pass through Shakti. Thus, in the Shaivite vision, Shakti is the doorway both to the world and also back to the spirit.

One might ask what does all this linguistic speculation have to do with *sadhana*? Perhaps not a lot, unless one adopts a technique like Abulafia's. However, Abhinavagupta, as we have already seen, is an aesthete as well as a yogi. Perhaps, his artistic nature joins his yogic side in his language mysticism. He holds the view that the universe is Shiva's vast work of art, His garland of letters. Seeing meaning and resonances everywhere, the Shiva yogi melts in devotion.

Baba Muktananda also gave a lot of importance to the concept of *matrika*, though in a less aesthetic and more practical way. He urged the yogi to become aware of the subtle play of *matrika* though careful Self-observation. Seeing how *matrika* works in his inner world to create his experience of life, the yogi slowly learns to control *matrika* and turn it in the right direction.

He writes:

> Just as *matrika* helps us to contract, it also helps us to expand ourselves. The moment one understands the *matrika shakti* and its

work, one is no longer a human being. When the *matrika shakti* expands within, in this very body one becomes Shiva.

Sit quietly and watch the play of *matrika shakti*. Watch how the *matrika* gives rise to letters, how the letters compose words, how the meaning of the words create images in the mind; watch how you become involved in these images.

The yogi pursues *matrika shakti;* he watches it and makes it steady. He brings it under his control, he manipulates it any way he likes. He turns evil thoughts into good thoughts. The *matrika shakti* works according to his will. Such a yogi is called a conqueror of the senses.

Another aphorism in the *Shiva Sutras*, II.7, says:

Matrika chakra sambodhah
When the Guru is pleased he grants full knowledge of *matrika*.

Very naturally as one pursues spiritual development under the tutelage of a true Guru, one's inner energy awakens. As an aspirant draws closer to the Self he understands the play of *matrika* within himself. Through meditation, Self-inquiry, and penetrating wisdom he is no longer the victim of *matrika*, but truly, a Lord of Matrika.

At the highest level we are talking about mantra. A phrase like *Om Namah Shivaya* has no external meaning, no outer world referent. It comes from within and connects us to the Divine. We can use numinous language like mantra or G-Statements to uplift us, and we can also edit our own brain. When our *matrika* or self-talk is separative, when our language is, 'I hate this person. I am no good', we should edit our minds and move towards higher awareness.

This is the science of *matrika*. Language takes us up and pulls us down. Sometimes you speak to someone and as a result you get a bad feeling. It is worthwhile to ask, 'Why is that happening?' Something is wrong. You begin to see that you manifest a certain level of awareness through your speech and through your thought. This is *matrika*. It is the subtext, the hidden conversation behind the outer conversation.

A Shaivite sage says:

No notion exists in the world unassociated with speech. All knowledge manifests as if it were pervaded by speech.

Another way of saying, 'everything is Consciousness' is to say, 'everything is speech'. Some speech is beyond language, it is pure meaningfulness. God is pure radiant meaning, awareness itself.

The scholar-yogi Paul Muller-Ortega says:

> In the secret Heart of reality, Shiva continuously explicates himself. His rumbling vibratory monologue to Himself unfolds to become the delightful and enlightening dialogue of Bhairava and Devi, the Goddess.

This is a wonderful picture: Shiva sitting on Mount Kailas, rumbling to Himself. He is burbling. Or He is going 'Om'. He recites the mantra. Our earthly language is not very effective. I say, 'Pass the salt', and I am likely to get it, but, then, I might not. Shiva has perfectly effective language. He is not stuck in the limitations of action and will. He can do whatever He wants.

He begins talking to Himself inside of Himself, playing two parts as the student and the teacher or as Shiva and Shakti. 'Hmm, why are things like this?' 'Well here's why'. Becoming both, He has a dialogue within Himself. When we turn within we can still hear that rumbling, vibratory monologue. It is the fundamental vibration of the mind within.

Whatever is in Shiva is in you, whatever divine powers are in God are in you. To truly get there you have to become unlimited. You have to let go of limitation, you have to let go of ego, you have to let go of ignorance. It is not a trivial process.

The *Mahartamanjari* says:

> This is the way that the error of ordinary persons who think, 'I am not the Lord', is dissipated. This is an error with respect to the Self who shines always as the 'I'. One repeats to them, 'You are Shiva, gifted with the free power of Consciousness and activity: this world depends on you as a kingdom on its king. It is in you that the world shines, in you that it resides. It is you as Consciousness that the world has as its basis: from which it arises and into which it is reabsorbed.

There is no world here without you. Only your awareness makes the world so for you. Contemplate this until conviction dawns. The *Shiva Sutras* say that such conviction is realisation of the Self. *Shivo'ham. I am Shiva. All this arises and has its being in my awareness!*

MEDITATION II: MATRIKA

See if you can watch the flow of matrika *within your mind. Become a Lord of Matrika: bend it to your will. Notice the effect of the thoughts you are having, and if you don't like those effects, change the thought. Particularly notice if your inner work uplifts your inner experience. Positive* matrikas *hold much more energy than negative ones. They will put you in touch with the current of energy at the base of your mind, that vibratory murmur. There is the experience of 'I am Shiva'. See if you can find it and stay with it. Meditate for 10 minutes.*

Chapter 19

Language Mysticism in Shaivism II: Self-Inquiry

> The yogi renounces seeing the Self in that which is not the Self. And now the Supreme Self also dissolves the error which sees the not Self in the Self. Thus, when this pair of illusions has been torn up from the very root, that supreme yogi has attained his goal.

> Abhinavagupta, *Paramarthasara*, Verses 39-40

While Self-inquiry has come to be associated with the teaching work of the great sage Ramana Maharshi, it also forms the heart of Shaivite *sadhana*.

Abhinavagupta says:

> Inquiry is the highest branch of yoga since it distinguishes between what is to be rejected and what is to be chosen. Therefore, the wise person should practise inquiry.

He calls inquiry 'the wish-fulfilling cow', which surpasses all other methods, and he says that it is 'a finely sharpened axe which cuts the root of the tree of duality'.

As the name suggests, the essential tool of inquiry is the question. Whatever field we are involved in, we strive to understand it by seeking the answer to a series of questions. Questions always come first. 'What material should I use to build that bridge?' What would happen if I combined this with that?' 'What's the fastest way to get to Paris?' A question is a focusing device. It brings the whole power of Consciousness to bear on a small area, a single issue. Everything else is eliminated from the mental field and the focus is entirely on the question in front of us. Very naturally, we use inquiry in the mundane sphere of our lives. When we turn that same inquiry inside, it becomes Self-inquiry.

Questions like, 'What should I wear?', 'What job should I look for?', 'What course should I take?', 'Who should I marry?' are all forms of self-inquiry, but should probably be written with a small 's'. Capital 'S' Self-inquiry begins when we use it spiritually, to investigate the Self. Though the archetypal question is Ramana's 'Who am I?', it can take many forms. In the Shiva Process Self-inquiry normal questions include, 'Why do I feel contracted?' 'What do I need to do to overcome this contraction?' 'How can I get closer to the Self/God?' and so on. Inquiry dives deeper and deeper into the inner truth.

You might ask: 'I understand asking questions, but who answers?' Shaivism holds that perfect wisdom is within each one of us as the inner Self. You are probably aware that when you ask yourself a question like, 'Should I marry him or her?' some sort of response comes from within. It might be a clear 'yes' or 'no' or it might be a feeling of confusion. Sometimes when we inquire within, a complex and murky response happens and we drop the whole inquiry, or put it in the 'too hard basket'. In all these cases the 'right answer' is bubbling up from the Self. But for any number of reasons (pride, negative emotion, preconceptions, prejudice, judgment, weakness of the mind or mental agitation), our reception of the answer is blocked or obscured.

Ramana's inquiry does not look for a verbal response at all. He was justifiably suspicious of any answer that might come in the form of words. His 'Who am I?' inquiry aimed at putting the meditator in touch with a feeling sense of the Self. The Tantric scriptures are usually set up as a dialogue between Shiva and Shakti. Shakti asks questions and Shiva answers them. Of course, in the Shakta Tantras, a more realistic scenario takes place: Shiva asks questions and Shakti answers them. These dialogues are really an objectified form of Self-inquiry—Shiva and Shakti are one and become two in order to dialogue for the sake of humanity. When we use Self-inquiry in our meditation, it is good to think of yourself as Shakti inquiring of Shiva, or the disciple inquiring of the inner Guru.

In areas of life where we are confused, our inquiry will have to peel away layers of illusion and reach the essence that lies beneath. Ultimately, that is Shiva or supreme Consciousness. But on the way to that ultimate level, many important understandings and decisions relevant to practical life are there to be discovered.

Abhinavagupta writes:

> After rejecting the fixation of the heart on a path which is to be rejected because it is concerned with a particular wish, he should, by means of inquiry, gradually arrive at the level which is exempt from ill.

Here he describes what actually occurs in Shiva Process Self-inquiry. When contraction or limitation arises in a participant, it is always because of a 'particular wish', that is, the play of the ego. By inquiry, the truth behind that wish, the desire behind the desire, is arrived at. 'That which is exempt from ill' is the Self, because only the Self can neither be added to nor removed, only the Self is not affected by success or failure, gain or loss.

Any spiritually inclined person will perform informal Self-inquiry as a natural part of his inner process. At the Shiva School a method of Shaiva Self-inquiry is the core of our practice. First let us look at an ancient analogue of the modern Shiva Process group.

THE KULA-CHAKRA GROUP RITUAL

There is a remarkable passage in *Tantraloka* in which Abhinavagupta talks about the *kula-chakra*, the group ritual, practised in some schools of Shaivism:

> Consciousness, which is composed of all things, enters into a state of contraction due to the differences generated by separate bodies, but it returns to a state of oneness, to a state of expansion, when all of its components are able to reflect back on each other. The totality of our own rays of Consciousness are reflected back one on the other when, overflowing in the individual consciousness of all present as if in so many mirrors, and without any effort whatsoever in an intense fashion, it becomes universal. For this reason, when a group of people gather together during the performance of a dance or of song, etc., there will be true enjoyment when they are concentrated and immersed in the spectacle all together and not one by one. Consciousness which is overflowing with bliss, even when considered individually, attains in these spectacles a state of unity and, because of that, a state of full and perfect blissfulness. The absence of causes of contraction such as jealousy, hate, etc., allows Consciousness in such moments to fully expand without obstacles in a fullness of bliss, but if even one of those present is not concentrated and absorbed, then Consciousness remains

offended as at the touch of a surface full of depressions and protuberances because he stands out there as a heterogeneous element.

This is the reason why during the rites of adoration of the circle (chakra) one must remain attentive and not allow anyone to enter whose consciousness is in a dispersed state and not concentrated and absorbed, because he will be a source of contraction. In the practice of the circle (chakra) one must adore all the bodies of all those present because since they have all penetrated in the fullness of Consciousness they are in reality as if they were our own body. If through some negligence a stranger succeeds in entering, the initiated ritual may proceed together with him provided that he does not enter in a state of contraction. Such a one, if divine grace falls upon him, will become concentrated and absorbed with the various rituals, but if he is struck by a sinister and malevolent power of the Lord, he will criticise the group.

In his comments on this passage, Muller-Ortega makes the point that though there were sexual rites practised within the Kula tradition of Shaivism, the emphasis here is on expansion of Consciousness. Even sexual rituals would have been undertaken as a method of Consciousness expansion.

Shiva Process group work is a contemporary form of *kula-chakra sans* any sexual element. Even if one wanted to follow Abhinavagupta in this latter aspect, his writings are rather too obscure to work out his method exactly.

Let's look at what this passage tells us about Consciousness. Abhinavagupta says that when Consciousness enters individual bodies it becomes contracted. This is obvious: there is identification with the body and the ego which personalises Consciousness and diminishes it. The *malas* create sheaths—the causal, subtle and physical bodies, which cloak the Self. He points out, however, that when a group gathers for some sort of performance, the individuals become immersed in the collective and are lifted out of their personal limitations.

Abhinavagupta says, 'Consciousness, which is overflowing with bliss, even when considered individually, attains in these spectacles a state of unity and, because of that, a state of full and perfect blissfulness'. The first part of this sentence is reminiscent of the narrator's point of view described earlier: even individual consciousness is full of bliss. How much more perfect is that bliss during the depersonalised experience of a performance? Every rock performer, indeed every public speaker, knows the phenomenon of the 'performance high'. Here is the first explanation of it I have ever seen. It is actually *Lokananda samadhi sukham*: The bliss inherent in people (*Shiva Sutras* I.18).

Abhinavagupta goes on, 'The absence of causes of contraction such as jealousy, hate, etc., allows Consciousness in such moments to fully expand without obstacles in a fullness of bliss'. Just as the heady experience of falling in love lifts a person (temporarily) beyond jealousy and base emotions, so a gripping performance gives us access to the nobler regions of our soul for a while. With the contracting elements of egoic life absent, because of the depersonalising effect of a performance, bliss expands. The individuals present create a mirroring effect and the light of Consciousness is increased. This very same phenomenon takes place during spiritual *satsang*. Consciousness radiates between the teacher and the audience and expands and multiplies.

The phenomenon is not essentially different from what happens during a rock concert, except that Consciousness is more fully aware of itself in *satsang* than in a rock concert where it is only dimly understood. A yogi will understand the vibrating *spanda* of *satsang* to be an experience of the Self and will nurture and enhance it through spiritual practice and contemplation, while a rock musician may find it hard to contain, and will seek to dissipate it, numb it or throw it off, even violently. Then too, in *satsang*, refined and harmonious *(sattvic)* elements will generally be in the ascendency, not the destructive and passionate elements *(tamasic* and *rajasic)* that are likely to be in a rock performance and make its 'taste' less peaceful and calming.

Any performer knows that members of the audience who don't open or give their grace to the performance create an obstacle. Abhinavagupta's comment is memorable, 'but if even one of those present is not concentrated and absorbed, then Consciousness remains offended as at the touch of a surface full of depressions and protuberances because he stands out there as a heterogeneous element'. In his work on aesthetics, Abhinavagupta talks about *sahridaya,* or 'like-heartedness'. Here the sensitive open audience responds to the performer and in their relationship the energy of the performance expands and flows. Abhinavagupta suggests that members of the *kula-chakra* be on the alert for people whose awareness is contracted or separative, and keep them from participation.

SHIVA PROCESS SELF-INQUIRY GROUP

Shiva Process group work presents many of the same features. A circle is formed for the purpose of going deeper in Self-inquiry and observing and expanding group energy. Consciousness flows, but when a particular participant is blocked, it prevents the mirroring effect from taking place. To be blocked means to be unable to fully participate because mental and emotional energy is bound elsewhere. Such a participant is said to be 'not present' and the task of the group is to bring him present.

Consciousness remains confined to a lower level by means of its weakest link. An apt metaphor is that of an electrical circuit with appliances attached. Each appliance will have a resistance. The higher the resistance, the more energy it diverts from the circuit. Each individual participant in the chakra has both a divine potential and personal elements. When the personal elements impede expansion of awareness, we have Abhinavagupta's 'surface full of depressions and protuberances'—the energy of the group is disharmonious, blocked, flat or jarring.

In the Shiva Process work, rather than excluding such a person from the circle, a technology is available to help him unblock and overcome his obstacles. A certain preliminary commitment to the work along with some understanding of the work is required but at the same time it is understood that in any group of qualified participants, a number of them are likely, at any particular time, to be manifesting egoic qualities which will create resistance.

When Consciousness contracts it becomes thicker, slower, more dense, darker, more stupid and heavier. When we desire something or oppose something, when we experience attachment and aversion, when we overanalyse situations, or become fixed and inflexible, second force builds up. All of these create blocks. Since Consciousness, despite its thickening, is essentially the most fluid and plastic substance, blocks are amenable to being shifted.

SHAIVISM AND EMOTION

A Western student of Indian yogic disciplines might be surprised at the apparent lack of much discussion of the emotions in the texts. Shaivism too talks endlessly about *iccha, jnana, kriya*—will, knowledge and action—without mentioning the affections. This however, is only apparently the case. Deeper study shows that the emotions have a prominent role in Kashmir Shaivism even apart from the theory of *rasas*.

The five divine *shaktis* are *chit, ananda, iccha, jnana, kriya. Ananda* is bliss, therefore one of the prime characteristics of supreme Consciousness is that it is full of bliss. Moreover, *iccha,* or willpower, actually indicates the emotions. The Shaivite authors make much of the fact that God is *svatantrya*, supremely independent. The *Shiva Sutras* say, *Siddhah svatantrabhavah*: A *Siddha*, a realised being, is supremely free (*Shiva Sutras* III.13). *Svatantrya* is a blissful sense of independence and in the truest sense it belongs only to the Lord or the Self-realised sage.

The modern Shaivite Acharya, Amritavagbhava says:

> Only God is truly independent because He alone shines independently through the luminosity of His own pure Consciousness. All other forms of life, from Brahma (the creator) to a lowly plant, operate under His *vilasa* (His play, i.e., at the effect of His will).

The *iccha* Shakti or willpower of the Lord has to do with emotion. In contemporary terms, *svatantrya* is supreme self-empowerment and therefore indicates the most perfect feeling states. Disempowerment is the condition that an individual finds in himself when his willpower is at the effect of another person or external events. This is the opposite of *svatantrya* and, in Shaivite terms, the cause of all negative emotion. These observations are confirmed in Shiva Process work when negative feeling states are again and again coupled with vitiated will and lack of independence, and upward shifts, joy and empowerment all flow from being centred in Self.

Shiva is always the subject and can never be the object. To be the object is to be disempowered; to be the subject is always to stand in power. Abhinavagupta said that however many *tattvas* you decided there were, Paramashiva, supreme Shiva, would be *tattva* (n + 1). As soon as a *tattva* becomes an object you know that it is not Shiva since Shiva is eternally the subject. If there are 36 *tattvas*, Shiva is the 37th, if there are 39 *tattvas*, Shiva is the 40th and so on.

RELATIONSHIP BETWEEN THOUGHT AND FEELING

Perhaps the reason that the Indian sages do not speak about emotion in the way we do, is that they may have seen thought and feeling as inextricably connected, even as the same. When a person walks around with a bounce in his step, feeling good, there is not the slightest doubt that his thoughts are positive. Conversely, when someone is depressed and feeling despair, his thoughts are black and negative. It never happens that a depressed person is thinking positive thoughts.

Thought and feeling are two sides of the same coin: you might say that a negative feeling, for example, is the fruit of negative thinking. In Shiva Process work we take it as a working hypothesis that if a person is depressed, there is some negative thought pattern, however unconscious of it he may be, holding his depression in place.

Thought and feeling are the only two inhabitants of our inner world. The thought aspect gives strength and invulnerability, while the feeling aspect softens and humanises. Thought and feeling are two poles in the polarity of truth and kindness. Both truth without kindness and kindness without truth should be avoided.

When a person sets up his inner world so that he is aware only of his thought and ignores his feeling, he may become very strong. He may be able to live and even sacrifice himself for an ideal. On the other hand, a person who emphasises his feeling far beyond thought will shift and change like the sand in a desert windstorm.

Thought should be strong and based in the strongest of all thought: the G-Statement, but even then it should stay in touch with feeling. Feeling grounds and humanises thought. Some spiritual paths stress the primacy of thought and the denigration of feeling. Even when their system of thought is noble, such paths tend to become dry, cold and somewhat ruthless. Practitioners of such paths often have to spend time reintegrating with their feeling side before attaining perfection.

Gurdjieff says that mere *knowledge* is a function of only one centre, the intellectual centre, while real *understanding* is a function of three centres: the intellectual, the emotional and the moving, or vital centre. The Shiva Process work, therefore, always attempts to bring thought and feeling together and to move them towards action. A person's understanding is expressed in action that flows from harmonised thought and feeling.

GROUP PRACTICE

Like Abhinavagupta's *kula-chakra*, the Shiva Process Self-inquiry cannot be fully explained in an essay but has to be learned from a competent teacher. Nonetheless, some of its elements can be described. The overarching metaphor of the group is the ancient Vedic *yagna*. There, Brahmin priests sit in a circle around the sacred flame. They offer mantras and foodstuffs into the fire. When ghee is poured on the flame, it leaps up. Shiva Process participants are like Brahmins offering their statements into the fire of Consciousness. There is no physical fire, but the centre of the circle represents the fire of awareness, and that can leap up when the statements of the participants uplift Consciousness.

My metaphor of the Vedic fire brightening with the ghee of Consciousness is analogous to Abhinavagupta's metaphor of mirroring in the *kula* ritual. A wonderful passage from Corinthians (3.18) brings in a corresponding Biblical parallel:

> Now this Lord is the spirit,
> And where the Spirit of the Lord is, there is freedom.
> And we, with our unveiled faces reflecting like mirrors the brightness of the Lord,
> All grow brighter and brighter as we are renewed into the image that we reflect;
> This is the work of the Lord who is Spirit.

Participants in the Self-inquiry group carefully observe the play of *matrika* against the background of feeling. They watch upward and downward shifts of feeling and they try to see how these shifts are related to thought-process. They might observe that awareness is destabilised by tearing thoughts (self-hatred), attack thoughts, inflating thoughts, self-pity and the like. They observe that awareness is stabilised by A-Statements and expanded by B- and G-Statements. During all of this inquiry they become more and more aware of the intimate connection between thought and feeling. What we think and how we think changes the structure of the brain.

Bhagawan Nityananda says:

> There are various tests to which a devotee is subjected: they could be of the mind, or the intellect, or the body, and so on. A number of such tests are there. In fact, God is conducting tests all the time; every occurrence in life is a test. Every thought that crops up in the mind is in itself a test to see what one's reaction will be. Hence one must be always alert and aloof, conducting oneself with a spirit of detachment, viewing everything as an opportunity afforded to gain experience, to improve oneself and go on to a higher stage.

When a block is found through introspection, the blocked participant is offered A-, B- and G-Statements to unblock his contracted feeling. In this way the work flows around the room finding the block or the weakest link and releasing it. It is difficult and dangerous work and not always uniformly successful. The unfoldment of the group is a bit like a detective story. Contraction is investigated, seeking what is underneath. Things are rarely what they seem, and underneath it all is the promise of a just and happy resolution. At times the group enters a kind of darkness or maya in which the best it can do is bear witness to present experience.

Kshemaraja says:

> Let people of great intelligence closely understand the Goddess Consciousness who is simultaneously of the nature of both revelation *(unmesha)* and concealment *(nimesha)*.

The best attitude is to regard everything that happens in the group as the play of *Chiti*. Revelation is Shiva and confusion is also Shiva. However, there is always recourse to A-Statements, statements of present feeling.

An A-Statement (I feel mad, sad, bad, scared or glad), is already at a higher level than a statement in which the A-Statement is not acknowledged or expressed. A person might be angry and not know it. That anger will colour all his opinions and attitudes and distort them. The simple statement, 'I am angry', is much closer to the truth and also much less destructive.

Making A-Statements keeps thought closely tied to feeling. If thought wanders away from feeling, that is, if it is unconscious of the feeling underlying it, it can and does create universes of delusion. When thought is tied to feeling, it becomes much more trustworthy.

If I were to look for a scriptural justification of the concept of the A-Statement, I would point to the remarkable verse (I.4) from *Spanda Karikas:*

> I am happy, I am miserable, I am attached—these and other cognitions have their being evidently in another in which the states of happiness, misery, etc., are strung together.

Notice the A-Statements (I am happy, etc.). Of course, the point that Vasugupta is making has to do with the old debate with the Buddhists. He is saying that these cognitions or A-Statements must exist within an underlying context, the Self. The Buddhist logicians denied the existence of a continuous Self, saying that each mind moment was essentially unrelated to every other one. Leaving that debate aside, the verse suggests the close connection of the A-Statement with the Self. The participant in Shiva Process work makes an A-Statement, understanding that with it he comes to the doorway of the Self, which underlies it.

I think of the A-Statement as a kind of Shaivite devotional ritual. The Shaiva yogi sacramentalises every movement and gesture of life and by making a perfect articulation of present feeling, he performs his sacrament to the presence of divinity in that moment.

Once the A-Statements are found, expansion takes place via B-Statements, any statements that uplift, and G-Statements, those B-Statements that are scriptural or come from higher Consciousness. Without G-Statements the inquiry might be merely psychological, or rooted in the mundane. Without A-Statements we are building an edifice on shaky foundations. Balance is needed.

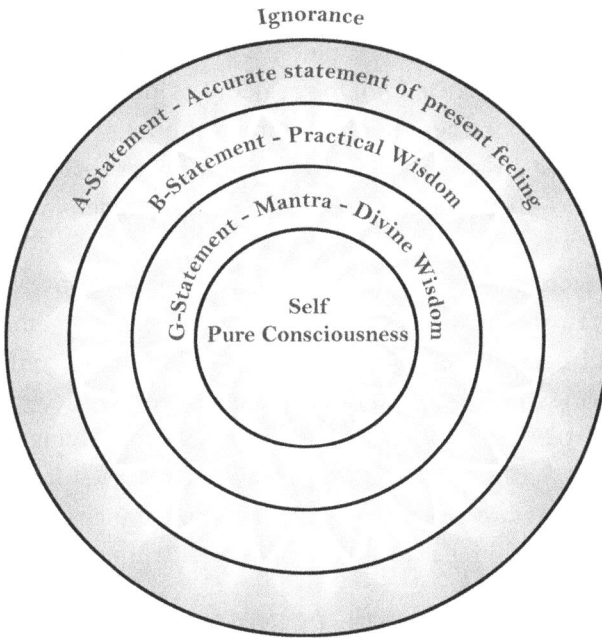

Ignorance

A-Statement – Accurate statement of present feeling

B-Statement – Practical Wisdom

G-Statement – Mantra – Divine Wisdom

Self
Pure Consciousness

Mandala of the Hierarchy of Statements. Self-inquiry leads to more subtle and profound understanding. A-Statements set the foundation of present feeling, B-Statements draw on inner wisdom and G-Statements lift the inquiry to higher Consciousness.

Each dharma, each religion, each philosophy, is really a fund of G-Statements that puts adherents more in touch with the divine Self. Incidentally, the use of 'statements' suggests that Shiva Process work is centred in *shaktopaya*. I think that is a fair assessment, although magical moments of *shambhavopaya* and even *anupaya* abound.

Though Abhinavagupta proposed to exclude members of the *kula-chakra* who were contracted, he knew that blocked members of an audience of a play or dance performance could not similarly be excluded. He suggests what can be done to remove the obstacles they experience. Clearly it is not enough of a technique to tell a blocked person to live life more fully or do *sadhana*. With the Shiva Process technique, blocks are removed right in the moment. No doubt some blocks can only be overcome after many years and perhaps many lifetimes of work.

A person who 'plays', or is the subject of a Shiva Process inquiry, experiences his state of being through his speech. That speech carries cognitive and emotional energy that enters the circle of Consciousness and the sensitive hearts of the listeners. They can now introspect on that very feeling and offer statements in empathy with it.

Participants are instructed not to speak out of judgment or anger but to temper truth with kindness and strengthen kindness with truth. When participants are in an open state of sympathy—the *sahridaya* of Abhinavagupta—they can give feedback that helps the player to become present.

Effective work moves in the direction of greater Consciousness and light. But even ineffective work can bring new understandings. Any intentional, direct study of Consciousness and its laws of contraction and expansion brings rewards. In the Shaivite meditative technique called *layabhavana*, gross *tattvas* are dissolved into their underlying, more subtle *tattvas*. Shaivite Self-inquiry is a kind of *layabhavana* meditation, a peeling of the onion of awareness so that surface appearances are continually stripped away, revealing a deeper resonance of truth underneath.

CONTEMPLATION: DOING SELF-INQUIRY

1. Close your eyes and turn your attention to your inner world.

2. Notice where you hold tension in your body.

3. Explore the emotion connected with the tension. Ask yourself:

   - Could this tension be anger (or from the anger family: frustration, impatience, resentment)?

   - Could this tension be fear (or from the fear family: anxiety, worry, stress)?

   - Could this tension be sadness (or from the sadness family: grief, nostalgia, disappointment)?

Try other statements that lead you to pinpoint your feeling state. Watch your inner response to each statement. An easing of tension, or a feeling of peace indicates your present feeling.

4. Make an (accurate) A-Statement:

   ♦ I feel angry.

   ♦ I feel scared.

   ♦ I feel sad.

Accurate statements lead to a story, an event that occurred or a reaction to something in your life. Keep making statements until the tension eases. When you feel a shift then:

5. Make a (beneficial) B-Statement that increases the upward shift. Some suggestions are:

   ♦ I let go.

   ♦ I forgive myself.

   ♦ I forgive others.

   ♦ Wisdom, love and strength are in me.

Or any other statements that are empowering.

6. Make a G-Statement:

   ♦ I am Shiva.

   ♦ Everything is *Chiti*.

   ♦ I have divine power within me.

7. When you get a shift in the direction of peace, plunge into meditation. One positive shift is enough and limiting yourself to that prevents overanalysis.

THE ART OF YOGIC THINKING

Strongly related to Shiva Process work is the art of 'yogic thinking'. Following the upward shift of feeling, the yogi should retrain his mental process to be an ally—and not an enemy—in his quest for peace. When a situation causes him to feel more and more contracted, he should be able to see that there is nothing inherent in the situation that is the real cause of that contraction, but only *the way he thinks about the situation*. The way he thinks about the situation may be the result of past tendencies, habitual patterns or present negative emotions.

A true yogi gives himself the freedom to *choose* how he thinks about any situation, based on the inner feeling result of such thinking. If everything is Shiva, then it is irrational to think in such a way as to cause yourself suffering, and it is only rational to think in such a way as to uplift yourself. It takes great strength of mind to freely choose how you think along those lines, but it can be done. Instead of reacting with anger, yogic thinking might include, 'He didn't really mean that, he's having a bad day', or 'I don't need to take that personally, that really has nothing to do with me', or even 'That person is a fool. Why should I take anything he says seriously?'

If the result of our thinking about a situation leads us to peace, then we can say that our thinking is harmonious with our yoga in that case. Such thinking is undoubtedly familiar to you: all of us use it in a wide variety of situations. This is automatic: if a five-year-old says something to us that would be insulting if said by a 30-year-old, we instantly factor in that he is a child, and don't react. There will always, however, be certain situations in which this kind of thinking is not natural. These will be our challenges, and it is precisely in those cases where effort is necessary.

It is no small matter to be able to habitually think yogically, and it is usually the fruit of a lot of meditation and Self-inquiry. Some possible A-Statements that aid the process might be: 'My thinking about this situation is wrong', or 'God wants me to think differently about this', or, 'May I find a way to hold this situation that gives me peace'.

'THINKING IT THROUGH' MEDITATION

Applying yogic thinking to meditation gives excellent results in a technique I call 'thinking it through' meditation. Since Patanjali has given us the classical definition that 'meditation is to still the thought waves of the mind', and in *shambhavopaya* we learn that high-class meditation goes beyond the mind to Consciousness Itself, it seems politically correct for a meditator to castigate the thinking mind.

However, there are times when life issues bubble up in the mind with emotional intensity. They are crying out to be dealt with and understood. In such cases, to still the mind by force of will would not achieve a desirable goal. First, the peace derived would be only temporary and cost a lot of effort, and second, the life issue would not go away. When this happens to me, I let my mind be where it wants to be. Respecting its divine capacity, I ask it what it wants to tell me. I try to listen deeply to what it is really saying. That means, noticing feeling as well as thought. I don't try to force it into my concept, but work with it from where it is.

When such a situation is at hand, the adroit meditator would do well to use his meditation for contemplation of the issue. In truth, thinking is a noble capacity of a human being and should not be denigrated. The mind should be worshipped as the dancing ground of the Goddess Chiti. Quite remarkably, each of us has a voice speaking to us within our head. When the mind and the heart are clear, that voice speaks with perfect reliablity. It is the voice of the Self.

There are times when a person has to clean, to lift, to dig, to move; there is also a time to think. The problem with thinking is only that we are not skilled at it. It is not so much that we lack intelligence, but that we sometimes 'think ourselves down'. That is, our thought-process leads us into a greater state of contraction and anxiety than we were in at the beginning. Such thinking is shoddy in the spiritual sense.

Good thinking, from a spiritual point of view, will resolve the issue towards God or the Self and produce an upward shift of feeling. Therefore, the 'thinking it through' meditation begins with a decision to think through a specific issue (note that this decision can come about spontaneously after you have begun to meditate, when you discover that your mind is agitated). Now the meditator thinks about the issue with part of his attention always on his inner feeling.

As a chess player, I learned to analyse lines of possibility: if I go here, he goes there, then I go there—that's good for me. Or, if I go there, he goes there, then I go here—that's bad for me. A chess player guides his analysis by how favourable the resulting position seems. In the 'thinking it through' meditation, the meditator should make a similar analysis but stay closely in touch with how each alternative feels. Thus, affect, and not intellectual cleverness, is the deciding factor. He tries to keep moving the situation in his mind towards peace and harmony.

A person who uses this form of meditation has to have two attributes. He has to be able to be objective and also patient. A clear solution doesn't always come right away, often because preferences and prejudices obscure it. It is good to repeat this contemplation more than once.

Chapter 20

Language Mysticism in Shaivism III: Mantra

> As long as you repeat the mantra on the gross level, you experience it
> as sounds and syllables. But through the Guru's grace, you pass beyond
> this state, and the inner divine nature of the letters is revealed.
>
> Baba Muktananda, *I Am That*

S ome spiritual seekers undervalue the practice of mantra, thinking
of it as a kind of blue collar *sadhana*. They prefer more intellectual
and glamorous methods. In my opinion, this is a serious mistake. Mantra
practice lays the groundwork for real understanding of the path of
knowledge, and it is a powerful and relatively easy method in its own
right. Every meditator should keep the mantra as an arrow in his spiritual
quiver. There will come times when he will be thankful he has, when no
other method serves him as well.

During a particularly difficult period of my *sadhana*, while at my Guru's
ashram in Ganeshpuri, India, I was flooded with negative emotion. I
became overwhelmed by fear and completely disempowered. Neither
inquiry, nor wisdom, nor service, nor scriptural study helped me. My
meditations were not meditations at all, but concentrated panic attacks.
My misery was such that I could not even go to my teacher to discuss my
predicament. Then one day while I was doing my ashram work in the
garden, he came up to me and inches from my face he imparted to me the
supreme mantra of Shiva, *Om Namah Shivaya*. *Om Namah Shivaya* can be
translated as 'I bow to the Self'. He told me to repeat it silently 24 hours a

day (he may have been exaggerating) and also to meditate on it with full focus for four hours a day. Although I had not told him about my condition, it was clear that he had intuited it and was reaching out to help me. And help me he did: within two days of beginning my practice, I had shifted from the depression that had haunted me for weeks and I felt my inner joy bubbling again.

CHAITANYA MANTRA

Baba had received that same mantra, *Om Namah Shivaya*, from his Guru, Bhagawan Nityananda, on the day of his initiation in 1947. Just so, in our tradition the mantra is passed on from Guru to disciple in an unbroken chain, going back thousands of years. Such a mantra is called a *chaitanya mantra* because it is infused with the conscious power of a living tradition. By contrast, a mantra received from a book is considered *jada*, inert.

The *Kularnava Tantra* (15.61) says:

> Without Consciousness the mantras are mere letters; they do not bear fruit even after being repeated a million times.

A mantra is a curious piece of language whose reference is to the internal world only. It has no outer meaning. Its tendrils reach inward to the depths of the Self and create a bridge to inner Consciousness. It is a thought that is much more intense and full of energy than ordinary thought.

The notion of an alive, conscious mantra has to do with the function of the Guru. Scripture says, 'The Guru is the grace-bestowing power of God'. If Lord Shiva performs the five functions—creation, sustenance, dissolution, grace and concealment—it is the Sadguru, the true Guru, who is the specialist in the fourth of these.

Abhinavagupta said, 'The Guru is only Consciousness'. Baba had attempted every kind of yoga available to him and none had given him the authentic experience of the Divine until his decisive encounter with his Guru. In my own *sadhana* I recognised the Guru as my homing device. Spontaneously my orientation in life shifted and *came into relationship with him.* The Self-realised Guru is the doorway to Shiva, the embodiment of that uplifting *spanda*. The seeker draws that power to himself when his relationship with the Guru is appropriate.

In the state of separation, or *jivahood,* a human being wanders the world alone. He may have a wider identification with his family, nation, ethnic or religious group and these give him a relatively higher purpose. The

Guru is one who is in integral relationship with the whole universe. He has attained Shiva *samavesha* and stands at the very centre of Consciousness. The connection with such a Guru gives a seeker a reliable reference point to Consciousness. An intelligent seeker will let the nuances of his relationship with the Guru show him when he is moving towards oneness, and when he is moving towards separation.

Traditionally, a student had to earn a mantra from a realised Guru. He served the teacher for 12 years, receiving *mantra diksha,* mantra initiation, at the end of that period. In such a case, receiving the mantra whispered in the ear by the Guru might be the actual moment of *shaktipat* awakening. He would be triumphant, and perhaps return to his ordinary life with the great gift in his hand. The mantra was regarded as a verbal form of the Guru or of Shiva. Having the Guru mantra, the seeker felt liberated, or at least that liberation was inevitable. Now he would never again be separate from the Guru in a spiritual sense. He would always have the Guru with him in the form of the Guru mantra. In every moment the single spiritual action was repetition of the mantra. It set the world right.

THE MIND IS MANTRA

As we have seen, in the discussion of *matrika* and the four levels of speech, outer language has its hidden source in inner language, ultimately in the wordless language of pure awareness.

The *Shiva Sutras* II.1 says:

> *Chittam mantrah*
> The mind is mantra.

At the deepest level of mind, is the profound vibration of the Self. As speech becomes more external, more lost in objects and outer things, it becomes weaker. It separates itself from emotion and intuition. It becomes dry and hollow.

The true form of the mind is mantra. External language is associated with objects and mental activity, and is bound by conventions. Mantras are intermediate between the objective world and pure awareness. As language turns in on itself through mantra, it seeks its own source. First the essence of mind is revealed, and then mind itself becomes one with Consciousness. Mantra leads language to the source of the Word.

Objects

Spoken Words

Thoughts

Mantra

Great Lake of
Consciousness
Self

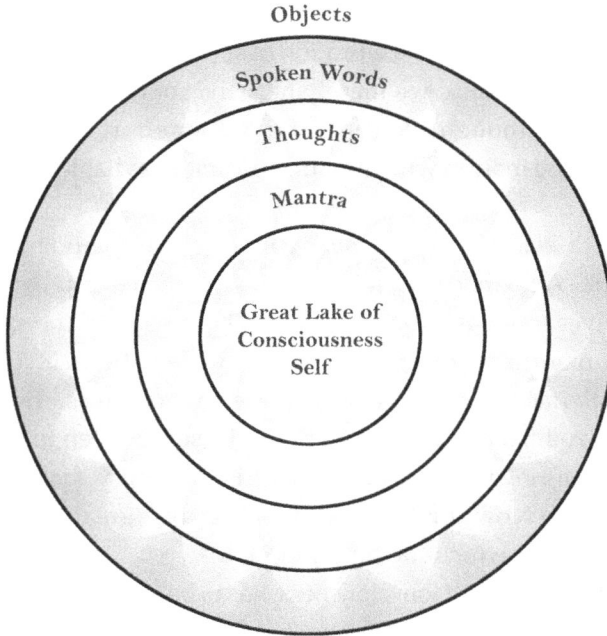

Mantra Mandala. Repeating the mantra directs spoken word and thought towards the experience of pure Consciousness.

Earlier, I cited *Shiva Sutras* III.27, *Katha japah*: His casual conversation is mantra (referring to a Self-realised yogi). A being who is permanently established in the heart of Consciousness, does not become disconnected from his source. Thus even his offhand remarks are treasured and pondered over by his students, who consider them to be mysterious reflections of the Divine. As language moves closer to the source, it reflects equally the qualities of *satya* and *ahimsa*, truth and compassion or truth and kindness. Truth and kindness create a continuum. A person who speaks with a lot of truth but little kindness, will speak harsh and hurtful words. A person who speaks in a kindly way with little truth, will speak weak and passive words. At the juncture point where truth and kindness meet in equal measure, is empowered speech.

Shiva Sutras I.22 says:

> *Mahahradanu sandhananmantra viryanubhavah*
> By mystically uniting with the great lake, the infinite reservoir of divine energy, the yogi experiences the vibrant source of mantra.

A mantra like *Om Namah Shivaya* has its source in *Chiti*. Mantra turns speech back to the source, the vibration of supreme Consciousness. If while repeating such a mantra, we merely hear the sounds of the syllables and allow extraneous thoughts to come and go, our effort is weak. Rather, we should repeat the mantra with attention, riding its syllables inward, feeling them deeply.

In the sutra, *anusandhana* implies a concentrated, one-pointed awareness of the mantra. A textbook we read may be full of meaning, but if we don't exert ourselves to focus properly, we can't access it. In the same way the power of a mantra will escape us unless we exert ourselves to meet it. Thus *Shiva Sutras* II.2 says, 'A seeker is one who makes effort'. A potent mantra received from a realised Guru, and a seeker keen to practise is the right combination. When *mantra shakti* is joined by *sadhana shakti*, the practice kindles. Now the seeker experiences the 'great lake', the infinite source of Shakti to which the mantra is a link.

So perhaps *chaitanya*, Consciousness, has to be on both ends—the mantra has to be empowered and the seeker has to give his attention. It might be that the seeker is really the decisive factor. If you were to receive the same mantra from a book that you receive from a good Guru, conventional wisdom says that the book mantra would be ineffective. That might simply be because a mantra lightly received is lightly abandoned. A real, human relationship with a Guru or a lineage ensures that the seeker will stick to his practice. If you had, for some reason, deep faith in a book-received mantra it would undoubtedly be efficacious.

Language that plunges inward, gathers power in the same way that externalised speech dissipates power. As we move with the mantra inward, we get in touch with subtler levels of speech. We undergo a series of shifts as we move from *madhyama* to *pashyanti* and finally to *para* levels of speech.

Mantravirya is the 'virility', the potency, of mantra. The power of mantra is always divine energy, the power of Consciousness. Mantras can be used to achieve any goal, from material ends right up to spiritual liberation. Mantras are effective and energetic speech.

This possibility—using mantras for worldly ends—might come as a surprise to Western seekers who typically learn of mantra through their spiritual quest. In India, however, you can get a mantra for anything: to acquire a husband or wife, to cure a disease, to ward off calamity, to kill an enemy. One is reminded of Sheikh Nasruddin's acquisition of a mantra to control his wife, the wilful Fatima. It didn't work because, he discovered, she already had one to control him! In India, so comfortable with inner things, it is not unusual to try to control outer events by inner actions. Perhaps such an approach eventually transforms itself into true spirituality in which the Self is the goal.

Another Shiva sutra (II.3) says that 'the secret of mantra is the being of the body of knowledge'. The being whose body is knowledge is the Lord. Mantra draws on the energy, luminosity and wisdom of the unfathomable depth of universal Consciousness, the power of *matrika*. It draws wisdom-energy and bliss-energy to the practitioner. The feeling of energy that arises is harmonious, holistic and uplifting. It is bright with Shakti.

Spanda Karikas II.1 says:

> *Tadakramya balam mantrah sarvajnabalashalinah*
> *Pravartante 'dhikaraya karananiva dehinam*

Baba Muktananda's colourful and informal translation of this aphorism was, 'The mantra is the power of everything and everyone. The mantra is all-knowing and can do anything'. Jaideva Singh's translation is, 'Mantras derive their power from the *spanda* principle and finally dissolve in it'. For Baba, mantra was a method for tapping the deep source of inner energy and bringing its life to the surface of things. He considered the repetition of a mantra received from an awakened teacher to be a streamlined, easy and almost effortless path.

There is tremendous emotional power in language. In fact, thought and feeling are two sides of the same coin. Thought or language is a container of feeling: words and ideas shape emotion and create upliftment or contraction. The wrong kind of language (or thought) pinches feeling and creates emotional pain, while the right kind of language is a fitting vehicle of feeling, and given such a vehicle, feeling becomes free to expand and soar. Language has the binding power of ignorance (*Shiva Sutras* I.2: *Jnanam bandhah*: Knowledge is bondage) and also the mysterious freeing power of the master of *matrika*. Mantra is a key method for liberating the practitioner from illusion. Do not underestimate it.

The word *mantra* is traditionally derived from *manana*, 'mind, to think', and *tranam*, 'to save/protect'. Thus mantra shapes the mind in such a way as to make it a fit vessel for divine Shakti and to protect it from the forces of negativity. Viewed mechanically, the mantra calms the agitation of the mind by excluding unwanted thoughts. Mystically considered, the mantra is a vehicle of the root power of Consciousness Itself. Mantra is the preeminent methodology of Tantric yoga, to which Shaivism belongs. The Tantric approach is extremely practical, providing not just philosophy but methodology as well. The practice of mantra gives immediate results.

Japa ('muttering') is the continuous recitation of mantra whether in or out of meditation. All over India you will encounter people murmuring to themselves—they are doing *japa*. Because the subtle and inner is always considered more powerful than the gross and external, silent repetition of mantra is more effective than verbalised or whispered mantra. For the same reason, *Vijnanabhairava* Verse 145 says that the real *japa* is the contemplation of Consciousness over and over again. Since mantra is a linguistic vehicle that carries us to Consciousness, the highest form of *japa* is to repeatedly connect with Consciousness with or without using a verbal mantra.

The Shaivite yogi knows that all the *tattvas* or levels of experience are present everywhere. He knows that through *samavesha*, absorption in the Divine, he can discover Shiva anywhere. The yogi of *nadabrahma* can ride music to the Self. The *tantra vamacharya* can ride sensual experience to the Self. The wisdom yogi and the mantra yogi can ride language and inquiry to the Self. Every object, every thought, every emotion, every experience is a doorway in the Shaiva universe to higher Consciousness. The Shaivite yogi is simply one who recognises these doorways, opens them and walks through. O yogi! Do not neglect the mantra.

MEDITATION: OM NAMAH SHIVAYA

Sit quietly and repeat the mantra, Om Namah Shivaya *silently to yourself. It is pronounced* OM na—MA shee—VY—ah. *Find a comfortable rate of speed. If you like, you can join the mantra to the breath, one repetition on the inbreath and one repetition on the outbreath. To help concentration you can visualise the letters or listen carefully inwardly to each repetition. If other thoughts intrude, let them go and calmly return to the mantra without condemning yourself. Repeat the mantra for 10 minutes.*

Chapter 21

Being Present: Deconstructing Time and Space

A yogi climbing the ladder of the *tattvas* step by step, one-pointed on the essence which transcends everything, achieves the ascension right up to the ultimate principle and in the end identifies himself as Shiva.

Abhinavagupta, *Paramarthasara*, Verse 97

In Shiva, knowledge is perfect, will is perfect, ability is perfect, feeling is perfect. In Shiva there is no time but only eternity. In Shiva too, there is no space as we know it, but only omnipresence. There is total freedom, *svatantrya*. There is no sequence of events, no steps, nothing outside of Shiva Himself. There is no cause and effect. Everything is known at once in its totality. In Shiva, past and future do not exist separately from the present. In Shiva, other places do not exist separately from this place. In Shiva there is no 'there and then', only 'here and now'.

The early Shaivite masters measured time with thought. They held that the smallest unit of time is the 'moment', which is the time it takes to have one thought. A meditator soon discovers that past and future are products of his mind alone. He sees that meditation is a struggle to become present. When the mind moves towards future possibilities or broods over past events there occurs a subtle but real diminution of energy. But when the mind stays present, energy is enhanced and uplifted. In every activity in life our enjoyment and our efficiency are increased the more present we are. Whether the activity is watching a movie, playing a sport or making love—the more present we are, the more vivid, full and enjoyable it is. Being present clearly has something to do with our interest in whatever we are doing, and that can affect our emotional engagement with it. Although the Self is ultimately the source of all love and interest, it takes a while to truly focus on it because we are beguiled by false possibilities and superficial goals.

Early in my *sadhana* I grappled with the issue of being present. I practised a Buddhist meditation in which I mentally noted everything I was doing as I did it. When I went for a meditative walk, I watched my feet rise and fall and I would say to myself, 'Lifting, lifting, lifting, stepping, placing, placing, lifting, lifting'. When I ate, I would say, 'Chewing, chewing, swallowing, swallowing. Lifting the food, opening the mouth, chewing, chewing'. Because this is one-remove from reality in the sense that I was providing a commentary on what I was doing, I still felt blocked from being truly present.

An early teacher of mine used to challenge new students to focus their attention on the second hand of a watch as it swept around. He wagered that they would not be able to stay with it without a break for one full minute. In the vast majority of cases he won. To focus the mind in the present is not trivial, so strong is its tendency to wander.

In the same vein, I worked with the interesting Buddhist concept of 'mind moments'. Each thought is seen simply as a moment of mind. It exists in itself unconnected to past or future. Taking this point of view, I tried to become strongly present. In this practice there is no struggle because whatever arises is simply what arises in the moment, only to change in the next moment.

During this period, I attempted to stop my mind by force of will. I inwardly froze my third eye in such a way that I temporarily blocked thoughts. The fruit of this practice was double-edged. I achieved a few states of *samadhi* or inner absorption, but the effort rebounded against me and I found it difficult to meditate that way consistently.

Later, when I was with Baba I became strongly influenced by the description of his extraordinary meditation experiences. I had difficulty meditating and I gradually became aware that every time I sat, I was subtly straining to be in some altered state, to have the experience that I thought I should have. Again this yielded some fruit in the form of a vision of blue light on a number of occasions, but essentially I felt blocked.

Baba himself, in full career, provided me with a powerful model of being present. He seemed to meet everything as it arose. He carried no baggage, no ghosts from the past. I never noticed him seeming to be focused elsewhere or wool-gathering, but always dynamically interacting with what the moment offered. The phrase, 'takes no prisoners', used to arise as I watched him.

Inspired by him I tried to be as present as possible in my meditation. I struggled against my mind's tendency to take me away. I tried to hear inwardly each mantra I repeated in meditation and I tried to carefully watch the rise and fall of every breath, with no breaks. On other occasions I would try to stay present to the feeling of 'I' or 'I am'; holding my third eye open, not letting it contract into thoughts. I experimented with the Aurobindian technique of imagining a fence around my mind and vigilantly attempting to keep all thoughts outside.

Then one day sitting in Baba's presence, I had a transforming insight. I realised I might not be able to have the meditation I want to have, but I can *always* have the meditation I am having. Instantly, my approach changed. With the lens of this insight, I saw how much I had been at war with myself and at war with reality. I saw that I had to surrender to what was so, respecting it all as Shiva. The insights of Shaivism had perhaps precipitated this moment. If every thought, every feeling, every sensation, every thing were Shiva, why would you reject something and seek something else? In doing so, you would be dishonouring Shiva, you would be killing Shiva to get to Shiva.

When I sat to meditate, I now thought, 'Begin where you are'. But to begin where I was, I had to first know where I was. Locating yourself is the first thing. Once, a traveller in Ireland asked a local farmer, 'How do I get to Dublin from here?' The farmer thought and thought. He contorted his face. Finally, he said, 'You can't get there from here!'

Of course, we know that we can get there from here. We can get *anywhere* from here, but it is essential to know where *here* is. A golfer knows that wherever he is: in the woods, in sand, behind a tree, he can get to the green. His route may be circuitous and difficult, but he can always get home. The one indispensable thing is that he must locate his ball.

I started to surrender into each moment in meditation. I told myself 'Be present, everything is Shiva'. My war-cry became, 'Be with what is'. I felt that I had to transcend time by entering more fully into the present moment. To do this, I minutely observed my experience in the moment. I saw that while thought might lead me away from being present, feeling was a reliable indicator of presentness, since it could never be of the past or future.

When I sat to meditate, I examined feeling within my body. I noticed that it tended to cluster in various chakras, like the navel, the heart and the third eye. From this inquiry the A-Statement developed as a technique for becoming present (I feel sad, I feel glad). Getting in touch with the present moment is indispensable in true meditation, because the present moment is the doorway to the infinite. Making an A-Statement, we enter that doorway.

Once we have become aware of the situation as it is in the moment, we are ready to go deeper. To stop time, we must stop thought. Since we have defined the basic unit of time as the amount of time necessary for one thought, time and thought are in this sense one. By stopping thought you stop time and enter eternity.

The great compendium, *Vijnanabhairava,* gives many methods of reaching the thought-free state. This one is the most direct:

> Having freed the mind of all support, one should refrain from all thought constructs. Then, O gazelle eyed one, there will be the state of Shiva, the absolute Self. (Dharana 84)

The 'gazelle-eyed one' is the supreme Shakti, the student as well as the consort and the very Self of Shiva who is speaking. By 'support' Shiva is referring to any thought-form arising from within or generated in reaction to external events.

Certainly, it is not easy to free the mind from all thought-constructs. For that, I recommend one of my favourite *dharanas* in the *Vijnanabhairava*:

> One should contemplate thus: 'Within me the inner psychic apparatus consisting of *chitta*, etc. does not exist'. (Dharana 71)

The meditator contemplates, 'I have no mind', or 'I am a body with no mind in it', or 'There is an empty space in my head'. It is very effective.

Kshemaraja quotes the *Svacchanda Tantra:*

> One established in the supreme principle is not harassed by all forms of Time. One should regard everything as of the form of Shiva and Shakti . . . One who has this conviction is liberated while living. Time can never throttle him who always contemplates on Shiva.

From the perspective of the *upayas,* the *shambhavopaya* technique for stopping time is intense focus on pure Consciousness and the *shaktopaya* technique is to use a single thought as a springboard to go beyond thought. Starting in time with a single idea, the meditator tries to transcend time. He might say, 'Now, now, now', or 'Be present', or 'I am present', and use such thoughts to bring himself into the moment. In my meditation courses, I teach a 'being present' meditation in which the meditators focus on present sound, present sensation, present breath, present thought and present feeling.

In this universe everything is vividly present *except* the mind. We dream the past and the future. Indeed, one could say that every person carries three dreams within himself, two of which prevent him from being present to his real life.

The first dream is the dream of glory. Here he will be 'discovered', become fabulously rich and famous, meet Mr or Ms Right. In most cases, this dream is simply not going to be fully consummated. Still, one type of person will ceaselessly try to push towards this dream, becoming frustrated and angry in the process.

The second dream is the nightmare dream of disaster. Here everything horrible happens: disease, financial ruin, romantic tragedy. In most cases, this dream does not take place, at least, in its full horror. This dreamer spends all his time brooding about, warding off and being in terror about this dream. He has no energy to pursue the first dream. Still another type of person moves from dreams of glory to despair—inflation to deflation on a regular basis. Such a one becomes extravagantly hopeful and then extravagantly depressed.

The third dream is the yogic dream of being present. It is not a dream at all, but an awakening. It marries the dream to what actually is. It sees Shiva in every moment and accepts with maturity the difficulties of life. This yogic vision sacramentalises life and can truly be achieved only by inner work.

In meditation, as well as in life, whatever the situation, it is good to accept it as though you have chosen it. That way, you make the present moment your ally, not your enemy. Use every bit of your power to come into harmony with present time, or to search for the harmony that is hidden in present time.

MEDITATION I: BEING PRESENT

In karate it is said that the *yoi* or ready stance is the most important stance. In this stance one is alert, aware and attentive. There are a lot of parallels from the world of sport. One can think of the intense focus of a batsman in baseball or cricket as the ball is being thrown, or equally, of the third baseman or silly-point fielder who must be ready for a batted ball that could come towards him like a shot. Or the boxer whose life depends on dealing with any punch that comes.

The common feature of all these postures is that the athlete is open and ready for whatever arises. His mind should be in the no-thought or *avikalpa* state because if he cherishes any expectations, he might be surprised by something else.

The *being present* meditation is less intense. The meditator should be aware and present, moment to moment, watching whatever arises and continually wiping out what has passed. At the beginning, it will be difficult to keep the attention focused for more than a few minutes, but the effort is worthwhile. Use present feeling to ground you in the moment.

Close your eyes, and bring your mind to the present moment. The past is behind you, the future has not arrived. Experience the present moment in as many ways as you can: listen to the sounds, feel the sensations, be aware of the breath, notice the mind thinking, notice your mood. Now, scan the body for points of tension. Be present to them and try to release them. When thoughts come into your mind, let them go. Eventually, you will come into contact with the current of presentness and you will be able to stay effortlessly in the now, letting go each moment's manifestation in the next. The present moment is the sacrificial fire and every thought and feeling should be offered into it in every moment.

SHIVA PROCESS AND LAYABHAVANA

In Self-inquiry practice, the meditator brings himself present by focusing on the sensation in his navel, throat, heart and third eye. Then he goes deeper by means of *layabhavana*.

I have already briefly mentioned *layabhavana*, the meditative technique where gross *tattvas* are resolved into subtle *tattvas*. In a sense, *layabhavana* is an archetypal Shaivite *anavopaya* method of meditation, delving deeper and deeper into reality. It is a method by which we peel back the external and superficial levels of being until we merge in the underlying truth. The *Maharthamanjari* says:

> This *pashu* (bound soul) should try to go beyond the four energies—
> *khechari, gochari, dikchari, bhuchari*—reabsorbing them one into the
> other in turn, and should plunge the limited self into the great lake
> (*vameshvari*), the conscious Self.

Shiva Process Self-inquiry is a form of *layabhavana*. We encounter a contraction in meditation. We delve into it with the faith that underlying it is hidden the peace and joy of the Self. In effect we resolve it into higher *tattvas*: reactive ignorance is resolved into A-Statements; A-Statements are resolved into B-Statements; B-Statements are resolved into G-Statements. And G-Statements take us to *samavesha*, absorption in divine Consciousness.

A text from the Krama School of Shaivism, the *Mahanayaprakasha*, vividly depicts *layabhavana*:

> Objects are dissolved into the sense functions and these, in turn, into thought, then thought into Consciousness and this last one is finally absorbed into the supreme firmament (the Heart).

Shiva Sutras III.4 says more simply:

> The forces or *tattvas* in the body should be dissolved backwards into the Source.

The brilliant Nisargadatta Maharaj describes meditation in a way that is relevant to Shiva Process and *layabhavana*:

> The art of meditation is the art of shifting the focus of attention to ever subtler levels, without losing one's grip on the levels left behind . . . One begins with the lowest levels: social circumstances, customs and habits; physical surroundings, the posture and the breathing of the body; the senses, their sensations and perceptions; the mind, its thoughts and feelings; until the mechanism of personality is grasped and firmly held.

So far he is referring to the level of the A-Statement in which the personal truth is discovered and acknowledged. Here, *anavopaya* merges in *shaktopaya*. Maharaj goes on:

> The final stage of meditation is reached when the sense of identity goes beyond the 'I-am-so-and-so' [A-Statement], beyond 'so-I-am', beyond 'I-am-the-witness-only', beyond 'there-is' [G-Statements] beyond all ideas into the impersonally personal pure being [*shambhavopaya*].

There are two essential methods. One of these is to merge everything into the highest *tattva* in a single sweep. By saying, 'I am Shiva', meditating directly on Shiva *tattva*, the personal self merges in the highest. The second method is to laboriously, stage by stage merge each *tattva* into the one prior to it. I will not deny that the express-method is excellent. But a cautionary note: I have known many yogis who have leapt to the highest without doing the groundwork lower down. Consequently they could not hold their attainment.

Ramana Maharshi did his whole *sadhana* in half an hour, but his *samavesha* was so powerful that personal elements never pulled him down. Therefore do use the great G-Statements like 'I am Shiva', by all means, but at the same time do not overlook the humble *anavopaya*. Do the hard work: encounter everything, stand face to face with it, inquire into it, *understand* it. If you are the next Ramana you can ignore this caveat. However, the next Ramana probably won't be reading this book, and instead will emerge full-grown one day after having paid no previous attention at all to spirituality.

DECONSTRUCTING TIME

Time itself can be deconstructed, via *layabhavana*. *Vijnanabhairava* Dharana 33 says:

> One should contemplate step by step on the whole universe under the form of *bhuvana* and other *adhvas* (courses) as being dissolved successively from the gross state into the subtle and from the subtle state into the supreme state till finally one's mind is dissolved in pure Consciousness.

The *sadadhvas*, or six courses or paths, is a system cobbled together by Abhinavagupta from scriptural materials. Basically, three of the *adhvas* refer to time and three to space. Time and space arise together as the two *kanchukas*, *kāla* and *niyati*. They are two sides of the same coin, as in the space-time continuum. Just as we are caught in time we are also caught in space or in the illusion of being confined to a body. The *sadadhvas* technique is a *layabhavana* in which gross time is resolved into subtle time, more subtle time and finally into supreme Consciousness. The same process takes place with space as well.

The meditator begins at the gross level, with time represented by the spoken word or *pada*. Spoken words link to other spoken words and enmesh us in complex relationships with things and people. Often they lead us into depletion. Going deeper, the meditator resolves *pada* into mantra. He experiences that the word is a vitiated form of mantra and the mantra is an empowered and a more subtle form of language. Mantra stores and replenishes energy—it connects us to the source of energy and it fights against time by going nowhere. It 'kills time' by repeating itself. While the mind normally ranges far from the Self, the mantra knocks at the door of the Self saying, 'I'm not going anywhere till you open!'

Going deeper still, the meditator finds the subtlest level of time with *varna*, the phoneme. A phoneme is pure energy in verbal form and is more subtle than mantra. As we go inward by means of language, things become more subtle and energised and we transcend time. When we get to the end of the process we become simply present and filled with divine *spanda*.

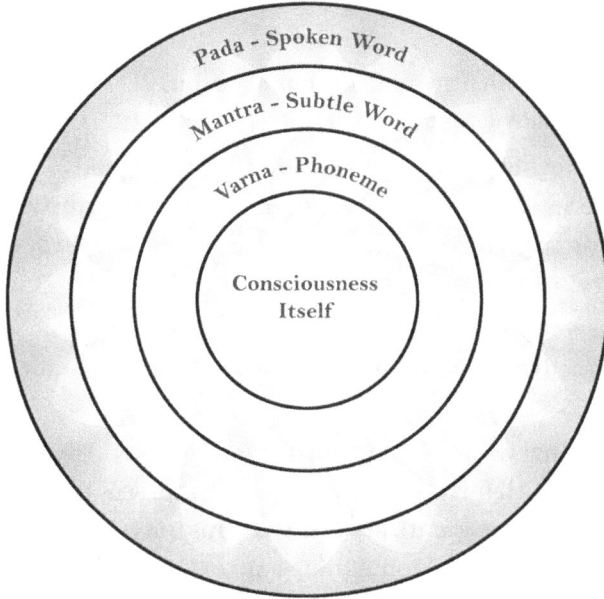

Deconstructing Time (Language) Mandala. The spoken word is resolved into mantra and mantra is resolved into the energy of phonemes, which resolves into Consciousness Itself.

MEDITATION II: SUBTLE LANGUAGE

Try this technique. Resolve language into mantra and then resolve mantra into the sound of phonemes. Finally, go beyond even that into pure shakti. This is a subtle meditation but worth trying.

DECONSTRUCTING SPACE

The *layabhavana* that I have given from the *Vijnanabhairava* deconstructs not only time but also space. It is most natural to identify with our bodies, and see the external world as separate from ourselves. Shaivism says that despite appearances, this is not correct. Through contemplation we can discover that it is not that 'I am in the room', but that 'the room is in me', that is, in my awareness.

Nisargadatta says:

> You are independent of space and time, space and time are in you, not you in them. It is your self-identification with the body, which, of course, is limited in space and time, that gives you the feeling of finiteness. In reality, you are infinite and eternal.

Vijnanabhairava Dharana 81 turns Nisargadatta's assertion into a meditation exercise:

> One should with firm mind contemplate thus . . . 'I am everywhere'. He will then enjoy (supernal) happiness.

Releasing himself from identification with the body, the meditator instead identifies with awareness. Awareness does not stop at the limits of the body, but is perfectly coterminous with whatever is seen or experienced.

Shiva Sutras I.14 says:

> *Drishyam shariram*
> The objective world around such a yogi appears to him as his own body.

Drishyam is that which is seen and *shariram* is body. The attitude here is *sarvam idam aham:* All this is myself. A Shaivite yogi sees the whole world as his own body for he identifies not with his physical body, but with Consciousness. And while some things are external to the physical body, nothing is external to the Consciousness body. Thus, when he looks around, he does not see objects as separate from himself but he sees objects *within* his own awareness. Seeing in this way, nothing is external to him and therefore nothing threatens him. He lives fearlessly. If blocks arise in his life or in his world, he knows they are actually inside his own Consciousness and performs *hathapaka* and *alamgrasa*, burning everything to sameness with Consciousness.

Doing the practice implied by *drishyam shariram,* a meditator realises that his experience of the world of space is not different from his own awareness. *Layabhavana* is therefore a method of uncreating the creation. Everything is folded back on itself and merges into the Self.

In the system of the *sadadhvas,* the meditator begins at the gross level with *bhuvana,* the world. He then penetrates to the deep structure of the world, the categories or the *tattvas.* Underlying this level, he finds *kalā*, cosmic energies. His quest ends eventually in the one underlying energy of the Self. This rather subtle idea can be represented as a diagram:

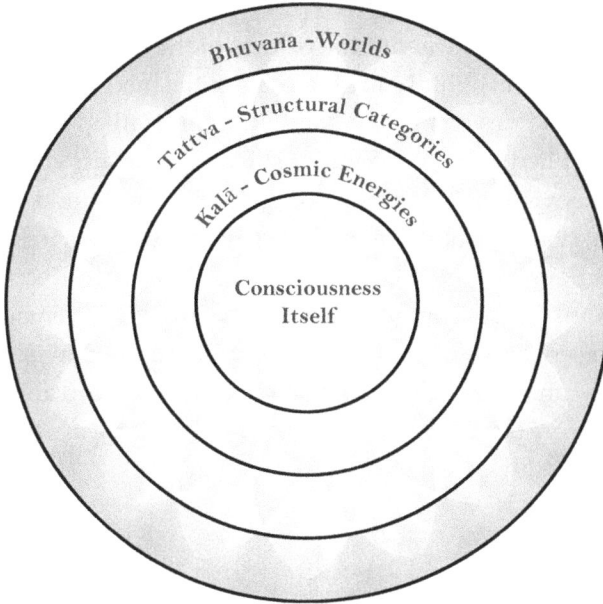

Deconstructing Space Mandala. On the space side of the sadadhvas *the meditator begins with the gross physical world and penetrates to the underlying structure and energies. Consciousness underlies it all.*

Another way to describe this inward movement is to note that the aspirant moves from his outer life in physical reality back through the bodies. He goes from the physical body to the subtle body. From there he goes to the causal body. His destination is the supracausal body, the abode of the Self. Rolling up the universe in this fashion, the yogi conquers time and space and consequently conquers death. He finds what is permanent at the core of all that decays. He achieves *samavesha* or absorption in Consciousness. Conquering the *kanchukas* he discovers to his amazement and delight, 'I am immortal and all-pervasive. I am Shiva, indeed!'

MEDITATION III: A VARIETY OF POSSIBILITIES

This chapter is a rich field of possible meditations. Layabhavana *is always a rewarding technique, dissolving the external gross into the underlying subtle. It can be practised in many ways and in many areas of life.*

Practise the dharanas *given here, especially 'I am everywhere', and* Sarvam idam aham, *'All this is myself'. I am also fond of contemplating, 'I have no mind'. Select one and meditate for 10 minutes.*

AN IMPORTANT HINT FOR THE MEDITATOR

In this chapter I spoke about the origins of the A-Statement, which are connected with the insight 'I can always have the meditation I am having'. Meditators sometimes complain that their mind is filled with thoughts or their system is filled with toxic feeling. This disempowers your meditation. The A-Statement is a tool of empowerment. When your mind is scattered or negative, you should silently make A-Statements to yourself. If done properly, this will calm your mind and take you to a new level. Keep making A-Statements until the inspiration comes to make B- or G-Statements. This will bring you present and eventually your mind will quiet down.

While you can't always have *nirvikalpa samadhi* you can always have the meditation you are having. In the same way, you can't always have a peaceful mind but you can always make an A-Statement.

Chapter 22

Shakti Chakra: The Collective Whole of Energies

> So the Lord who, by his own play, sets in motion this cosmic machine, the *shakti chakra*, is the 'I', the immaculate essence, situated in the place of the driver of the big wheel of the *shakti chakra*.
>
> Abhinavagupta, *Paramarthasara*, Verse 47

The chess master sits at the board. To his right is the chess clock. In front of him are 16 bits of wood with interesting shapes—the chess pieces. They will soon become enlivened by his thought and his imagination. He knows that if he directs them well, they will take on a scintillating power, and victory will be his. On the other hand, if he plays poorly, they will prove to be weak and ineffectual and he will lose. In themselves, they are nothing, but are brought to life by the heart and brain of the master.

In the same way, Lord Shiva sits as Consciousness at the core of the universe and projects His energies outward, creating His manifestation. The source is always in Shiva, in Consciousness.

The *shakti chakra*, a concept developed by the Krama School, is the wheel or assemblage of *shaktis* that accompany Shiva and perform various tasks. They create, sustain and destroy. They are the *shaktis* of knowledge, will and action. He sends mantras out to accomplish things: 'Let there be light', '*Om Tat Sat*'. Finally, He surveys His creation knowing that it is good: 'This is perfect, That is perfect, if you take the perfect from the perfect, the perfect remains'.

In the first sutra of the *Spanda Karikas*, the author says:

> We laud that Shankara (Shiva) by whose mere opening and shutting of the eyelids there is the appearance and dissolution of the world and who is the source of the glorious powers of the collective whole of the *shaktis (shakti chakra).*

The whole universe emanates from the heart of Shiva and He brings it into being with the mere opening of His eyes. The second sutra tells us that nothing can veil Shiva's true nature since the whole universe comes from Him and rests in Him. Unfortunately, though nothing can veil Him in the highest sense, in a relative sense He is very well hidden.

Similarly, in the microcosm the Self sits in the body surrounded by the *shakti chakra*—the circle of energies—at His disposal. Wherever the Self goes in the physical world, He is always accompanied by this assemblage of powers: the mind, the *prana*, the senses, the organs of action and the body. Wherever *you* go, you are accompanied by your posse—your mind, emotion, senses and body and you are always at the centre of those entities. Shaivism tells us in *Spanda Karikas*, I.6–8, that the senses are inert in themselves, like the chess pieces, and only derive energy from the Self.

This image of the Lord or the Self at the centre surrounded by an entourage of Shaktis is a compelling one. In a sense Shaivism's goal is to make us be aware of this position: the Self as the source is always the centre of all experience. Shaivism tells us that when we don't hold ourselves at the centre we lose energy or, in terms of this image, we lose control of our own *shaktis*. I call this the *Shiva position* or the *Shiva asana* (seat or posture). This *Shiva asana* is not different from Douglas Harding's headless one nor from Somananda's *Shiva drishti*. It is easily expressed by the Shaiva mandala (see opposite).

The various functional energies within the body are personified as deities by the Shaivite masters. Each of the *shaktis* has her own characteristics and especially her own positive and negative ways of manifesting. *Vameshvari, khechari, gochari, dikchari* and *bhuchari* are the group of *shaktis* that accompany the individual. *Vameshvari* is the presiding *shakti*, she 'vomits' the universe out of the Absolute. *Vama* also means 'left-handed' or 'contrary' and she is called this because she creates multiplicity rather than unity. *Khechari shaktis* reside in the subject, or *purusha*. *Gochari* are the *shaktis* of the mind. *Dikchari shaktis* have to do with the senses and *bhuchari shaktis* have to do with the external world.

As we have seen, *Pratyabhijnahridayam* Sutra 12 says:

Tadaparijnane svashaktibhir vyamohitata samsaritvam
To be a transmigratory being means being deluded by one's own
shaktis because of the ignorance of the authorship of the fivefold act.

Each of the *shaktis* has a dual nature. She can work positively towards
the liberation of the person or negatively to increase his bondage. When
the *gochari shaktis* work properly, for example, the mind and intellect of a
yogi turns all his thoughts and experiences towards the Self. He accesses
his fund of G-Statements and is committed to always move in the direction
of peace and divinity. When the *gochari shaktis* work negatively, however,
then the person is tortured by tearing thoughts and negativity. He indulges
his sense of victimisation and hopelessness and gravitates towards negative
emotions and disempowerment.

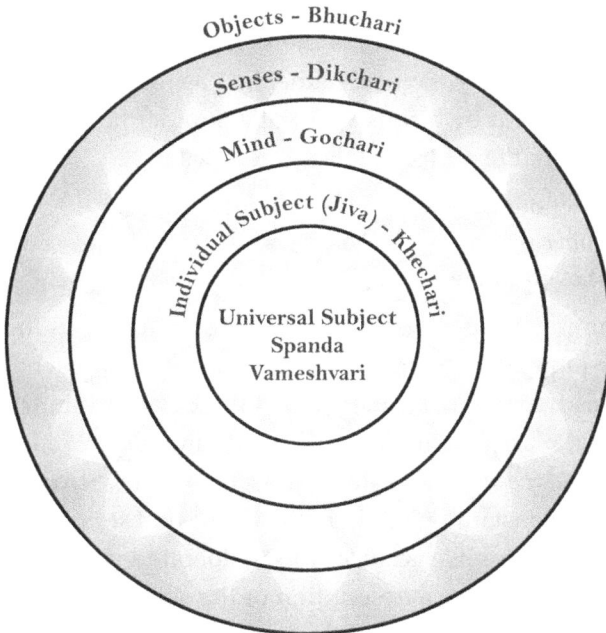

Mandala of the Shakti Chakra. *In the* Shiva asana *the various* shaktis
surround the Self.

The 'authorship of the fivefold act' refers to the five processes, which I
have discussed previously. Kshemaraja's key idea here is that we become

deluded by our own *shaktis* when we don't realise that we, as Shiva, are at the creative source of our own experience. We lose our *Shiva asana*, we regard ourselves as victims at the effect of external forces and then become deluded. In the model of liberation suggested by the concept of the *shakti chakra*, a disempowered Lord Shiva has lost control of his *shaktis* and must reclaim his lost status.

Shiva Sutras I.6 says:

> *Shaktichakra sandhane vishvasamharah*
> The destruction of the universe takes place through meditation on the group of *shaktis* or powers.

When a yogi gains the understanding of the *shakti chakra* he sees that the universe is an alive reflection of his own powers. By intensely focusing on the universe as Shakti, he brings everything into union with Consciousness.

The great text *Spanda Karikas* is the second text in Kashmir Shaivism after the *Shiva Sutras*. It was written either by Vasugupta himself (the author of the *Shiva Sutras*) or by his disciple Kallata under his close supervision. Sutra I.21 from that text is particularly significant.

> Therefore, one should be always on the alert for the discernment of the *spanda* principle. Such a person attains his essential state (as *spanda*) even in the waking condition in a short time.

This commitment to *unmesha*, the upward shift, marks the method of Shaivite Self-inquiry. The yogi of Self-inquiry will always be looking for the trail of breadcrumbs in the forest, and it is the upward shift, the vibration of the Self, that marks them. When the meditator sits in *Shiva asana* at the centre of the *shakti chakra* he realises himself as Shiva. Strong in this point of view, he is in constant union with the Divine and sees everything as the play of Consciousness. He is a *jivanmukta*, liberated while still alive (II.5).

The *Spanda Karikas* are a description of the struggle to attain and hold the Shiva position. The Lord and the individual are surrounded by their entourage of *shaktis*, but the individual struggles for control. Indeed sometimes the *shaktis* seem to take on a separate and malevolent existence. Though they belong to the experient, they turn against him.

Spanda Karikas I.20 says:

> These energies, intent on veiling their real nature push the people of unawakened intellect into the terrible ocean of transmigratory existence, from which it is difficult to pull them out.

Our old nemesis *matrika* is once again at play. The wrong use of self-talk, inner language, limiting ideas, is the cause of bondage. These ideas are the direct result of the loss of control of the *shakti chakra*. The individual becomes bound because he is the victim of the language *shaktis* (*Spanda Karikas* III.13). He loses his independence because of limiting ideas that arise in his mind, destroying inner bliss (III.14). The language powers are not only capable of creating bondage and suffering for the person, but they are positively eager to do so (III.15). These malevolent *shaktis* are related to our self-talk and when our *shaktis* have gone negative they will always show up as an unpleasant tension in the chakras.

By centring himself in the *Shiva asana,* and thereby identifying with the Self, the yogi gathers these scattered and treacherous energies and brings about harmony. He 'infuses them with the light of his Consciousness', that is, he recognises them to be one with his Consciousness, and 'deposits everything in the one place'. He knows that the Self is the source of everything (III.11–12).

At the end of the *Spanda Karikas,* the yogi emerges from bondage by establishing himself in the spanda principle, taking possession of the *shakti chakra. Spanda Karikas* III.19 says:

> When the yogi is centred in the supreme *spanda* principle he becomes the real enjoyer and Lord of the Shakti Chakra.

Again, *Pratyabhijnahridayam* Sutra 20 says:

> When one enters the Self, which is light and bliss, one attains Lordship over the *shakti chakra* that creates and dissolves the universe.

The first time I saw Swami Muktananda was in Delhi in February 1971. He was giving programmes in a large tent on the lawn of a big estate. He sat like a king on his throne and drew everyone's attention to him. I recognised him as the Lord of the Shakti Chakra, although I did not have that terminology then.

This impression was heightened by two vigorous and intelligent young Indian men, Markandeya and Professor Jain, clad in orange, who attended him. Baba would beckon one of them, who would quickly come to his side. Baba would whisper something in his ear and the disciple would be off, running across the ground with great intensity of purpose. Though Baba's manner was simple, matter-of-fact, and even slightly amused, no one I had ever seen was so much at the centre of his own universe and had so much command.

I once heard someone refer deprecatingly to another, saying, 'She leaves a trail'. He meant that the woman in question created karma by her emotional reactions. I thought it was a harsh assessment, yet a colourful image. One thinks of a woodsman moving silently through the woods without disturbing a blade of grass, or a yogi living his life, acting like a knife through water without leaving a ripple. The Lord of the Shakti Chakra is, on the contrary, not afraid to 'leave a trail'. But he wants to make certain that it is a trail of love, vibrancy and luminosity and not one of confusion and hurt.

The depiction of the universe as a rich collection of energies radiating out from its central source in the Lord is vivid. As always in Shaivism we must apply that vision to ourselves personally. Just like Lord Shiva, we are actually at the centre of our experience of life unless we abdicate that position and 'lose our *asana*'.

The process of *sadhana* finds a good metaphor in the myth of the Journey of the Hero. On his quest the hero begins in disempowerment and through a series of strengthening encounters, he moves towards empowerment. The questing yogi is disempowered because he feels himself a victim of forces outside of himself. He doesn't realise that these apparently external forces are really his own *shaktis* that have turned against him because of his lack of mastery.

As he grows he quits the victim attitude and 'takes responsibility' for his own situation. In esoteric Shaivism external objects are known as the moon, the Self is known as fire, and the instruments of perception—the mind and the senses—are known as the sun. Objects, like the moon, have only a reflected light, the sun (the mind) illumines them. But even the sun is not the fundamental power because it is fire—the Self—that illumines the sun.

When a person is under the sway of external objects he is controlled by the moon and its fluctuating phases and emotions. In an interesting parallel, Gurdjieff called the condition of being disempowered by externals, 'being eaten by the moon'. When the yogi becomes the Lord of the Shakti Chakra he takes his stand in the fire of the Self and reaches the Shaivite goal of freedom, *svatantrya*. He is then under the control of no other person, thing or event and is Self-empowered. To achieve this he must fight a war, not with an external enemy, but with unconscious tendencies within himself, which are like neural circuits and patterns in Consciousness that have been formed over a long time. He must uncover them and then defeat them.

The author of the *Spanda Karikas* depicts the Self as the Lord and the controller of the *shakti chakra*. Anyone who has worked with Shakti knows that it is not always possible to establish such control.The most complex and powerful group of *shaktis* that we encounter, other than the ones inside our own mind, is other people.

Spanda Karikas II.3–4 says:

> Because of the knowledge of all subjects, he has the feeling of identity with them all (all others).

Other people are a special kind of object—they are objects that are subjects in their own right. They reflect you to you. They are you.

As we know very well, other people share the dual nature of the *shaktis*. The loving wife of the honeymoon becomes the snarling monster of the divorce; the adorable three-year-old becomes the vile, rebellious teenager. To handle these *shaktis* is indeed a formidable task. This type of Shakti is a Shiva in his or her own right and must be respected as such.

Sometimes, rather than trying to control the Shakti, it is much more appropriate to take the stance of a devotee and worship the Shakti. The Indian mind was capable of great flexibility. In the writings on statesmanship for example, it is recommended that a ruler be adept in four methods from opposite poles. These were propitiation and negotiation, force, gifts and sedition—both hard and soft means.

It is possible for Shiva—knowing that He is Shiva—to adopt the *bhavana* or attitude of the devotee. This kind of sport, of course, is not a disempowerment but a *rasa lila,* a love sport. The hard means of discipline, mental control, renunciation and physical austerity, as well as the soft means of prayer, puja, devotional chanting, and all-embracing love must be applied appropriately.

There are two *bhavanas*: the *Shiva asana* whose G-Statements are 'I am Shiva', I am the Self', 'I am the Lord of the Shakti Chakra'; and the *Shakti asana,* the attitude of the devotee. The G-Statements from the *Shakti asana* are prayer and praise ('Lord, please grant me money and Self-realisation', 'Lord, your bewitching smile pierces my heart').

The Shakti, universal Consciousness, is all-knowing and all-powerful. When the yogi tunes inwardly to the Shakti in his heart, subtle secrets become available to him, but his attitude must be reverent.

Baba says:

> Believe that the Shakti is real, that the Shakti actually exists. If you have such firm faith, Shakti will guide you wherever you may be,

Shakti will take the form of the Guru, or Shakti will give you messages from within. I always worship Shakti with great reverence within my being, and as a result of that I receive messages from Her from time to time.

A meditator should cultivate the awareness that when he turns inside he is gazing into living Consciousness, Consciousness so alive and responsive that it records and responds to every nuance of his thought and feeling. The answer to every legitimate question and the solution to every problem is available to him.

For the devotee, prayer is empowered speech. If we insist on holding the *Shiva asana* under all conditions, we tend to become hard and arrogant. In Douglas Harding's terms, we should be able to have both the expanded head of the headless one and the little head of the devotee. A great yogi should have the flexibility to move from one to the other as situations demand. Too rigid or too yielding: our inner feeling will tell us when to take another tack. Only the true Lord of the Shakti Chakra, who mixes perfect love with perfect discipline and perfect wisdom, can achieve this goal in its fullness.

MEDITATIONS ON THE SHAKTI CHAKRA

Shiva Sutras I.21 says:

Through the appearance of pure wisdom, the yogi attains mastery over the *shakti chakra*.

The best way to assimilate the understandings of the *shakti chakra* and make them experiential is through meditation.

Eyes Open
Sit comfortably with your eyes open. Look around the room. Reflect 'I am Shiva and I am at the centre of all this. All this occurs within my awareness'. Fully understand that while you are at the centre right now, if you moved across the room you would still be at the centre, and even if you went into another room, you would still be at the centre.

Vameshvari Shakti (the supreme Shakti)
Close your eyes. Feel the life-force and energy running through you. Say to yourself, 'O supreme energy, you create my whole universe. O my Shakti, you are supremely free and powerful'.

Khechari Shakti (the individual self)
Feel your 'I'. Where in your body does it reside? Contemplate that even though

272

you usually identify this with your personal Self, it is really Shiva's 'I'. Consider this deeply: the 'I' you feel is not 'you' but Shiva. Or, rather, you are Shiva but you didn't know it. You will have a sense of your own vastness.

Gochari Shakti *(the mind)*

The gochari shaktis *are the shaktis of the mind. Talk to your mind lovingly. Say 'O Goddess of my mind, please think beautiful thoughts. Please see everything with divine understanding. Please give up anger, fear, jealousy, self-pity and tearing thoughts. O Goddess, please remember the Lord'.*

Dikchari Shakti *(the senses)*

The dikchari shakti *moves in the senses. Speak to your senses. 'O Goddesses of my senses, you exist within me. I love to see, to hear, to feel, to smell and to taste. What a rich world you let me experience. You make me want to forget myself in you. Although you tempt me, I will never forget the Self'.*

Bhuchari Shakti *(the outer world)*

Bhuchari shakti *moves in the outer world. Say to her, 'O Goddess of everything I perceive, you exist only because I am here to observe you. Though you seem separate from me, you exist within me as Consciousness Itself. Though you try to separate from me to delude me, I am on to your trick. You are my own Self'.*

Abhinavagupta, writing from the point of view of the Self, says, 'Even without body and organs, I see, I hear, I feel'. He is saying that the Self encompasses and is prior to the mind, senses and so on. The Self contains all their qualities and abilities. These things are shaktis *of the Self and can never usurp Him. Meditate on one of these* shaktis *for 10 minutes.*

Chapter 23

Anupaya

> He who has broken the bonds of ignorance, who has conquered doubt
> and error, in whom good and bad actions have been annihilated, this
> one is liberated even though he remains in the body.

> Abhinavagupta, Paramarthasara, Verse 61

Kashmir Shaivism has interesting things to say about the nature of
the universe—cosmology, ontology and teleology as philosophers
might say. Because my real interest was always in self-development, the
quest for Self-realisation, the feature of Shaivism that most gripped me was
the *upayas*, the methods of *sadhana*. The discussion of the *upayas* opened my
understanding of the path.

To swiftly review the three *upayas*, they are *anavopaya*, the method based
on bodily action; *shaktopaya*, the method based on the mind; and
shambhavopaya, the method emphasising immersion in awareness itself. I
have held back the best for last, the mysterious fourth *upaya*, *anupaya*, the
'non-way'. In this *upaya* the Guru explains the truth and the aspirant grasps
it at once. It is also called the way of divine *recognition* and is marked by a
ripe student and a powerful transmission of grace.

Ramana Maharshi was renowned for asking seekers to meditate on 'Who
am I?'. What has not been appreciated is how often he told seekers—before
he prescribed the 'Who Am I' inquiry—'Why not remain as you are?'. This
instruction flowed from Ramana's divine vision, his *Shiva drishti*. A great
being sees the world as shimmering Consciousness, inherently perfect.

Similarly, he sees each person radiating the light of the Self. Each one is a unique manifestation of Shiva and is to be honoured and respected.

So Ramana's first line of instruction was often to invite the seeker to share his vision: 'You are Shiva just as you are. Why change? Why do *sadhana?* Just understand who you are, be who you are, and celebrate who you are.' (Although perhaps 'celebrate' is too strong a word for Ramana's low-key personality).

This was an invitation to *anupaya*. Only after the bewildered seeker demonstrated that he did not understand this instruction, would Ramana go down an *upaya* or two and ask them to inquire, 'Who am I' or say a mantra. Though you could scarcely call Ramana a Shaivite—both his personality and the tone of his teaching were intensely Vedantic—in this one thing, Ramana acted like a Shaivite since he followed the method of offering the highest *upaya* first.

Ramana's method gives a clear understanding about the way the *upayas* work. Imagine a Shaivite sage being approached by a seeker who asks to be taught. The sage, like Ramana says, 'Remain as you are. You are Shiva. There is nothing wrong', offering *anupaya*.

The seeker says, 'I can't do that, I need a practice'.

Sage: Okay, focus on pure awareness. Use your will to stay present to Consciousness Itself. Now he is offering *shambhavopaya*.

The seeker says, 'I can't do that'.

The sage says, 'Why not?'

Seeker: My mind keeps coming in and pulling me away.

Sage: Okay. Purify your mind. Focus on the thought 'I am Consciousness', repeat the mantra. Now he is offering *shaktopaya*.

Seeker: I can't do that either.

Sage: Why not?

Seeker: I am obsessed by sex and money and worldly ambition.

Sage: Okay. Get married. Get a good job. Give some money to the ashram. Do hatha yoga, do breath exercises and meditate on the form of your Guru or deity. Now he is offering *anavopaya*.

Seeker: Thank you. O Master, please give me your blessing.

Each *upaya* solves the difficulty the seeker has with the one above it.

I have mentioned earlier in the book the odd Tantric principle whereby the lowest becomes the highest. What really happens is this: in Zen there is an old witticism that says, 'Before practising Zen, the mountains are mountains and the rivers are rivers. During the practice of Zen, the mountains are no longer mountains and the rivers are no longer rivers. And when the goal of Zen is reached, the mountains are once again mountains and the rivers are once again rivers'.

Early in my stay at my Guru's ashram, I felt that all of my old values were being replaced with an entirely new set of values. These were not only spiritual ideas, but even aesthetic standards. An unusual feature of the yoga of my generation's seekers was that we went outside our culture for instruction, and this had an immense impact. Sometimes I felt that my new hierarchy of good and bad seemed one hundred percent opposite to my previous value system. But as my Guru liked to say, this was really 'a thorn to remove a thorn'. It was a temporary madness to counteract lifetimes of delusion.

Later, things shifted again and I felt myself return to myself: the same in some ways, but profoundly different. *Atma vyapti*, which is the conventional yoga of inwardness where the seeker turns away from the world to realise the Self, involves a certain measure of distortion. The process reaches its fruition in *Shiva vyapti* when the inner knowledge gained in *atma vyapti* is applied to the world in extrovert meditation, the yoga of awareness in ordinary life. The mountains are once again mountains: things again are simply as they are.

Abhinavagupta says:

> There is no need here of spiritual progress or of contemplation, neither of discourses nor discussion, neither of meditation nor of concentration, nor recitation of mantra, no practising anything, no making effort, nothing. What is then, tell me, the supreme Reality which is absolutely certain? Listen: neither reject nor accept (anything), share joyfully in everything, being as you are.

This extraordinary attitude is familiar to us from the great *jnanis*. It is inherent in a monistic approach. The equation reads: if everything is God (or Consciousness) what can possibly be wrong that we should change it? It is all divine will, divine experience, the play of Consciousness.

Spanda Karikas I.2 says:

> Inasmuch as nothing can veil His nature, there cannot be His obstruction anywhere in whom all this world rests and from whom it has come forth.

Of course, it is all so obvious after we have awakened. Before that happens, this sutra and others that say the same thing, make no sense at all.

Kamalakar Mishra further quotes Abhinavagupta in *Tantraloka*:

> There is no attainment of the Self, for it is eternally present.
> There is no question of making it known, for it is self-illumined.
> There is no question of uncovering or discovering it, for it cannot be covered by anything whatsoever.
> There is no entering into it, for there is nobody separate from it who would enter into it.

Anupaya is nothing but the *sahaja* state of the *Siddhas*. The world is already transformed; nothing has to be done. God is fully manifest. One thinks of the story of Sri Ramakrishna leaving his carriage to dance in ecstasy with some drunkards. To his vision, their bibulous ecstasy reminded him of his own spiritual ecstasy—and brought it on

The world itself becomes the goal of yoga as well as the method of yoga. Utpaladeva writes:

> Where even pain transforms into pleasure
> And poison into nectar,
> Where the world itself becomes liberation,
> That is the path of Shankara.

Vijnanabhairava Dharana 99 reads:

> The reality of [Shiva] is apparent everywhere—even among common folk (who do not possess any particular sense of discrimination). One who knows thus, 'There is nothing other than He', attains the nondual condition.

How can it be that the reality of Shiva is apparent even for ordinary people? The commentary points out that everyone uses the pronoun 'I'. Jaideva Singh says: 'Even ignoramuses are conscious of this 'I'. The *Maharthamanjari* tells us that even 'portresses of water' (that is, unevolved people) know Him.

What a noble vision of the world. How conditioned we are to see faults, to reduce everything to maya and ego! In a world transformed by vision, ego does not exist. Ego is simply a throb of Self. We do not try to turn a stream into the ocean by widening its banks or having it repeat a mantra. It is fine as it is, it is made of the same stuff as the ocean, it is beautiful and useful in its own way, and ultimately it flows into the ocean.

In the *Vijnanabhairava*, many different methods are used. Most are *shaktopaya* techniques with a few *anavopaya* and *shambhavopaya* ones. As for *anupaya* meditations there are only two, the one just given (Dharana 99) and Dharana 110:

> There is neither bondage nor liberation for me. These (bondage and liberation) are only bogies for those who are terrified (on account of the ignorance of their essential nature).

Bondage and liberation have no objective existence, but are simply attitudes held within the mind. Once a famous rabbi noticed that a member of his congregation looked very grim and upset. When this continued for a few weeks, he took the man aside and spoke to him. 'Heschel! What's the matter? You look terrible.'

'Rabbi, it's true. I am having a very hard time. My mother-in-law is visiting us and though I try very hard to be kind to her, everything she does rubs me the wrong way and pushes all my buttons. Rabbi! I can't sleep at night. I can't eat. I feel like I have no space *in my own house*. I should have talked to you long ago. What can I do?'

'Heschel', said the rabbi, 'that's an easy one. Do what I say and I'll fix it right up'.

'Anything, Rabbi.'

'Okay, go home and bring your cows into the house. Then come back next week and report to me.'

He came back next week.

'How is it now, Heschel?' asked the rabbi.

'Terrible. Now my mother-in-law is still her obnoxious self and the cows are making filth everywhere.'

'Good', said the rabbi, 'now bring the goats in and come back next week and report to me'.

Next week Heschel came back and the rabbi said, 'So, Heschel, how is it now?'

'Hideous!' said Heschel. 'The cows are roaming, my mother-in-law is complaining and the goats are stinking.'

'Wonderful!' said the rabbi. 'Now bring in the horses and the chickens.' Weeks went by like this. Now Heschel had his whole barnyard in the house with him. Everything was covered by filth and feathers and the din was horrific. He returned for another visit to the rabbi. The rabbi said, 'Heschel, everything is going according to plan. Now go back, take out the cows, take out the horses, take out the chickens, take out the goats, take out everything but leave your mother-in-law, and come back next week to report'.

Next week, the rabbi asked, 'How is it now, Heschel?'

Heschel said, 'O Rabbi, it's wonderful. There's so much space. There's so much peace and quiet. You've saved my life. How can I thank you!'

In the natural state of *anupaya*, even bondage and liberation are seen to be illusions of the mind. When grace descends through *anupaya*, this very universe is utterly transformed. Nothing happens to the universe, only to the viewer. All conceptual systems fall away and things are simply as they are. Once a Jewish seeker said, 'I don't go to hear the Rebbe speak on abstruse matters of philosophy, I go to watch him tie his shoelaces'.

One of the main features of my *sadhana* at my Guru's ashram—if not the main feature—was simply watching Baba. It was evident to me that he brought divinity into the most mundane actions. I watched him and watched him, trying to soak up this knowledge that could not be articulated. *Anupaya* is yoga not by practice, not by doctrine, but by osmosis.

My Guru used to say that realising the Self was, 'Getting rid of what you haven't got'. Really speaking, this is easy to understand but much harder to realise. There was a young man who came to the ashram in Ganeshpuri who had been self-educated in Vedanta. He told everyone, 'everything is Ram', and consequently, we began to call him 'Ram-Ram'. He became a bit of a problem since whenever an ashram manager would tell him to observe the ashram discipline, he would say, 'Everything is Ram, man. Why are you so uptight?' Needless to say, he was not enjoying *Shiva drishti*, the divine vision of Shiva, but instead spiritual delusion based on ego. He was using the few Vedantic shibboleths that he knew to gain power and status. The real *Shiva drishti* is simply a matter of fact and is uplifting for everyone. It is not to gain power.

A few years later, one of my Ganeshpuri friends found himself rooming with Ram-Ram in San Francisco. Ram-Ram had created a mini-ashram in his apartment and all the roommates had to surrender to him as to God. My friend was troubled by this arrangement and he came for my advice. I told him he should tell Baba about it on the *darshan* line that night. He did. What he said was, 'Baba, I'm living with a fellow who claims that he is a realised being and it doesn't feel right. What should I do?'

Baba said, 'You should always avoid realised beings. They are very bad!'

There was uproarious laughter at this response but my friend moved out at once. Half-baked *advaitins* like Ram-Ram love to proclaim that there is nothing to be attained. That may very well be true, but it is well worth spending your whole life working hard to attain that nothing.

Nonetheless, the notions of bondage and liberation are a drama of bondage. Even the idea of *Siddhahood* is a 'golden handcuff', according to Baba. When a person experiences his own Self he attains equal vision. He does not see himself as different from others. Some people may exclaim how extraordinary he is. He simply watches these karmas unfold. Others are equally likely to abuse or ignore him, but they are merely in the throes of the peculiar process we call *sadhana*, which will ultimately take them to the Self. The process is peculiar because it is so subtle, so elusive, like wrestling with our own shadow. And the result is to see that this process—as inevitable as it is—was unnecessary.

True *anupaya* is free of ego assertion. It is marked by living freely and naturally in harmony with the divine will. Since all human effort is limited and the Self is unlimited, it is impossible for the unlimited to be reached via limitation. Hence, only by penetrating recognition does the quest end.

Abhinavagupta says:

> This recognition occurs in the cosmic heart—which is also the heart of man—always hidden and universally apparent, always new and yet ancient.

The key ingredient in *anupaya* is to live in *satsang* with a great being. Hence *Shiva Sutras* II.6 says, *Gururupaya*: The Guru is the means. This is an interesting aphorism, since although the *Shiva Sutras* are divided into three sections, for the three *upayas*, this is the only time an *upaya* is specifically named. Do we then have a fifth *upaya*? I don't think so. I believe that *gururupaya* is the doorway to *anupaya*. When I met Baba, I had the intuitive understanding that simply living in association with him would do everything. Whatever tests I needed to undergo, whatever situations I needed to encounter, whatever realisations I need to have, would naturally happen.

Soon after I arrived at the Ganeshpuri Ashram, my first spiritual teacher, Ram Dass, visited for a few weeks. He told me, 'This is a fierce place. If you stay here a few months, you will be transformed'. I remember thinking that was an odd statement for I had already decided never to leave. I had understood this *anupaya*, the *sahaja* yoga of living with a *Siddha*, although I would not then have been able to formulate it.

A realised being is in union with the divine will. All his actions and behaviours mirror the perfection of that union. Whatever such a being does becomes his yoga, his teaching device. Even though Muktananda taught many conventional yogic techniques, he really didn't need to. His life was his yoga and to join him in his life, was to join your will to the divine will.

When Ram Dass spoke to me I thought, to take myself away from such a being would be to assert my personal will and separate me from God. Why would I do that? I could only leave such a being under his direct command or when, through my yoga with him, I had become established in the divine will myself. Though it sounds easy, to live in such an association is extremely difficult. That very impulse to separate yourself from that association is the greatest obstacle to the yoga of *anupaya*.

Shaivism holds that the decisive factor in *sadhana* is the descent of divine grace, *shaktipat*. This is an infusion of Consciousness that, operating on matter and ignorance within an individual, decisively alters the shape of his life and lifts him permanently towards the light. The way of grace is mysterious, coming as it does, from the freedom of the divine will. One would think that qualified aspirants who have done a lot of practice would be the ones to receive grace but this is not always the case.

My Guru gave *shaktipat* liberally. People received the awakening with little or no background or even prior interest in spirituality. Of course, you could say that despite that they were destined to receive grace at just that time. I vividly remember one woman who had visited Baba at the urging of a friend and had received *shaktipat*, much to her dismay. She would endlessly complain to me and ask if it could be taken away. Though it made me feel unkind, I always laughed. How many people were desperate for that awakening!

While we try to fit these things into neat categories, probably only the most general remarks are true: the unmotivated descent of the grace of the Lord is the central fact of yoga.

The Guru is the agent of that grace. Kshemaraja, in his commentary to *Shiva Sutras* II.6, The Guru is the means, says:

> *Gurur va parameshvari anugrahika shatih*
> The Guru is the grace-bestowing power of God.

He goes on to quote the *Malinivijaya Tantra:*

> The power of grace has been said to be the collective whole of *shaktis*, that has been said to be the mouth of the Guru.

Thus, the Guru's word, that is, his teaching and the mantra that he gives, conveys his Shakti-power, the gracious power of awakening. Grace, the fifth of the five cosmic processes, acts on the fourth process—concealment—to undo it. The Lord's *shaktipat* destroys the *malas* that cloak the individual soul.

Some commentators say that the primary *mala, anava mala*, which has been called the 'limitation of smallness', because it makes Shiva feel like a separate and impotent individual, can only be overcome by grace. The other two *malas* can be worked on through yogic practice. In fact, it is felt that *shaktipat* initiation actually destroys *anava mala*, but not necessarily *mayiya* and *karma mala*.

Whether or not that is literally true, in my case, once I had walked through the gates of the Ganeshpuri Ashram, I felt connected to the source in a permanent way. I was no longer small and alone and never would be again. That is not to say that there was not a lot of work and suffering ahead, but an essential emptiness in my soul had been removed.

If we keep ourselves in *satsang*, everything does happen as it should. One time I was sitting in the hall in the Oakland Ashram during a long chant. Baba was soon to come in and bring the chant to an end and give a talk. At this point the senior Oakland swami came in to take his seat, prior to Baba's arrival. The two home-swamis sat in the first row, but now the junior swami was, for some reason, sitting in the senior man's usual seat. When the senior came in, the junior man saw him and silently offered to give him his seat. The senior man responded (again wordlessly) that it was okay for him to continue to sit there and sat down in the second seat. I was sitting in the row behind, chanting and casually observing this sequence of events. At the very moment that the senior swami refused his junior partner's offer, my Consciousness exploded. I entered an altered reality of divine ecstasy. I sat in that for the remainder of the programme and during Baba's talk. When the programme ended, after Baba had left the hall, I walked around greeting various devotees in the most extraordinary state of Consciousness. I went back to the swami-dorm and told a few of the swamis what had happened. The experience lasted for hours.

One analysis was that somehow the Shakti was supporting or pointing out to me the swamis' attitude of noble humility. But my actual experience was that what had happened was a pure act of grace with no cause. I had had absolutely no thoughts about it. I didn't think, how nice of the junior swami to offer his seat, or how humble of the senior swami to take the lesser seat. I simply sat as a witness enjoying the chanting. Thus it seemed to me a pure example of *anupaya*. I absorbed the apparent lesson, but it was clear to me that the grace was far beyond any specific lesson.

Such an experience is dramatic and memorable of course, but the *anupaya* of *satsang* with a *Siddha* is usually gradual and nearly invisible. More and more, Consciousness becomes the context of awareness. The focus shifts from the passing conceptual and emotional states to the abiding background. The seeker 'collapses into Consciousness' in a natural way. He finds he is living from a completely different perspective

Baba often gave the spiritual instruction, 'See God in each other'. *Lokanandah samadhisukham (Shiva Sutras* I.18), points to the state of *anupaya* or *sahaja samadhi*. Unlike the other *upayas*, *anupaya* is not a practice but a state. *Lokanandah samadhisukham:* The bliss you experience in people is exactly the same bliss that is on offer in deep meditation. Here the yogi need not do special practices to realise the Self, but seeing the Self in every person, he attains the same *samadhi* state that strenuous yogis do.

Abhinavagupta says:

> Just as juice, syrup, sugar-candy, molasses, pieces of sugar are equally sugarcane juice, in the same way the various states all belong to Shiva.

Just as the narrator in the *Pratyabhijnahridayam* was, even in the darkest hour of the soul's journey, aware that divine Consciousness was present, so in life our natural yoga has to keep this understanding in our minds. Shiva permeates everything, even our negative experiences and our negative states. If we forget this and live only in mundane reality, our Consciousness contracts. If, on the other hand, like Ram-Ram, we try to avoid mundane reality by ignoring it in favour of spiritual principles, we miss the point as well.

We should learn the art of dealing seriously with life issues, while keeping the higher awareness in our minds. Shiva is always there in depression as well as joy, in boredom as well as excitement. In this attitude, is perfect self-acceptance. Any attempt to 'attain' Shiva is in some sense an affront to

Shiva. Where is Shiva not? What condition or state is not Shiva? Why strive to become that which you already are? Seeking special states is antithetical to the vision of Shiva. Thus, *anupaya* is the perfect flowering of the Shaivite vision.

True spirituality begins with the awakening by *shaktipat*, the descent of grace. The seeker feels flooded with awe and wonder. As he does his *sadhana* and attains the goal, he stands face-to-face with the beloved: the Guru, the deity or Consciousness Itself. The emotion that he feels is reverence. Now in the third phase, he feels that God has become completely intimate to him. He relaxes and is simply himself in the divine presence. He feels he can say anything and do anything, for he and the Lord cannot be separated. Every word and action, and even every breath he takes, embodies the divine sport of his relationship with God. This is the final state.

MEDITATION: DIVINE ACCEPTANCE

Anupaya, *recognition*, sahaja samadhi—*these are many names for the same state. Let's do the meditation of divine acceptance. Everything, exactly as it is, is Shiva. It is not that Shiva will appear when the world is purified. It is not that Shiva will manifest when the avatar comes or the Age of Aquarius dawns. It is not that you will experience Shiva when your kundalini reaches your brain.*

Close your eyes. Now, now, now. This, this, this—it is all Shiva. My contraction is Shiva, my sorrow is Shiva, my depression is Shiva. My thoughts are Shiva, my overactive mind is Shiva. Shiva and Shiva alone is. This is perfect Shaivite meditation and it cannot fail because failure too is Shiva and Shiva alone. Meditate for 10 minutes.

Chapter 24

Love

> The 'first person'
> Is distinguished from the 'second person'
> And the 'third person' as well.
> You alone are the Great Person,
> The refuge of all persons.
>
> Utpaladeva, *Shivastotravali*, Third Song, Verse 15

H aving realised the Self within himself by *atma vyapti* the Shaivite sage turns to the world. He experiences *Shiva vyapti*. He lives in the natural state seeing Shiva everywhere. The state he attains is not the dry embodiment of a concept, but is full of love. Wherever he looks, he sees his beloved. Whomever he speaks to, it is the beloved. Even trees and rocks, mountains and rivers are lovable and intimate.

Abhinavagupta in his work on language mysticism, *Paratrishika Vivarana*, says that everything in the universe is of the form of the Trika, the three. It is *Shiva*, *Shakti* and *nara* (*nara*—the individual, and everything that is not Shiva and Shakti). This triad is reflected in the grammatical structure first person (I), second person (you) and third person (he, she or it). Abhinava says that the first person is always Shiva. When the first person has a counterpart and becomes dual, then the second person is always Shakti. When the two become many, the third person is always *nara*. The first person is of primary importance, the second next, and then the third.

Abhinavagupta quotes *Tantrasamucchaya*:

This universe is established always and is in every way involved in third person *(nara),* second person (Shakti) and first person (Shiva) both in the dealings of worms and the all-knowing.

Anavopaya is related to the third person, *shaktopaya* is related to the second person (notice the word 'Shakti') and *shambhavopaya* is related to the first person.

Abhinavagupta continues:

> This all-inclusive order of experience consisting of the third, second and first person has been manifested by the free will of the highest Lord.

As I read Abhinava's words, I thought of Douglas Harding's teachings. The headless one is Shiva—the first person. When we think of ourselves as the third person, we lose Shakti. But Shiva recognises other people as a special kind of object. While he does not directly know them from within, he intuitively feels that they, like him, have interiority. They are Shiva in their own universe. In this sense, another person is one with ourself. Feeling this identity there is a flow of love, as we imaginatively enter the space of another. It is love of the Self by the Self

Dharana 106 in the *Vijnanabhairava* says:

> On the occasion of the assertion, 'I am; this is mine, etc.,' the thought goes to that which does not depend on any support (i.e., the Self or pure Awareness). [Then] one attains peace.

This is a charming explanation of the capitalist urge to possess. The pen on my desk is merely an object in itself, however, because I regard it as 'mine', it acquires lovability by its association with my Self. Whatever I own thus becomes, for me, part of me, and is infused with my energy. The *Siddha* who experiences the attitude 'All this is mine, all this is my own being', sees himself everywhere and experiences that love everywhere.

If I am the subject and you are a conscious object, you must be Shakti, my own dear one. Hence arises the grammatical second person. The second person is suffused with love and intimacy. When we have a relationship with someone, that person becomes second person to us. People hunger for relationships so they can explore the intimacy of Shakti, the second person.

Douglas Harding is aware of second personism and in his characteristically witty way, says that when we are face-to-face with another, we are actually face-to-no-face: our face disappears and we hold the other's face in our awareness. There can be no greater love or greater surrender than to give way entirely to Shakti in this way.

Even more involved in the ecstasy of the second person was the Hasidic sage, Martin Buber. He defined two primary human attitudes: *I-Thou* and *I-It*. We easily recognise these as second and third person. While the *I-It* has to do with objective life and functioning, the *I-Thou* expresses relationship and mutual recognition. Buber said that while the 'It' is named and defined, the 'Thou' is *addressed*. Thus while the 'It' can be approached rather coldly and held at a distance through the intellect, the 'Thou' must be approached directly and immediately through the heart. In addition, Buber felt that God can never be objectified but must always be a 'Thou'. He felt that God was the *'Thou of Thous'* and each particular 'Thou' that we encounter in life is a spark of the Divine.

To his two primary attitudes, I would add a third: the *I-I* relationship. In meditation (*I-I*) we approach the Self directly. One remove, further out (*I-Thou*) are our primary relationships in life. They are still redolent of divinity. When our primary relationships go off the rails, it is not fundamentally different from having a meditation where the mind chatters and the emotions are depressed. Buber's point of view is very close to Shaivism. My Guru had two aspects to his teaching: meditate on the Self and find God within; and also see God in others. These correspond to *atma vyapti* and *Shiva vyapti*.

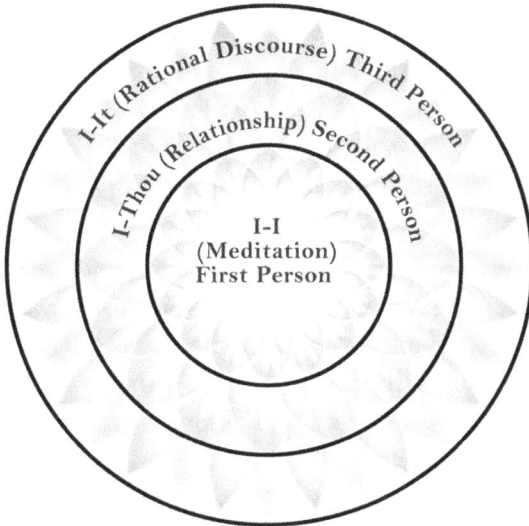

Three-Personed God Mandala. *The three persons of grammar represent three levels of relationships.*

These insights give us strong clues to practise. If we speak *of* God we make Him into the third person and there is not much life in it. If we speak *to* God then we enter relationship and we experience Him. Thus in our heart of hearts, prayer should be intimate and personal. Closest, of course, is to *be* one with God in meditation.

When a person dies, the heartbreak comes because we feel that we've lost the intimacy of our second-person relationship with him or her. This wisdom shows us that we should not turn the one we've lost into an object or third person. Instead we should speak loving words to that person, secretly inside our heart. We will discover that the relationship has not been lost. Shakti is eternal.

Since Kashmir Shaivism is strongly monistic and the seeker is enjoined to discover his Shiva nature, where then is the place for devotion? The great Shaivite sages like Abhinavagupta and Utpaladeva had no problem with expressing their ecstatic devotion to the Lord.

Once the Sufi saint, Baba Musa, appointed a successor. In doing so, he overlooked a disciple of great attainment named Aqbal. A friend asked him, 'O Aqbal, don't you feel hurt to be overlooked as Baba Musa's successor?'

Aqbal said, 'I don't want to be Baba Musa's successor, I want to attain *samavesha* with him. I want to *be* Baba Musa!'

Just then the cook from the kitchen burst out, 'O Aqbal, you are a fool! Why become either the successor or even Baba Musa himself, when to love him is so sweet?'

Sri Ramakrishna perfectly expressed the *bhakta's* eternal argument for a dualistic point of view when he said, 'I want to *taste* sugar, I don't want to *become* sugar'.

Kashmir Shaivism is richly devotional. Here, Shiva as the meditator becomes Shakti the devotee and prays to God as Shiva. This is Shiva's 'controlled folly'. Knowing full well that he is Shiva, he becomes Shakti in certain relationships with God, with the Guru, with the beloved, to experience the softness and *rasa* of devotion.

A great poet saint wrote:

> This world was empty and harsh and filled with heartless objects with cold shiny surfaces. When I looked into my Guru's eyes he kindled a fire within me. Now the objects and people of the world are him and him alone and they are warm with the heart's intimacy.

HEART-TO-HEART MEDITATION

Here is a meditation you can use everyday for the rest of your life. Using the insights of Abhinavagupta, Douglas Harding and Martin Buber, go inside and speak intimately to God. Pour your heart out to Him in an unpremeditated, nonformulaic manner. Ask Him for what you want from the material to the sublime. Be a person to Him. Look for and follow the upward shift of feeling.

Do the same with a loved one who has died or is absent. You can also do this with someone from whom you have become alienated. In that case, speak heart-to-heart, ignoring the differences, which are at the level of personality. Abhinavagupta said, 'That is no speech that does not reach the heart directly'.

Chapter 25

Conclusion: The Living Spirit of Shaivism

> It is in me that this universe reveals itself, like vases and other objects in a spotless mirror. From me everything arises, just as the many different dreams arise from sleep. It is I whose form is this universe, just as a body has hands, feet, and sense organs. It is I who shines in everything, like a light shining in different forms.
>
> Abhinavagupta, *Paramarthasara*, Verses 48-9

The goal of the philosophy and yoga of Kashmir Shaivism is lofty. Abhinavagupta tells us it is:

... liberation of all beings in their lifetime, beings who have become entitled to this knowledge of the Absolute by the excellent descent of divine Shakti. This liberation consists of penetration of the essential nature of Bhairava with complete identity *(samavesha)* and union with perfect I-Consciousness, the delightful flash of one's own essential Self. A liberated one regards the entire multitude of created objects not as bondage, but merely as different aspects of his own sportfulness and as the expression of the abundance of his own delight.

Liberation involves a decisive movement towards the centre of our being. We have seen that as we move from gross to subtle we get closer to the Truth. As we go up the *tattvas* we are moving inward. We leave behind the appearances and experience what lies underneath. Gross language resolves into mantra and finally into meaning itself. Language becomes more truth-bearing as it goes inward. Every conversation contains what is said, and underneath that, what is meant and what is felt. Every contraction we experience within ourselves can be investigated and resolved, first into its causes, then beyond that, into peace and bliss. For as we approach Truth, we also approach bliss. *Chit* and *ananda* are essential aspects of the Self.

At the same time as we move from the object to the subject, we approach that same *Chit* and *ananda*.

Spanda Karikas I.14 says:

> Two aspects of the *spanda* principle are mentioned: the subject and the object. Of these two, the object decays but the subject is imperishable.

Gurdjieff said, 'Remember yourself!' That is, hold onto the subject. Douglas Harding tells us to live first-personism, become the headless one. Sri Nisargadatta tells us to hold the 'I am'.

Shaivism's conclusions are the same. Abhinavagupta says that *aham vimarsha*, supreme I-Consciousness, is our true nature. Kshemaraja teaches us to practise *shakti sankocha* and *vikasa*, to pull our energy to the Self, or hold the Self in *shambavi mudra*, even while experiencing the world. He tells us that when the mind moves inward it expands and becomes *Chiti*. Via *krama mudra* we move between subject and object, finally suffusing the objective world with the bliss of the subject. We crack the code of *vikalpas*, thought- forms, and enter the silent world of mantra, *matrika*, and *Chiti* that lies beneath.

All these journeys: from object to subject, from gross to subtle, from outer world to inner world are the same journey. They are fully expressed in Shaivism's first sutra, *The Self is Consciousness.*

Two of the *kanchukas* that occur when Shiva is limited, when He enters physical reality and becomes a person, are time and space: eternity contracts to time; omnipresence contracts to space. Language unfolds in time. Objects are held in space. Language is of the inner world, space is of the outer world.

The yogi performs Self-inquiry via *layabhavana*. Gross language is resolved into subtle language. Gross physicality is resolved into the subtle. The universe is folded in on itself to discover *Chiti* at its centre. But just here is the supreme Shaivite moment. Shiva himself has made the opposite journey from the Self to other, from subject to object, from the one to the many, from subtle to gross, from silence to the world, from Consciousness to matter. So the Shaivite yogi-hero joins him. He realises the inner and with it, consecrates the outer. He transforms the material into the Divine. He suffuses the gross with the *chitananda* of the subtle. He lives in Shiva's garden right in worldly life.

As I contemplated the sweep of these grand ideas while I was in Ganeshpuri, inquiry began to arise in me. When I felt an obstacle in my meditation, I would try to trace it back to its source and resolve it into Consciousness. During one period, I encountered a big obstacle. I felt a painful contraction. Late in the afternoon after my ashram work was complete, I would bathe and then sit in the meditation hall and work on it. I focused on the feeling. It centred in my heart. There was a burning sensation and a feeling of spiritual dryness and emptiness. I inquired into it. I asked myself if this was a familiar feeling. Did I recognise the emotion? What was the underlying cause? Did it lie in the obscurity of my youth or had something recent happened that brought it about. Had my thoughts changed direction?

After a few days of inquiry, I felt that I had isolated the cause. It was enmity. I simply hated most of the other ashramites. Back in America, I had become expert in seeing ego everywhere. This was a vestige of that. I was looking with jaundiced eye at every ashramite and seeing their secret motivations. This one only likes to feel important. This one is sucking up to be close to Baba. That one loves to hold power over others. That one is stupid and lazy.

Why was I so critical? Was I jealous? I tried to let the feeling speak to me and tell me its story, even suggest a solution. No matter how hard I worked, I couldn't get to the bottom of it. On this particular day, I gave up, left the meditation hall and stood in front of Baba. It was a beautiful time of day. The wife of the owner of the chai shop next door made *idhlis* (ricecakes) every evening for Baba to distribute. We went up one by one and he firmly pressed half an *idhli* into each of our hands. You could smell the perfume of his heena scent and the intense love of his immediate presence. As I watched the scene, new thoughts came to me. 'You are completely stupid. These are not horrible people. They are great souls. They have left their comfortable middle-class existence in the West to do austerities in search of the Truth in an ashram in India. They have not only left their comforts, but their families, friends and jobs. It is not they who are sinners: your vision is skewed.'

Standing in front of Baba, I saw this very clearly. The ashramites were mostly people I would not be friendly with back in my old life. Yet, where were the people from my old life? Certainly not here. The one thing all of us in the ahsram had in common was our dedication to the spiritual quest.

These understandings came with great clarity, but I still was in misery. Nothing had shifted. In an inspired moment, I prayed inwardly, 'Baba, shift my vision. Let me see them with your eyes. Let me see their divinity'. In that moment the bell rang for the evening chant. Baba got up from his perch and hunched down to go through the little door into his apartment, and I was not what I had been a moment before. My awareness expanded. I moved quickly into the hall and began doing my evening duty of handing out the chanting books. Before my eyes, the ashramites had morphed into gods and goddesses. This was not conceptual, but visionary: I was seeing it and feeling it and I was filled with bliss. I laughed to myself, how easy it all is.

Shaivism is the path of the heart. It is the embodiment of the *rasa* of love and the quality of wisdom. It is not disgusted with the world—though it concedes that disgust, too, is Shiva. It rejects nothing, it celebrates the essential divinity of life and of every person. It worships not only Shiva, the impersonal Absolute, but also Shakti, the manifest universe in all its variety and paradox. Shaivism tells us that beneath our mundane view of life lies a greater possibility. It tells us that beneath our dryness, our depression, barely hidden from our view, is another kind of experience: vast energy and abundant love.

Shaivism does not tell us to reject the world and go to a mountain cave or a forest hermitage. It tells us to live a fully human life, but that includes profound meditation and reflection. For a life to be fully human it must also be spiritual. The life of a Shiva yogi is a life of worship. He worships the world as a manifestation of Shakti. He unfolds the Shakti within himself.

Baba says:

> We should not regard our mundane life as different from Shakti. It is an aspect of the same Shakti we are trying to attain through meditation. The outer world is the external sport of Shakti. Yoga is the inner sport of Shakti. The two should not be looked upon as different from one another. Wherever you are you will receive guidance from Shakti, because Shakti Herself manifests in your worldly life.

In my own case, the *rasa* of disgust drove me from my worldly life. I hated the vanity of ordinary existence, with a few fleeting pleasures and an occasional stroking of the ego. When I left for India, I was finished with the emptiness of that kind of life. When, through the grace of my Guru and his divine Shaivite vision, I was taken into the world of the Spirit, I discovered that the world I had left behind had come with me. And it had taken on a new meaning, rich with divinity.

Shaivism encourages us not to be satisfied with appearances but to always go deeper. What we find in the depths of our heart and our spirit will be the intersection of our humanity with the Divine. Shaivism says, 'I am Shiva'. It says as well, 'All these are Shiva, too'. Ultimately it is our own choice. Are the people sinners or Shiva Himself? The distinction is held entirely in the attitude of the onlooker. The Guru himself can be seen as a flawed human being or the incarnation of Shiva.

Your awareness holds the transforming key. Use it, and life is no longer an endless trial of pain, loss and sorrow but the blissful abode of divinity. There is Shiva and nothing but Shiva. There is no high or low, no sacred or profane. There is only God. Every breath, every moment, every experience discloses His presence. Then we ask with Narayanabhatta:

> What is the path by which You cannot be reached? What is the word that does not speak of You? What is the meditation of which You are not the object? What, indeed are You not, O Lord?

This, finally, is the saving message of Shaivism: cultivate *Shiva drishti*, the divine eye. One who has done that, is a true Shaivite, a true yogi. He is a supreme *Siddha* and his life is constant communion with the Divine.

MAY THERE BE WELFARE FOR ALL!

The great Shaiva yogis wrote their works and gave their teachings in the spirit of blessing. At the end of their works, they reveal their motivation. Scripture says, *shaktipat eva diksha:* Only that initiation is the true initiation which is accompanied by the descent of the grace of the Lord.

At the end of the *Pratyabhijnahridayam*, Kshemaraja says:

> Whatever has been said in the text is Shiva, because it is a means to the attainment of Shiva. It is Shiva also, because it has come from Shiva, because it is not different from the true nature of Shiva, and because it is indeed Shiva.

I had been searching for the broadest, most inclusive vision of life and I had found it in the Trika. The entire corpus of the teachings of Kashmir Shaivism is, like the mantra received from a Self-realised Guru, infused with divine Shakti. It is a teaching transmitted from Guru to disciple and it cannot fail to awaken the student. Kshemaraja tells us that the teaching is given 'for the welfare of all', and in that spirit, it is a teaching with no restrictions of sex, caste or race. It is a teaching that embraces all of life as the play of the Divine and affirms that our divine Self is not something new that we have to acquire, but something that we have always had that we must simply *recognise*.

Many times over the years, I have heard seekers bear witness to the transforming power of Shaivism. One man told me how the sutras appeared to him in meditation as living entities and revealed their secrets to him. On one occasion, I recommended that one of my students memorise the *Shiva Sutras* to help her with her emotional problems. She worked hard at the memorisation, not concerning herself too much with the meaning. She told me that the practice has been of immense help in her meditation. Now when she finds her mind wandering, she simply repeats the sutras to herself and they take her into deep states of meditation. I have noticed that, while in the West, we shun rote knowledge and focus on the essence and meaning of things, in India, there is no such bias. Indian students are taught to memorise sutras and chunks of scripture and then are drilled on them, with little concern for the meaning. Perhaps the story I have just told gives an explanation.

Yet another student told me that she had been awakened with a start during the night and had a mild panic attack. To calm herself, she told me that she 'contemplated Shaivism', not, she said, specific sutras or concepts, 'but Shaivism as a whole'. It reminded me of *Shiva Sutras* II.3:

> *Vidyasharira-satta mantrarahasyam*
> The secret of mantra is the being of the body of knowledge.

Vidya is knowledge, *sharira* is body and *satta* is being. I have always felt this phrase referred to Shaivism itself. Just as the mantra is considered to be the 'sound body' of God, the Divine incarnated as words, so Shaivism as a whole is a deity—the divine wisdom-body of knowledge. As such, it can be entered anywhere. It can never be exhausted. It yields a feeling of richness, Shakti and upliftment. Shaivism is part of the grace-bestowing power of Shiva. As we have seen, two of Shiva's five processes are concealment and grace, and things in the universe tend to move towards one or the other. Among instruments of grace in this world, there are few as luminous as Shaivism.

This, then, is the promise of Kashmir Shaivism. Even when we approach it in the manner of a western intellectual—out of curiosity or scholarly or philosophical interest, it has its own energy. Kashmir Shaivism, like the other great yogic philosophies, is not fundamentally an intellectual system, but one that has sprung from the direct visionary experience of the sages. It begins in that experience and its goal is that experience. It has the power to lift one to that experience. Kashmir Shaivism is a saving knowledge. It will have its effect on our inner being.

When I first encountered these teachings in the words of my Guru, I was thrilled by their clarity and relevance. I felt sure that they would speak directly to the mind and heart of the Western world. Finally, after many years of deep involvement and appreciation of this path, I have written this book to inspire aspirants. Surely, it is only the dawning of this knowledge.

In my younger days, I was in the world of scholarship. I left that world to seek a higher truth. Today, most of the students of Kashmir Shaivism are scholars. They are learned in Sanskrit and take great pains to analyse every nuance of doctrine. I am no Sanskritist, and in this phase of my life, I can make no claims as a scholar. My one advantage is to have imbibed the living spirit of Shaivism from one who radiated it through every cell of his body.

Substituting Muktananda for Somananda, I can say with Abhinavagupta:

> I have written this work after (fully) reflecting on the doctrine of Somananda which has spontaneously entered my heart which shares that pure state of truth taught by my Guru.

And join Kshemaraja in giving this blessing to all:

> May you all cross quickly the ocean of transmigratory existence and be established firmly in the highest state full of eternal light and delight. Ponder deeply over these sutras, enunciated by Shiva, radiant with mystic truth. Taught by an excellent Guru, they shine forth vigorously and joyfully enlighten the inner understanding.

Appendix A

Shiva Sutras

I.1   *Caitanyamātmā*
The Self is Consciousness.

I.2   *Jñānam bandhaḥ*
Limited knowledge is bondage.

I.3   *Yonivargaḥ kalāśarīram*
Maya with its associated principles and *kalā,* which gives origin to
bodies and worlds, are bondage.

1.4   *Jñānādhiṣṭhānam mātṛkā*
The letters of the alphabet from *a* to *ksha* are the basis of limited
knowledge.

I.5   *Udyamao Bhairavaḥ*
The sudden flash of divine Consciousness is the Lord   (Bhairava =
Shiva).

I.6   *Śakticakrasandhāne viśvasaṁhāraḥ*
The destruction of the universe takes place through meditation
on the group of *shaktis,* or powers.

I.7   *Jāgratsvapnasuṣuptabhede turyābhogasambhavaḥ*
The bliss of *turiya,* or the fourth state of Consciousness, arises even
during the different states of waking, dream and deep sleep.

I.8   *Jñānaṁ jāgrat*
The waking state is perception. It is the state in which the Self is in
direct contact with the objective world.

I.9   *Svapno vikalpāḥ*
The dream state is mental activity. Its contents consist of the mental
processes which occur in isolation from the objective world.

I.10   *Aviveko māyāsauṣuptam*
The deep sleep state is the inability to discriminate, which is
caused by the power of illusion. This state is characterised by the
absence of perception since the knowing faculty has ceased to
function.

I.11   *Tritayabhoktā vīreśaḥ*
The supreme Lord Shiva is the witness or enjoyer of the three states of waking, dream and deep sleep.

I.12   *Vismayo yogabhūmikāḥ*
The different stages attained in the course of yogic practice are filled with wonder.

I.13   *Icchā śaktir umā kumārī*
The power of will is the maiden *Uma*.

I.14   *Dṛśyaṁ śarīram*
The objective world around such a yogi appears to him as his own body.

I.15   *Hṛdaye cittasaṁghaṭṭād dṛśyasvāpadarśanam*
When the mind becomes united with the heart, one sees everything as a form of Consciousness.

I.16   *Śuddha-tattva-sandhānād vā apaśuśaktiḥ*
By contemplation of the pure principle of the Supreme Reality the yogi is freed from bondage.

I.17   *Vitarka ātmajñānam*
The knowledge of the Self is conviction.

I.18   *Lokānandaḥ samādhisukham*
The bliss of *loka* is the ecstasy of *samadhi*. The yogi becomes aware of the bliss that pervades all the manifested worlds.

I.19   *Śaktisandhāne śarīrotpattiḥ*
Through the meditative union with Shakti, *siddhis*, like the creation of bodies, become possible.

I.20   *Bhūtasandhāna-bhūtapṛthaktva-viśvasaṁghaṭṭāḥ*
The yogi gains the ability to unite the gross elements, to separate them, and to know how and with which elements objects in the universe are composed.

I.21   *Śuddhavidyodayāccakreśatva-siddhiḥ*
Through the appearance of pure wisdom, the yogi attains mastery over the *shakti chakra*.

I:22 *Mahāhradānusandhānānmantravīryānubhavaḥ*
By mystically uniting with the great lake, the infinite reservoir of divine energy, the yogi experiences the vibrant source of mantra.

SECTION II

II.1 *Cittam mantraḥ*
The mind is mantra.

II.2 *Prayatnaḥ sādhakaḥ*
Right effort is the means; a seeker is one who makes effort.

II.3 *Vidyāśarira-sattā mantrarahasyam*
The secret of mantra is the being of the body of knowledge.

II.4 *Garbhe cittavikāso 'viśiṣṭavidyāsvapnaḥ*
Ordinary knowledge, or limited expansion of consciousness, which develops through the mind within the realm of maya is dreamlike and purely imaginary.

II.5 *Vidyāsamutthāne śvābhāvike khecarī Śivāvasthā*
Through the natural unfoldment of pure knowledge, *khechari*, the state of Shiva, is attained.

II.6 *Gururupāyaḥ*
The Guru is the means.

II.7 *Mātṛkācakrasambodhaḥ*
When the Guru is pleased he grants full knowledge of *matrika* (the letters of the alphabet).

II.8 *Śariraṁ haviḥ*
The body is the offering.

II.9 *Jñānam annam*
Knowledge is food.

II.10 *Vidyāsaṁhāre taduttha-svapna-darśanam*
When pure knowledge is destroyed due to the pride or carelessness of the seeker, there arise visions or manifestations of illusory, dreamlike worlds.

SECTION III

III.1   *Atmā cittam*
The individual self is the mind.

III.2   *Jñānam bandhaḥ*
Limited knowledge is bondage.

III.3   *Kalādināṁ tattvānām aviveko māyā*
The ignorance of the true nature of *kala* and the other *tattvas*, which are characterised by limitation, is maya.

III.4   *Śarīre saṁhāraḥ kalānām*
The forces or *tattvas* in the body should be dissolved backwards into the Source.

III.5   *Nāḍī-saṁhāra-bhūtajaya-bhūtakaivalya-bhūtapṛthaktvāni*
Stoppage of the *nadis* (control of *prana*), conquest (control) of the elements, withdrawal of the mind from the elements, separation from the elements into Consciousness should all be brought about by yoga.

III.6   *Mohāvaraṇāt siddhiḥ*
Supernormal power is due to a veil drawn by ignorance.

III.7   *Mohajayād anantābhogāt sahajavidyājayaḥ*
The knowledge of Reality is attained only on conquering that delusion completely.

III.8   *Jāgrat-dvitīya-karaḥ*
He is awake who sees the outer world as his own light.

III.9   *Nartaka ātmā*
The Self is the dancer.

III.10   *Raṅgo'ntarātmā*
The inner Self is the stage.

III.11   *Prekṣakāṇi indriyāṇi*
The senses are the spectators.

III.12   *Dhīvaśāt sattva-siddhiḥ*
The truth is realised by pure intellect.

III.13 *Siddhaḥ svatantrabhāvaḥ*
A *Siddha* is supremely free.

III.14 *Yathā tatra tathā anyatra*
As here, so elsewhere.

III.15 *Bījāvadhānam*
He should focus on the seed, the source.

III.16 *Āsanasthaḥ sukhaṁ hrade nimajjati*
Established in concentration on the Self alone, he easily plunges into the ocean of bliss.

III.17 *Svamātrānirmāṇam āpādayati*
Such a yogi can bring about the manifestation of objects according to his capacity.

III.18 *Vidyā-avināśe janma-vināśaḥ*
When limited knowledge is destroyed, the cycle of births comes to an end.

III.19 *Kavargādiṣu māheśvaryādyāḥ paśu-mātaraḥ*
The yogi should beware of the different ruling *shaktis*, Maheshwari and others, who are inherent in the different groups of alphabets such as the *ka*-group, through ignorance he may still be deceived by these *shaktis*.

III.20 *Triṣu caturthaṁ tailavad āsecyam*
The three states of waking, dream and deep sleep should be poured into the fourth state, or *turiya*, like the uninterrupted flow of oil.

III.21 *Magnaḥ svacittena praviśet*
The yogi should plunge his mind into the Self

III.22 *Prāṇa-samācāre samadarśanam*
When the *prana* is balanced, one attains equal vision.

III.23 *Madhye'vara-prasavaḥ*
If the yogi who has attained the *turiya* state remains satisfied with the delight he experiences at the beginning and end of that state and does not proceed to the state beyond *turiya*, his consciousness can revert to the lower states in the middle.

III.24 *Mātrā-svapratyaya-sandhāne naṣṭasya punarutthānam*
Even if such a fall occurs, if the yogi eliminates this intermediate state by constant contemplation of pure Consciousness, he can permanently regain steadiness in the *turiya* state.

III.25 *Śiva-tulyo jāyate*
The realised yogi becomes like Shiva.

III.26 *Śarīravṛttir vratam*
Such a Self-realised yogi performs all his physical activities as acts of worship.

III.27 *Kathā japaḥ*
His common speech is like mantra.

III.28 *Dānam ātmajñānam*
His (charitable) gift is knowledge of the Self.

III.29 *Yo'vipastho jñāhetuśca*
He who is established in Shakti becomes an agent of wisdom (i.e., a *Sadguru*).

III.30 *Svaśakti-pracayo'sya viśvam*
The universe is the unfoldment of his Shakti (power).

III.31 *Sthiti-layau*
Maintenance and reabsorption are also a manifestation of his own Shakti.

III.32 *Tat pravṛttau api anirāsaḥ saṁvetṛ-bhāvāt*
Even though he is engaged in such activities, he remains unmoved because he is established in the awareness of the supreme Self.

III.33 *Sukha-duḥkhayor bahirmananam*
The experiences of pleasure and pain in the life of such a Self-realised yogi are confined to the periphery of his consciousness and do not affect his inner being.

III.34 *Tadvimuktastu kevalī*
One who is free of the influence of pleasure and pain is a liberated soul.

III.35 *Mohapratisaṁhatas tu karmātmā*
One who has become a compact mass of delusion is subject to karma, good and bad actions.

III.36 *Bheda-tiraskāre sargāntara-karmatvam*
When a yogi ceases to see differences, he attains the power to create a new universe.

III.37 *Karaṇaśaktiḥ svato'nubhavāt*
The power to create extraordinary things exists in him naturally on account of his experience of the divine power.

III.38 *Tripad ādy anuprāṇanam*
Turiya, the fourth state, should enliven and interpenetrate the other three states (waking, dreaming and deep sleep).

III.39 *Cittasthitivat śarīra-karaṇa-bāhyeṣu*
Just as the mind is fixed in *turiya* during introspective meditation, so too during the ordinary conscious life of the body, senses and objects, one should remain established in the inner consciousness, even though the mind is turned outward.

III.40 *Abhilāṣāt bahirgatiḥ saṁvāhyasya*
When the *jiva* does not experience this state of *turiya*, he goes out on account of desire for objects and is carried from birth to birth.

III.41 *Tadārūḍhapramites tatkṣayāj jīvasaṁkṣayaḥ*
When one is established in *turiya*, all one's desires are destroyed; hence, one's existence as a limited individual being also comes to an end simultaneously.

III.42 *Bhūta-kañcukī tadā vimukto bhūyaḥ patisamaḥ paraḥ*
With the ending of desire, the body is seen simply as a covering and the yogi becomes liberated and attains the state of Shiva.

III.43 *Naisargikaḥ prāṇasambandhaḥ*
The connection of pure Consciousness with *prana* is natural.

III.44 *Nāsikā-antarmadhya-saṁyamāt, kimatra, savyāpasavya-sauṣumneṣu*
The *prana shakti* flows in the left (*ida*), right (*pingala*) and the central (*sushumna*) *nadis*. By constant awareness it abides in the *sushumna*, the centre, which is supreme Consciousness.

III.45 *Bhūyaḥ syāt pratimīlanam*
The yogi will again be united with his true Self; that is, he will be reabsorbed into Shiva.

Appendix B

Pratyabhijnahridayam

1 *Citiḥ svatantrā viśvasiddhihetuḥ*
   Supremely independent *Chiti* (universal Consciousness) is the
   cause of the universe.

2 *Svecchayā svabhittau viśvam unmīlayati*
   Of its own free will *Chiti* unfolds the universe on its own screen.

3 *Tan nānā anurūpa grāhya grāhaka bhedāt*
   That universe is manifold because of the differentiation of
   reciprocally adapted objects and subjects.

4 *Citi saṁkocātmā cetano'pi saṁkucita viśvamayaḥ*
   The individual experiencer also, in whom *Chiti* or Consciousness is
   contracted, has the universe as his body in a contracted form.

5 *Citireva cetanapadādavarūḍhācetyasaṁkocinī cittam*
   Chiti Herself, descending from the plane of pure Consciousness,
   becomes the mind by contracting in accordance with the object
   perceived.

6 *Tanmayo māyā pramātā*
   The empirical self, governed by maya, consists of *chitta* (the mind).

7 *Sa caiko dvirūpas trimayaś caturātmā sapta pancaka svabhāvaḥ*
   Though it (Self) is one, it becomes twofold, threefold, fourfold, and
   of the nature of seven pentads.

8 *Tad bhūmikāhā sarva darśana sthitayaḥ*
   The positions of the various systems of philosophy are only various
   roles of that Consciousness or Self.

9 *Cidvat tacchaktisaṁkocāt malā vṛtaḥ saṁsārī*
   In consequence of its limitation of Shakti, Reality, which is all
   Consciousness, becomes the *mala*-covered transmigrating
   individual soul.

10 *Tathāpi tadvat pañcakṛtyāni karoti*
   Even in this limited condition the individual soul performs the
   fivefold act as He (Shiva) does.

11   *Ābhāsana rakti vimarśana bījāvasthāpana vilāpanatastāni*
      As manifesting, relishing, experiencing as Self, settling of the seed,
      dissolution, these.

12   *Tadaparijnāne svaśaktibhir vyāmohitatā saṁsāritvam*
      To be a transmigratory being means being deluded by one's own
      powers (*shaktis*) because of the ignorance of the authorship of the
      fivefold act.

13   *Tat parijñāne cittam eva antarmukhī bhāvena cetanapadādhyārohāt
      citiḥ*
      Acquiring full knowledge of it (i.e., of the authorship of the fivefold
      act of the Self) *chitta* itself by inward movement becomes *Chiti* by
      rising to the status of universal Consciousness.

14   *Citivanhi ravarohapade ccanno'pi mātrayā meyendhanaṁ pluṣyati*
      The fire of *Chiti* even when it descends to the lower stage, though
      covered by maya, partly burns the fuel of the known.

15   *Balalābhe viśvam ātmasāt karoti*
      By acquiring the inherent power of *Chiti*, the aspirant assimilates
      the universe to himself.

16   *Cidānanda lābhe dehādiṣu cetyamāneṣvapi cidaikātmya pratipatti
      dardhyamjivanmuktiḥ*
      When the bliss of *Chit* is attained, the Consciousness of identity
      with *Chit* remains stable even while the body, etc., is being
      experienced. This state is *jivanmukti*, liberation even while one is
      alive.

17   *Madhyavikāsāt cidānandalābhaḥ*
      By the unfoldment of the centre there is acquisition of the bliss of
      the *Chit*.

18   *Vikalpa kṣaya śakti saṁkoca vikāsa vāhacchedādyanta koti
      nibhālanādaya ihopāyāḥ*
      Herein, for that unfoldment of the centre, the means are:
      i.   Dissolution of all thoughts.
      ii. Withdrawing of Consciousness that rushes out through the
           gates of the senses and turning it inwardly towards the Self.
      iii. Holding the Consciousness steadily within, while the senses are
           allowed to perceive their objects.

    iv. Cessation of *prana* and *apana*.

    v. Practice of fixing the mind at the time of the rising of *prana* and its coming to an end between the heart and the *anta* at the distance of twelve fingers from the heart, etc.

19   *Samādhi saṁskāravati vyutthāne bhuyo bhuyaś cidaikyāmarśānnityodita samādhi lābhaḥ*

In the post-*samadhi* state called *vyutthana*, which is full of the aftereffects of *samadhi*, there is the attainment of permanent awareness of the Self by dwelling on one's identity with the universal Consciousness over and over again.

20   *Tadā prakāśānanda sāra mahā mantra vīryātmaka pūrnāhantā veśāt sadā sarva sarga saṁhāra kāri nija saṁvid deyatā cakreśvaratā prāptirbhavatiti śivam*

Then, as a result of entering into the perfect I-Consciousness or Self, which is in essence light and bliss and of the nature of the power of the great mantra, there accrues the attainment of lordship over one's group of deities *(shakti chalua)* of Consciousness that brings about all emanation and reabsorption of the universe. All this is of the nature of Shiva.

Appendix C

Spanda Karikas

I.1   *Yasyonmeṣanimeṣābhyāṁ jagataḥ pralayodayau /*
Taṁ Śakticakravibhavaprabhavaṁ Śaṅkaraṁ stumaḥ //
We laud that Shankara by whose mere opening and shutting of the
eyelids there is the appearance and dissolution of the world and
who is the source of the glorious powers of the collective whole of
the *shaktis* (the divine energy in various forms).

I.2   *Yatra sthitam idaṁ sarvaṁ kāryaṁ yasmācca nirgataṁ /*
Tasyānāvṛtarūpatvān na nirodho' sti kutracit //
Inasmuch as nothing can veil His nature, there cannot be His
obstruction anywhere in whom all this world rests and from whom
it has come forth.

I.3   *Jāgradādivibhede'pi tadabhinne prasarpati /*
Nivartate nijānnaiva svabhāvādupalabdhṛtaḥ //
Even though differing states like waking, etc., occur, that *spanda*
principle remains identically the same, that *spanda* principle never
departs from its own nature as the identical experient (in all the
differing states.)

I.4   *Ahaṁ sukhī ca duḥkhī ca raktaśca ityādisamvidaḥ /*
sukhādyavasthānusyūte vartante 'nyatra tāḥ sphuṭaṁ //
I am happy, I am miserable, I am attached—these and other
cognitions have their being evidently in another in which the states
of happiness, misery, etc., are strung together.

I.5   *Na duḥkhaṁ na sukhaṁ yatra na grāhyaṁ grāhakaṁ na ca /*
Na cāsti mūḍhabhāvo' pi tadasti paramārthataḥ //
Wherein neither pain, nor pleasure, nor object, nor subject, exists,
nor wherein does even insentience exist—that, in the highest sense,
is that *spanda* principle.

I.6   *Yataḥ karaṇa-vargo 'yaṁ vimūḍho 'mūḍhavat svayam /*
Sahāntareṇa cakreṇa pravṛtti-sthiti-saṁhṛtīḥ //

I.7   *Labhate tatprayatnena parīkṣyaṁ tattvam ādarāt /*
Yataḥ svatantratā tasya sarvatreyam akṛtrimā //

That principle should be examined with great care and reverence by which this group of senses, though insentient, acts as a sentient force by itself, and along with the inner group of senses, goes towards objects, takes pleasure in their maintenance, and withdraws into itself, because this natural freedom of it prevails everywhere.

I.8   *Na hīcchānodanasyāyam prerakatvena vartate /*
        Api tvātmabalasparśāt puruṣastatsamo bhavet //
        The empirical individual cannot drive the goad of desire. But by coming in contact with the power of the Self, he becomes equal to that principle.

I.9   *Nijāśuddhyāsamarthasya kartavyeṣv abhilāṣiṇaḥ /*
        Yadā kṣobhaḥ pralīyeta tadā syāt paramaṁ padam //
        When there is no *kshoba*, mental agitation, then occurs the highest state.

I.10   *Tadāsyākṛtrimo dharmo jñatvakartṛtvalakṣaṇaḥ /*
        Yatas tadepsitaṁ sarvaṁ jānāti ca karoti ca //
        Then will flash forth his innate nature characterised by cognition and activity, by which he (the experient) then knows and does all that is desired (by him).

I.11   *Tam adhiṣṭhātṛbhāvena svabhāvam avalokayan /*
        Smayamāna ivāste yastasyeyaṁ kuṣṛtiḥ kutaḥ //
        How can this accursed way of life and death be his (any longer) who stands struck with amazement as he observes that nature (namely, *spanda*) which presides over all the activities of life (as I)?

I.12   *Nābhāvo bhāvyatāmeti na ca tatrāsty amūḍhatā /*
        Yato 'bhiyoga-saṁsparśāt tadāsid iti niścayaḥ //

I.13   *Atastatkṛtrimaṁ jñeyaṁ sauṣupta-padavat sadā /*
        Na tvevaṁ smaryamāṇatvaṁ tat tattvaṁ pratipadyate //
        Mere nonexistence cannot be an object of contemplation, nor can it be said there is no stupefaction in that state, because on account of the application of backward reference, it is certain that it (the experience of stupefaction) was there (in that state). Hence that artificial object of knowledge is always like sound sleep. It is not in this manner, (as a state of recollection) that the *spanda* principle is known.

I.14   *Avasthāyugalaṃ cātra kāryakartṛtva-śabditam /*
       Kāryatā kṣayiṇī tatra kartṛtvam punarakṣayaṃ //
       Of this *spanda* principle, two states are spoken about, the doer or the
       subject and the deed or the object. Of these two, the deed or the
       object is subject to decay but the doer or the subject is imperishable.

I.15   *Kāryonmukhaḥ prayatno yaḥ kevalaṃ so'tra lupyate /*
       Tasmin lupte vilupto'smityabudhaḥ pratipadyate //
       In the *samadhi* of void, only the effort that is directed towards
       objectivity disappears. It is only a fool who, on the disappearance
       of that effort, thinks, 'I have ceased to be'.

I.16   *Na tu yo'antarmukho bhāvaḥ sarvajñatva-guṇāspadam /*
       Tasya lopaḥ kadācitsyād anyasyānupalambhanāt //
       There can never be the disappearance of that inner nature which is
       the abode of the attribute of omniscience in the event of the
       nonperception of anything objective.

I.17   *Tasyopalabdhiḥ satataṃ tripadāvyabhicāriṇī /*
       Nityaṃ syāt suprabuddhasya tadādyante parasya tu //
       The fully enlightened has, always and incessantly, the undeviating
       knowledge of the Self in all the three states; the other one (namely, the
       partially enlightened) has it only at the beginning and end of each
       state.

I.18   *Jñānajñeya-svarūpiṇyā śaktyā paramayā yutaḥ /*
       Padadvaye vibhurbhāti tadanyatra tu cinmayaḥ //
       The all-pervading Lord, possessed of the supreme power in the
       form of knowledge and knowable (object of knowledge), appears in
       the two states of waking and dream as knowledge and objects of
       knowledge, and in the other than these two only as Consciousness.

I.19   *Guṇādispandaniṣyandāh sāmānyaspandasaṃśrayāt /*
       Labdhātmalābhāḥ satataṃ syur jñasyāparipanthinaḥ //
       The particular emanations of *spanda,* which begin with the *gunas,*
       and which acquire their existence by having recourse to generic
       spanda, can never stand in the way of the one who has realised his
       essential nature.

I.20   *Aprabudhadhiyas tvete svasthitisthaganodyatāḥ /*
       Pātayanti duruttāre ghore saṃsāra-vartmani //
       These (the *gunas,* etc.) however, intent on veiling their real nature,

push the people of unawakened intellect into the terrible ocean of transmigratory existence from which it is difficult to pull them out.

I.21   *Atah satatam udyuktah spanda-tattva-viviktaye /*
        Jāgradeva nijaṁ bhāvam acireṇādhigacchati //
        Therefore, one should be always on the alert for the discernment of the *spanda* principle. Such a person attains his essential state (as *spanda*) even in the waking condition in short time.

I.22   *Atikruddhaḥ prahṛṣṭo vā kiṁ karomi iti vā mṛśan /*
        Dhāvan vā yatpadaṁ gacchet tatra spandaḥ pratiṣṭhitaḥ //
        In that state is the *spanda* principle firmly established to which a person is reduced when he is greatly exasperated or overjoyed, or is in impasse reflecting what to do, or is running for life.

I.23   *Yām avasthāṁ samālambya yadayam mama vakṣyati /*
        Tadavaśyaṁ kariṣye'ham iti saṁkalpya tiṣṭhati //
I.24   *Tām āśrityordhvamārgeṇa candrasūryāvubhāvapi /*
        Sauṣumne' dhvanyastamito hitvā brahmāṇḍagocaram //
I.25   *Tadā tasmin mahāvyomni pralīnasaśibhāskare /*
        Sauṣupta-padavan mūḍhaḥ prabuddhaḥ syādanāvṛtaḥ //
        Taking firm hold of that *(spanda)* the awakened yogi remains firm with the resolution, 'I will surely carry out whatever it will tell me'. Resting on the experience of that *spanda*, both *prana* and *apana* get merged in the *sushumna* and by the upward path of *sushumna* they rise up to the great ether of universal Consciousness by abandoning the sphere of the body together with the *brahmarandhra* and are completely dissolved in it. There the unenlightened yogi by considering that state a kind of deep sleep remains stupefied, while the one who is not covered with the darkness of infatuation is established in that ether of universal Consciousness and abides as fully enlightened.

SECTION II

II.1   *Tadākramya balam mantrāḥ sarvajñabalaśālinaḥ /*
        Pravartante 'dhikārāya karaṇānīva deninām //
II.2   *Tatraiva saṁpralīyante śāntarūpā nirañjanāḥ /*
        Sahārādhaka-cittena tenaite śivadharmiṇaḥ //
        Resorting to that power (of *spanda tattva*), the divinities, mantra, etc, together with the sacred formulae, which serve as their indicators,

being endowed with the power of omniscience, proceed to carry out their assigned functions towards the embodied ones just as the senses of the embodied ones by resorting to the power of *spanda* proceed to carry out their (specific) functions. Freed of all limitations of office after having performed their assigned duties, their denotation as particular deities having ceased, they get dissolved together with the mind of their devotees in that very *spanda* principle. Hence they are of the nature of Shiva.

II.3 *Yasmāt sarvamayo jīvaḥ sarvabhāva-samudbhavāt /*
Tatsaṃvedanarūpeṇa tādātmya-pratipattitaḥ //

II.4 *Tasmācchabdārthacintāsu na sāvasthā na yā śivaḥ /*
Bhoktaiva bhogyabhāvena sadā sarvatra saṃsthitaḥ //

Since the limited individual self is identical with the whole universe, inasmuch as all entities arise from him, and because of the knowledge of all subjects, he has the feeling of identity with them all, hence whether in the word, object or thought, there is no state which is not Shiva. It is the experient himself who, always and everywhere, abides in the form of the experienced, that is, it is the divine Himself who is the essential experient, and it is He who abides in the form of the universe as His field of experience.

II.5 *Iti vā yasya saṃvittiḥ krīḍātvenākhilaṃ jagat /*
Sa paśyan satataṃ yukto jīvanmukto na saṃśayaḥ //

Or he, who has this realisation (identity of his Self with the whole universe), being constantly united with the divine, views the entire world as the play (of the Self identical with Shiva), and is liberated while alive. There is no doubt about this.

II.6 *Ayamevodayas tasya dhyeyasya dhyāyi-cetasi /*
Tadātmatā-samāpattir icchataḥ sādhakasya yā //

II.7 *Iyamevāmṛtaprāptir ayamev ātmano grahaḥ /*
Iyaṃ nirvāṇa-dīkṣā ca śiva-sadbhāvadāyinī //

This only is the manifestation of the object of meditation in the meditator's mind that the aspirant with resolute will has the realisation of his identity with the object of meditation. This alone is the acquisition of ambrosia leading to immortality; this alone is the realisation of Self; this alone is the initiation of liberation leading to identity with Shiva.

SECTION III

III.1 *Yathecchābhyarthito dhātā jāgrato'rthān hṛdi sthitān /*
Somasūryodayaṁ kṛtvā sampādayati dehinaḥ //

III.2 *Tathā svapne 'pyabhīṣṭārthān praṇayasyānatikramāt /*
Nityaṁ sphuṭataraṁ madhye sthito' vaśyaṁ prakāśayet //

As the sustainer of this universe (that is, Shiva), when eagerly entreated with desire, accomplishes all the desires abiding in the heart of the embodied yogi who is awake after causing the rise of the moon and the sun. So also in dream, by appearing in the central *nadi*, does He surely reveal always and more vividly his desired objects to him who never desists from his zealous prayer.

III.3 *Anyathā tu svatantrā syat sṛṣṭis taddharmakatvataḥ /*
Satataṁ Laukikasyeva jāgratsvapnapadadvaye //

Otherwise, the creative power of the Divine according to its characteristics, is free in manifesting always all kind of things (usual and unusual) (to the yogi also) both in waking and dream states as in the case of the common people of the world

III.4 *Yathā hi artho'sphuṭo dṛṣṭaḥ sāvadhāne' pi cetasi/*
Bhūyaḥ sphuṭataro bhāti svabalodyogabhāvitaḥ //

III.5 *Tathā yatparamārthena yena yatra yathā sthitam /*
Tattathā balam ākramya na cirāt sampravartate //

Indeed, just as a thing which, in spite of all the attentiveness of the mind, is perceived indistinctly at first, appears more distinctly later, when observed with the strenuous exercise of one's power. So when the yogi resorts to the power (of *spanda)*, then whatever thing actually exists in whichever form, in whichever place or time, in whichever state, that thing becomes at once manifest in that very way.

III.6 *Durbalo'pi tadākramya yataḥ kārye pravartate /*
Ācchādayed bubhukṣāṁ ca tathā yo'ti bubhukṣitaḥ //

Just as a feeble person also resorting to that power (of *spanda)* succeeds in doing what has to be done, even so one who is exceedingly hungry overcomes his hunger.

III.7 *Anenādhiṣṭhite dehe yathā sarvajñatādayaḥ /*
Tathā svātmany adhiṣṭhānāt sarvatraivaṁ bhaviṣyati //

Just as all knowability, etc., in respect of the body occurs when it is pervaded by that *spanda* principle, even so when the yogi is established in his essential Self, he will have omniscience, etc., everywhere.

III.8   *Glānir viluṇṭhikā dehe tasyāścājñānataḥ sṛtiḥ /*
Tadunmeṣa-viluptaṁ cet kutaḥ sā syād ahetukā //
Just as a plunderer carries away the valuables of the house, even so
depression saps away the vitality of the body. This depression
proceeds from ignorance. If that ignorance disappears by *unmesha*,
how can that depression last in the absence of its cause?

III.9   *Ekacintāprasaktasya yataḥ syādaparodayaḥ /*
Unmeṣaḥ sa tu vijñeyaḥ svayaṁ tam upalakṣayet //
That should be known as *unmesha* whence the rise of another
thought takes place in the mind of a man who is already engaged
in one thought, one should experience it introspectively for oneself.

III.10 *Ato vindur ato nādo rūpam asmād ato rasaḥ /*
Pravartante'cireṇaiva kṣobhakatvena dehinaḥ //
From this *(unmesha)* appear (supernormal) light, (supernormal)
sound, (supernormal) form, (supernormal) taste in a short time, to
the yogi who has not yet done away with the identification of the
Self with the body, which, however, are only a disturbing factor (in
the full realisation of the *spanda* principle).

III.11 *Didṛkṣayeva sarvārthān yadā vyāpyāvatiṣṭhate /*
Tadā kiṁ bahunoktena svayameva avabhotsyate //
When the yogi wishing to see all objects, abides in that state
pervading them all, infusing them all with the light of His
Consciousness, then what is the use of saying much, he will
experience for himself the splendour of that vision.

III.12 *Prabuddhaḥ sarvadā tiṣṭhej jñānenālokya gocaram /*
Ekatrāropayet sarvaṁ tato anyena na pīḍyate //
Observing all objective phenomena by knowledge, (by external
perception), one should always remain awake, and should deposit
everything in one place, that is, see everything as identical with
spanda, which is our own essential Self. Thus, he is never troubled
by another.

III.13 *Śabdarāśi-samutthasya śaktivargasya bhogyatām /*
Kalāvilupta-vibhavo gataḥ san sa paśuḥ smṛtaḥ //
Being deprived of his glory by *kalā,* he (the individual) becomes a
victim of the group of powers arising from the multitude of words,
and thus he is known as the bound one.

III.14 *Parāmṛtarasāpāyas tasya yaḥ pratyayodbhavaḥ /*
Tenāsvatantratām eti sa ca tanmātragocaraḥ //
The rise, in the bound soul, of all sorts of ideas marks the
disappearance of the bliss of supreme immortality. On account of
this, he loses his independence. The appearance of the ideas has its
sphere in sense-objects.

III.15 *Svarūpāvaraṇe cāsya śaktayaḥ satatotthitāḥ /*
Yataḥ śabdānuvedhena na vinā pratyayodbhavaḥ //
Brahmi and other powers are ever in readiness to conceal his real
nature, for without the association of words, ideas cannot arise.

III.16 *Seyaṁ kriyātmikā śaktiḥ śivasya paśuvartinī /*
Bandhayitrī svamārgasthā jñātā siddhyupapādikā //
That aforementioned operative power of Shiva existing in the
bound soul is a source of bondage; the same when realised as
residing in Him as the way of approach to one's own essential
reality brings about success (that is, the achievement of liberation).

III.17 *Tanmātrodaya-rūpeṇa manohaṁ-buddhivartinā /*
Puryaṣṭakena samṛuddhastadutthaṁ pratyayodbhavam //
III.18 *Bhuṅkte paravaśo bhogaṁ tadbhāvāt saṁsared ataḥ /*
Saṁsṛti-pralayasyāsya kāraṇaṁ sampracakṣmahe //
Besieged by *puryaṣṭaka,* which rises from *tanmatras* and exists in
mind, I-feeling, and the determinative faculty, he (the bound soul)
becomes subservient and undergoes the experiences that arise from
it in the form of ideas about certain objects and the pleasure or pain
that accrues from them. Owing to the continuance of the *purvastaka,*
he (the bound soul) leads a transmigratory existence. We are
therefore going to explain what causes the extirpation of this
transmigratory existence.

III.19 *Yadā tvekatra samrūḍhas tadā tasya layodayau /*
Niyacchan bhoktṛtām eti tataścakreśvaro bhavet //
When, however, he is firmly rooted in the supreme *spanda* principle,
then bringing the emergence and dissolution of the *purvastaka*
entirely under his control, he becomes the real enjoyer and
thenceforth the Lord of the collective whole of the *shaktis.*

SECTION IV

IV:1 *Agādhasaṁśayāmbhodhi-samuttaraṇatāriṇīm /*
Vande vicitrārthapadāṁ citrāṁ tāṁ gurubhāratīm //
I pay homage to that wonderful speech of my Guru, which is like a
boat for crossing the fathomless ocean of doubt and is full of words,
which yield wonderful meaning (in the case of the Guru). I offer my
reverential prayer to *spanda* in the form of *paravak*, the supreme
divine I-Consciousness, which acts like a boat in crossing the
fathomless ocean of doubt regarding my essential nature (in the
case of *spanda* in the form of *paravak).*

IV:2 *Labdhvāpy alabhyam etaj jñanadhanaṁ hṛdguhāntakrtanihiteḥ /*
Vasuguptavac chivāya hi bhavati sadā sarvalokasya //
As on the attainment of this treasure of knowledge which is
difficult of attainment, and on its being well-preserved in the cave
of the heart it has been for the good of Vasugupta, so also on the
attainment of this treasure of knowledge difficult of attainment and
on its being well preserved in the cave of the heart, it would always
be for the good of all.

Appendix D

G-Statements

- Everything is Consciousness.
- Consciousness is the dearest, most healing and desirable thing.
- I am Shiva.
- Every thought and feeling, even my blocks are Shiva.
- Wherever the mind goes is Shiva.
- The whole world is inside my own awareness.
- My thought-forms create my experience of life.
- I am the Lord of *matrika*.
- I am the Lord of my own *shaktis*.
- This universe is Shiva's grace.
- This universe is drenched in love.
- There is no distinction between worldly and spiritual.
- There is absolutely no problem.
- There is nothing outside of Consciousness.
- I am Shiva and my mind, senses and emotions are *shaktis*.
- Every other person is Shiva, too.
- The form of Consciousness never changes.
- All these people are Shiva in their universe.
- There is no obstruction to Shiva anywhere.
- Nothing veils Shiva—He is apparent.
- All my feelings are permutations of bliss.
- Whatever gives me peace or satisfaction shows me Shiva.
- My mind does not exist.
- I am everywhere.
- There is no bondage and no liberation.
- Everything is perfect as it is.
- Shiva's grace is the only thing I need.
- Everything is going according to Shiva's plan.
- The present state is Shiva in that form.
- Whatever meditation I am having is Shiva.
- The object is contained within the subject.
- No outer event can harm my true nature.
- Shiva is my most intimate inner space.
- O Shiva, give me your grace!
- O Shakti, O Mother, be kind to me!
- I open my heart completely to the experience of Shiva.
- Right now, exactly as I am, I am Shiva.

Selected Notes

Epigraph

p. 9   'He is a...' *Pratyabhijnahridayam*, p. 72

Introduction: Consciousness Itself (pp. 15–24)

p. 15   'This new and...' *Ishvara-Pratyabhijna* Tattva Sangrahadhikara 16, p. 229

p. 18   'All these three...' *Paratrishika Vivarana*, p. 267

Chapter 1: The Grace of Shiva (pp. 25–40)

p. 25   'In You, the...' *Paramarthasara* Verse 1

p. 26   'Now, what do...' *Siddha Meditation*, Swami Muktananda, pp. 7–8

p. 28   'My revered preceptor...' *Malinivijayavarttika* II:111–112, quoted in *Specific Principles of Kashmir Shaivism*, B.N.Pandit, p. 93

p. 32   'The most beautiful...' *Maharthamanjari* Sutra 9

p. 33   'I sat down...' *Play of Consciousness*, Swami Muktananda, p. 77

p. 35   'Just as an...' *Ishvara-Pratyabhijna* Tattva Sangrahadhikara 17, p. 230

p. 36   'to lie...' *Pratyabhijnahridayam*, p. 118

p. 36   'to cut asunder' Ibid.

p. 36   'Parashiva is full...' *Siddha Meditation*, Swami Muktananda, p. 66

p. 36   'The name Shiva' *Pratyabhijnahridayam*, p.118

p. 36   'O Lord, how...' Bhatta Nayaka, quoted in *Spanda Karikas*, p. 47

p. 37   'Shiva Himself full...' *Maharthamanjari* (personal notes)

p. 37   'The Goddess Shakti...' *Spanda Karikas*, p. 11

p. 37   '*Chiti* is supremely...' *Siddha Meditation*, Swami Muktananda, pp. 56–7

p. 38   'Self who is...' *Paratrishika Vivarana*, p. 48

Chapter 2: The Origins of Kashmir Shaivism (pp. 41–52)

p. 41   'When one follows...' *Paramarthasara* Verse 96

p. 46   'Having somehow realised...' *Ishvara-Pratyabhijna* Jnanadhikara I:1, p. 1

p. 46   'who made Trika...' *Doctrine of Vibration*, Mark Dyczkowski, p. 12

p. 48   'Thanks to him...' *The Oral Teachings of Swami Lakshmanjoo*, John Hughes, Foreword xi

Chapter 3: A Shaivite Overview (pp. 53–60)

p. 53   'Shiva pervades everything...' *Siddha Meditation*, Swami Muktananda, p. 74

p. 54   'The sage rests...' *Siddha Meditation*, Swami Muktananda, p. 37

p. 58   'Thus God is...' *Talks with Ramana Maharshi*, pp. 610–11

p. 58   'There is only...' *Tantraloka*, quoted in *The Stanzas on Vibration*, Mark Dyczkowski, p. 313

p. 59   'But if you...' *Ishvarapratyabhijna-Vimarshini* Kriyadhikara IV:20, p. 186

p. 59   'According to Vedanta...' *Siddha Meditation*, Swami Muktananda, p. 64

Chapter 4: Self-Realisation (pp. 61–74)

p. 61   'Nourishing Himself with...' *Paramarthasara* Verse 69

p. 62   'The perfected Sufi...' (personal notes)

Chapter 10: Malas and Upayas: Further Thoughts and Contemplations (pp. 128–139)

Chapter 11: The Five Processes and the Yoga of Self-inquiry (pp. 140–153)

Chapter 12: The Divine Narrator (pp. 154–168)

Selected Bibliography

Books by Swami Muktananda

Muktananda, Swami. *I Am That: The science of hamsa from Vijnana Bhairava (24)*. SYDA Foundation: South Fallsburg, NY (1978).

_____ , *Play of Consciousness (Chitshakti Vilas)*. SYDA Foundation: San Francisco (1978).

_____ , *Satsang With Baba*, Volume Three. Shree Gurudev Ashram: Maharashtra, India (1977).

_____ , *Satsang With Baba*, Volume Five. Gurudev Siddha Peeth: Maharashtra, India (1978).

_____ , *Secret of the Siddhas*. SYDA Foundation: South Fallsburg, NY (1980).

_____ , *Siddha Meditation, Commentaries on the Shiva Sutras and other Sacred Texts*. SYDA Foundation: South Fallsburg, NY (1975).

Primary Sources

Bailly, Constantina Rhodes. *Shaiva Devotional Songs of Kashmir, A Translation and Study of Utpaladeva's Shivastotravali*. SUNY: Albany, NY (1987).

Dyczkowski, Mark S.G. *The Aphorisms of Śiva, The ŚivaSūtra with Bhāskara's Commentary, the Vārttika*. SUNY: Albany, NY (1992).

_____ , *The Stanzas on Vibration*. SUNY: Albany, NY (1992).

Pandey, K.C. *Īśvarapratyabhijñā-Vimarśinī of Abhinavagupta, Doctrine of Divine Recognition*, Volume III. Motilal Banarsidass: Delhi, India (1986).

Singh, Jaideva. *Abhinavagupta, A Trident of Wisdom, Translation of Parātrīśikā Vivaraṇa*. SUNY: Albany, NY (1989).

_____ , *Pratyabhijñāhṛdayam* (Second Revised Edition). Motilal Banarsidass: Delhi, India (1977).

_____ , *Śiva Sūtras: The Yoga of Supreme Identity*. Motilal Banarsidass: Delhi, India (1979).

_____ , *Spanda Kārikās, The Divine Creative Pulsation*. Motilal Banarsidass: Delhi, India (1980).

_____ , *Vijñānabhairava or Divine Consciousness*. Motilal Banarsidass: Delhi, India (1979).

Secondary Sources

Chatterji, J.C. *Kashmir Shaivaism* (Reprint). Indological Book Corp.: Patna, India (1978).

Dyczkowski, Mark S.G. *The Doctrine of Vibration, An Analysis of the Doctrines and Practices of Kashmir Shaivism*. SUNY: Albany, NY (1987).

Hughes, John. *Self Realization in Kashmir Shaivism, The Oral Teachings of Swami Lakshmanjoo*. SUNY: Albany, NY (1994).

Lakshman Jee, Swami. *Kashmir Shaivism, The Secret Supreme*. SUNY: Albany, NY (1988).

Mishra, Kamalakar. *Kashmir Śaivism, The Central Philosophy of Tantrism*. Rudra Press: Portland, OR (1993).

Muller-Ortega, Paul Eduardo. *The Triadic Heart of Śiva, Kaula Tantricism of Abhinavagupta in the Non-Dual Shaivism of Kashmir*. SUNY: Albany, NY (1989).

Pandit, B.N. *Aspects of Kashmir Śaivism*. Utpal Publications: Srinagar, India (1977).

Pandit, B.N. *Specific Principles of Kashmir Śaivism*. Munshiram Manoharlal Publishers: New Delhi (1997).

Rastogi, Navjivan. *Introduction to the Tantrāloka*. Motilal Banarsidass: Delhi, India (1987).

Rudrappa, J. *Kashmir Śaivism*. Prasaranga: Mysore, India (1969).

SenSharma, Deba Brata. *The Philosophy of Sādhanā, With Special Reference to the Trika Philosophy of Kashmir*. SUNY: Albany, NY (1990).

Silburn, Lilian. *Kuṇḍalinī, The Energy of the Depths, A Comprehensive Study Based on the Scriptures of Nondualistic Kaśmir Śaivism*. SUNY: Albany, NY (1988).

Walimbe, Y.S. *Abhinavagupta on Indian Aesthetics*. Ajanta Publications: Delhi, India (1980).

Glossary

A to Ksha. In the Sanskrit alphabet, the first letter to the last letter, as in A to Z.

Abhanga. A devotional poem in the Marathi language.

Abhasana. (*lit.* shining forth) The manifesting or creative power of Shiva.

Agama. (*lit.* tradition) A spiritual text of the Tantric tradition said to be of divine authority.

Aghora shaktis. Uplifting energies.

Aham. (*lit.* I am) The inner Self, the experiencing subject, the innermost 'I'.

Aham Brahmasmi. (*lit.* I am Brahman) One of the great statements of the Vedas, meaning 'I am the Absolute'.

Aham vimarsha. (*lit.* I am supreme Self-awareness) The Self, our true nature.

Ahamkara. The ego.

Ahimsa. Compassion, kindness.

Alamgrasa. (*lit.* full swallowing) Yogic practice meaning the full swallowing of the world of differentiation and all karmic residue.

Ananda. Divine bliss.

Anava mala. Limiting impurity or contraction of will. See also *mala*.

Anavopaya. (*lit.* the means of the individual) Yogic action such as service, hatha yoga, *pranayama* and other techniques. See also *upaya*.

Anitya. Impermanence.

Anu. (*lit.* atom) A small, limited entity. Individual soul.

Anupaya. (*lit.* non means) The highest *upaya*, the path of divine grace, spontaneous recognition of the Self. See also *upaya*.

Anusandhana. Being inwardly or mentally united with higher Consciousness.

Apana. Inhalation, downward flowing breath.

Apara. See *para, apara, parapara*.

Arati. A ritual during which a flame is waved in front of an image of God.

Ashram. School of spiritual practice. The residence of a Guru.

A-Statement. Accurate statement of present feeling, such as 'I feel happy', 'I feel sad'. The first stage of the Shiva Process Self-inquiry technique.

Atma vyapti. Turning within to experience the Self. See also *Shiva vyapti*.

Atman. The inner Self identical with Consciousness.

Avikalpa. Thought-free state.

Ayurveda. (*lit. ayur* = life, *veda* = knowledge) An Indian tradition of medicine.

Bhairava. A name of Shiva or divine Consciousness.

Bhairavi mudra. A meditative posture in which the eyes are open and the attention is held inside focusing on pure awareness. See also *shambhavi mudra.*

Bhakta. *(lit.* devotee, devoted) A lover of God.

Bhakti. *(lit.* devotion) Love of God. Path of devotion.

Bhava. *(lit.* state, condition) Underlying emotional or intellectual attitude.

Bhogi. Pleasure-seeker.

Bhuvana. The world, sphere of existence.

Bija. *(lit.* seed) A primary mantra, also the vowels.

Brahman. Vedantic term for divine Consciousness.

Brahmarandra. The *sahasrara* chakra.

Brahmi. The presiding deity of a group of letters.

B-Statement. Beneficial statement designed to uplift and positively shift one's present state of being, such as 'I am content', or 'I can do what I need to do easily'. A stage of the Shiva Process Self-inquiry technique.

Buddhi. The intellect. *Tattva* 14.

Chaitanya. Consciousness.

Chaitanya mantra. A mantra infused with conscious power.

Chakra. *(lit.* wheel) An energy centre of the subtle body.

Chamatkara. Intuitive or sudden flash of delight.

Charya-krama. *(lit. charya* = activity, *krama* = succession) A practice of attaining higher Consciousness via the senses.

Chiti. Consciousness, the creative, dynamic aspect of God, pure awareness. Also *Chiti Shakti* and *Chitshakti.*

Chitta. The mind, contracted Consciousness.

Consciousness. The supremely independent divine awareness that creates, pervades and supports everything in the cosmos.

Dakshina. Gift, offering or alms.

Darshan. *(lit.* vision) Being in the presence of a great being. Internal or external vision of God.

Dharana. *(lit.* holding) A short meditative exercise.

Diksha. *(lit. di* = giving, *ksha* = destroying) Initiation, awakening, *shaktipat.*

Dualism. The philosophy that the universe consists of the two aspects of matter and Consciousness.

Dvadashanta. A point 12 finger-widths, from the tip of the nose or the heart, used as focus for meditation.

Dvesha. Aversion.

First Education. Conventional education of the intellect and personality.

Four levels of speech. From subtle to gross: *paravak,* transcendental or supreme speech, speech at the level of the Self, also called *paravani; pashyanti,* inner speech before language is formed, pure impulse of intuition; *madhyama (lit.* middling), subtle word or thought; *vaikari,* gross speech, the spoken word.

Ghora. The *shaktis* that lead to realisation.

Ghoratari shaktis. The energies that draw individuals in a downward path towards bondage.

Granthi. *(lit.* knot) A subtle or psychic contraction or knot of thought or feeling.

G-Statement. A Great statement, scriptural statement, God statement or Guru statement. A stage of the Shiva Process Self-inquiry technique.

Guna. One of three primary aspects of Consciousness. See also *rajas, sattva* and *tamas.*

Guru. *(lit. gu* = darkness, *ru* = light) A teacher, a Self-realised spiritual master.

Gururupaya. *(lit.* the path of the Guru) The spiritual path of discipleship and devotion to the Guru. See also *upaya.*

Hamsa. *(lit. ham* = I am, *sah* = That) A mantra used in meditation in combination with the breath.

Hatha yoga. Specific physical postures designed to keep the body fit for meditation and wellbeing.

Hathapaka. *(lit.* violent digestion) Yogic practice in which reality is devoured whole, in one gulp.

Hridaya. *(lit.* heart) Spiritual centre, heart.

Iccha. The power of will.

Ida. Subtle energy channel on the left side of the *sushumna,* or subtle spine, which carries the vital breath.

Internal considering. The tendency to see ourselves through others' eyes.

Ishvara tattva. Shiva's perfect knowledge. *Tattva* 4.

Jada. Inert.

Jagadananda. The bliss of the world.

Japa. *(lit.* muttering) Constant repetition of the mantra.

Jiva. *(lit.* living being) The individual soul. See also *purusha.*

Jivanmukti. Spiritual liberation while in the body.

Jnana. *(lit.* knowledge) Wisdom or knowledge.

Jnanendriyas. The senses of perception: hearing, touch, seeing, tasting, smelling. *Tattvas* 17 to 21.

Kāla. Time. One of the *kanchukas*. *Tattva* 10.

Kalā. Limited ability to do things. One of the *kanchukas*. *Tattva* 7.

Kama-kala. (*lit. kama* = desire) The force that brings two things together, as the tongue and delicious food. Also the sexual act.

Kanchuka. (*lit.* veil, covering) The covering or cloaking of ultimate Reality, a form of maya or principle of limitation. *Tattvas* 7 to 11: *kalā, vidya, raga, kalā, niyati*.

Karma. (*lit.* action) Cause and effect, the rewards or consequences of every thought and action, in this life or in a future life.

Karma mala. Limiting impurity or contraction of action. See also *mala*.

Karmendriyas. Powers of action, speaking (tongue), grasping (hand), movement (feet), excretion and procreation. *Tattvas* 22 to 26.

Kashmir Shaivism. A philosophy that recognises the entire universe as a manifestation of one Consciousness.

Krama mudra. (*lit.* succession) The practice, or gesture, of moving the attention from the outer world to the inner world and back again.

Kriya. (*lit.* movement) The power of action.

Kshoba. Mental agitation.

Kula-chakra. A group ritual to increase the experience of Consciousness.

Kundalini. (*lit.* coiled one) The inner divine power.

Layabhavana. (*lit. laya* = dissolution, *bhava* = attitude) The technique, or attitude in which gross elements, contractions or energies are dissolved into their underlying, more subtle and higher forms.

Lila. (*lit.* play) The divine play of Consciousness.

Lingam. See *Shivalingam*.

Loka. (*lit.* place, world) A plane of existence.

Madhyama. (*lit.* middling) Subtle word or thought. See also *four levels of speech*.

Mahabhutas. The gross elements of ether, air, fire, water and earth. *Tattvas* 32 to 36.

Mahahrada. (*lit.* divine lake) A metaphor that likens Consciousness to a lake.

Mahamelapa. Great festival of unification between the *Siddhas* and yoginis.

Mahasamadhi. (*lit.* the great *samadhi*) The final passing of a great being.

Maheshwari. One of the ruling *shaktis*.

Mala. Limiting impurity that contracts Shiva into an individual. There are three *malas*.

See also *anava mala, karma mala, mayiya mala.*

Man number one to seven. The sage Gurdjieff's hierarchy of spiritual attainment, with man number seven as the highest, such as the Buddha.

Manas. Lower mind. *Tattva* 16.

Mantra. *(lit. manana* = mind, *tranam* = that which protects) Divine sound invested with the power to transform the person who repeats it.

Mantravirya. The virility or potency of mantra.

Matrika. *(lit.* unknown mother) Letters and sounds, the inherent power of letters and words that give rise to language and knowledge.

Maya. The veiling power that creates separation and ignorance in the universe. In Shaivism, it is considered a *shakti* of Shiva. *Tattva* 6.

Mayiya mala. Limiting impurity or contraction of knowledge. See also *mala.*

Monism. The experience or philosophy that the universe is one Consciousness.

Muladhara. The *chakra,* or energy centre, at the base of spine.

Nadabrahma. *(lit.* sound of Brahman) Inner sound.

Nadi. *(lit.* nerve) Energy channel of the subtle body.

Nara. The individual, or *jiva.*

Nataraj. The image of the dancing Shiva.

Neelakantha. *(lit.* Blue-throated One) A name for Shiva. The one whose throat turned blue from swallowing the poison that contaminated the ocean.

Neti neti. *(lit.* not this, not this) A Vedantic attitude of negating the objective universe until only supreme Consciousness remains.

Nimesha. *(lit.* closing of the eyelid) Concealment of the essential nature of Consciousness.

Nirvikalpa. *(lit.* no thought-constructs) The state of mind that is free of thoughts.

Nirvikalpa samadhi. A deep experience of meditation in which the mind is free of thoughts.

Niyati. The limitation of space. One of the *kanchukas. Tattva* 11.

Nondualism. The experience or philosophy that the universe is not comprised of two aspects, matter and Consciousness, but is One Consciousness.

Om Namah Shivaya. An empowered Shaivite mantra.

Para, apara, parapara. Three goddesses or conditions: *para* = unity, *apara* = duality, *parapara* = unity in diversity.

Paramahamsa. *(lit.* supreme swan) A title for a person of great discrimination or realisation.

Parashakti. Supreme Consciousness or divine energy.

Paravak. Transcendental or supreme speech, speech at the level of the Self, also called *paravani*. See also *Four levels of speech.*

Pashu. A bound soul.

Pashyanti. Subtle speech, intuitive word. See also *Four levels of speech.*

Pati. The Lord.

Phoneme. Pure energy in verbal form, more subtle than mantra.

Pingala. Subtle energy channel on the right side of the *sushumna,* or subtle spine, which carries the vital breath.

Prakasha. *(lit.* light) The light of supreme Consciousness.

Prakriti. The outer world. *Tattva* 13.

Prana. The vital breath or energy, life-force.

Pranayama. Yogic breathing.

Pratyabhijna. *(lit.* recognition) A school or philosophy of Kashmir Shaivism that emphasises the process of recognising the divinity within.

Puja. *(lit.* worship) Ritual worship of God.

Purusha. Limited individual or *jiva. Tattva* 12.

Raga. Desire and the sense of lack. One of the *kanchukas. Tattva* 9.

Rajas. One of the three gunas, the principle of activity and passion.

Rasa. *(lit.* sap or juice of a plant) An aesthetic or emotional quality such as: *Adbhuta*: marvel, wonder; *bhayanaka*: terror, fear; *bibhatsa*: the odious, disgust; *hasya*: comedy, laughter; *karuna*: the pathetic, sorrow; *raudra*: fury, anger; *shanta*: tranquility, serenity; *shringara*: eroticism, love; *vira*: heroism, noble enthusiasm.

Rasa lila. Love sport, as in the attitude of a devotee.

Reincarnation. Cycle of birth and death repeated until Self-realisation is attained.

Rudraksha. *(lit.* tear of Rudra or Shiva) A bead made from the seed of a tree sacred to Shiva, used for repetition of mantra.

Sadadhva. A sixfold classification or analysis of the universe. Dissolving the gross into the more subtle until reaching pure Consciousness, such as dissolving *pada* (spoken word) into mantra, disssolving *kāla* (time) into *varna*, (phoneme of pure energy).

Sadashiva tattva. Shiva's pure will. *Tattva* 3.

Sadguru. *(lit.* true Guru) True teacher, Self-realised spiritual guide.

Sadhana. Spiritual practice, the yogic process of transformation.

Sadhana shastra. An enlightenment technique that maps the path to higher Consciousness.

Sadhu. (*lit.* good one) Holy one.

Sahaja. Natural, spontaneous.

Sahaja samadhi. The natural state of a Self-realised being living in harmony with the Self or God.

Sahasrara. The energy centre at the crown of the head.

Sahridaya. Sympathetic, open-hearted.

Sakala. Human being.

Samadhi. A meditative state of profound absorption.

Samavesha. Absorption in the Divine.

Samkhya. A system of philosophy that recognises two realities, matter and Consciousness.

Samsara. Transmigratory existence, the world process.

Samsarin. A transmigratory being.

Samskaras. Impressions of past thoughts, actions or experiences stored in the subtle body.

Satchitananda. (*lit. sat* = being, existence, *chit* = Consciousness, *ananda* = bliss) Ultimate Consciousness that underlies all as the absolute state of existence, dwelling in bliss.

Satsang. (*lit. sat* = truth, *sanga* = company) Gathering in the name of a great being or principle. Spending time with a realised being or a spiritually minded group or community.

Sattva. One of the three *gunas*, or primary aspects of Consciousness, the principle of purity and clarity.

Satya. Truth.

Second Education. Internal, or spiritual/psychological education.

Self. The divine conscious essence of a person. Underlying Consciousness that is everywhere.

Self-realisation. The goal of *sadhana*. Being permanently established in the state of connection with the inner Self.

Shaivite. A follower of Shiva, practitioner of Kashmir Shaivism.

Shakti. The divine energy that creates, maintains and dissolves the universe. Also, spiritual energy, the female or dynamic aspect of Consciousness.

Shakti chakra. The wheel or assemblage of *shaktis* (energies, powers) accompanying the individual in performing various tasks, such as the mind, the life-force, the senses and organs of action. *Vameshvari,* the presiding *shakti. Khechari, (lit. kha* = vast expanse of Consciousness), the *shaktis* of the individual self. *Gochari (lit. go* = sense), the *shaktis* of the mind. *Dikchari (lit. dik* = space), the *shaktis* of the senses. *Bhuchari, (lit. bhu* = existence), the *shaktis* of the external world.

Shaktipat. *(lit.* descent of grace) Initiation or spiritual awakening of the kundalini energy by the Guru.

Shaktis. Groups of energies or powers.

Shaktopaya. *(lit.* the means of Shakti) Using the highest thought and language such as mantra or prayer to sort out concepts, understandings and emotions. See also *upaya.*

Shambhavi mudra. Yogic state in which awareness is kept inside but the senses are open. See also *bhairavi mudra.*

Shambhavopaya. *(lit.* the means of Shiva) Using pure will to stay in the thought-free state of pure Consciousness. See also *upaya.*

Shastra. *(lit.* text) A teaching or body of knowledge usually in the form of a book.

Shiva. Ultimate Consciousness, the Absolute, or God. The male, or static aspect of Consciousness. Also the Lord of Yogis and the Hindu God of Dissolution.

Shiva asana. *(lit.* seat of Shiva) Being centred in the understanding that we are always at the center of our experience.

Shiva drishti. *(lit.* vision of Shiva) Seeing the universe as divine Consciousness.

Shiva Process. Form of Self-inquiry developed by Swami Shankarananda.

Shiva vyapti. Experiencing the Divine in the world. See also *atma vyapti.*

Shivalingam. The Shaivite symbol of a *lingam* (phallus) inserted in a *yoni* (vagina), representing the elevation of sexuality to the Divine and the cosmic marriage of opposites.

Shruti. *(lit.* that which is heard) Scriptures traditionally considered of divine revelation.

Shuddha-vidya. Shiva's perfect action/doership. *Tattva* 5.

Siddha. Enlightened being, perfected yogi who lives in the state of ultimate awareness and unity with Supreme Consciousness.

Siddhi. Supernatural power.

Spanda. The vibration of Consciousness.

Sushumna. The subtle spine, the middle energy channel of the body.

Sutra. A short aphoristic statement.

Svatantrya. Perfect freedom, independence.

Tamas. One of the three *gunas,* the principle of dullness and sloth.

Tanmatras. Subtle elements; sound in itself, touch in itself, form in itself, taste in itself and smell in itself. *Tattvas* 27 to 31.

Tantra. A divinely revealed text or path unrelated to the *Vedas,* generally stressing Shakti, the

Goddess, and offering both liberation and worldly enjoyment.

Tattva. In Shaivite cosmology, one of 36 levels of creation or Consciousness.

Tearing thought. A negative or limiting statement.

Thali. An Indian tray or platter for serving individual portions of many dishes.

Trika. *(lit.* three) Kashmir Shaivism is often known as the Trika for its threesomes, such as Shiva, Shakti and the individual; and Consciousness, contraction and the spiritual journey.

Turiya. *(lit.* fourth) The fourth state of Consciousness, beyond waking, dream and deep sleep.

Unmesha. *(lit.* unfoldment) Revelation of the essential nature of the Divine, the expansive upward shift of feeling when the Self is contacted.

Upaya. Spiritual or yogic method, means or path by which the individual soul returns to pure Consciousness. See also *anavopaya, anupaya, gururupaya, shaktopaya, shambhavopaya.*

Vaha-cheda. The cutting of the *vahas* (the flow of *prana*) by means of certain sounds.

Vaikari. Gross speech, the spoken word. See also *four levels of speech.*

Varna. A phoneme, or energy in verbal form.

Vedanta. Spiritual philosophy that Consciousness underlies the universe and the world is an illusion.

Vidya. Knowledge. Also one of the *kanchukas* meaning limitation of knowledge. *Tattva* 8.

Vikalpa. Thought-form.

Vimarsha. The eternal Self-awareness of divine Consciousness.

Vipassana. Buddhist meditation practice.

Vyutthana. *(lit.* rising) The aftereffects or intoxication of deep meditation.

Yamala. The divine couple, Shiva-Shakti.

Yoga. *(lit.* union) Spiritual practice, the path of spirituality.

Yoni. *(lit.* womb, vagina) Representation of female aspect of the universe, as in the *Shivalingam.*

Index

Abhinavagupta, and goal, 58, and
knower, known and knowledge,
181, and Kula School, 44, and
liberation, 61, and *Mailini-Vijaya*
Tantra, 46, and shape of Shaivism,
46, and *Svacchanda* Tantra, 46, and
synthesis of Shaivite schools, 46,
and *Tantraloka*, 46, and Trika, 58,
and *Vijnanabhairava* Tantra, 46 on
absence of contraction, 235, on *anupaya*,
32, on audience, 218, on awareness,
122, on bliss, 234, on bondage and
liberation, 87, on burning flame of
Consciousness, 140, on
Consciousness as reflection, 169–
170, on divine dialogue, 38, on
emotions, 28, on eternal presence,
277, on first personism, 285–286,
on four states of Consciousness, 196,
on grace of Shiva, 25, on group ritual,
234–235, on Guru, 296, on hiding
and revealing, 146, on identification
with Shiva, 253, on identity with
light, 169, on inquiry, 231, 233, on
joyful being, 276, on *kanchukas*, 105,
on *krama mudra*, 178, on liberation,
274, 290, on purifying thoughts, 121,
122, on recognition, 280, on removing
contraction, 129, on satisfaction, 219,
on seeing the Self, 231, on sexuality,
135, on *shakti chakra*, 265, on
shaktipat, 41, on Shiva as individual
soul, 117, on Shiva-Shakti-*nara*, 285–
286, on supreme unaffected by
maya, 128, on sutra, 18, on *tattvas*,
107, on the supreme *tattva*, 95, on
thought and awareness, 224, on
thought-free state, 122–123, 167, on
touch, 136, on transcendental point
of view, 154, on true nature, 291, on
universe revealed, 290, on violent
digestion, *hathapaka* and *alamgrasa*,
147–148, on wonder, 202, 217, on
work of art, 216, the *rasas*, art and
spirituality, 206–219, *See also Paratrishika*
Vivarana, Paramarthasara, Tantraloka
Absolute, as dynamic, 111, as God, 20
Abulafia, Abraham, language
mysticism, 226–227
Adyanta-koti nibhalana, hamsa technique,
179
Aham Brahmasmi, and 'I am Shiva', 46, 64
Alamgrasa, and *hathapaka*, 146–149,
burning it to sameness, 140–153
Amritavagbhava, on Truth, 71
Ananda, and five powers, 101, 106 *See*
also Bliss
Anava mala, affecting heart, 129–133,
and *kanchukas*, 130–131, and
samavesha, 135–136, and
shambhavopaya, 123–124, 136, and
tattvas, 131, as individuality, 128,
mandala of the *malas* and *upayas*,
119, three *malas* and three *upayas*,
117–127, two forms of, 185
Anavopaya, and *karma mala*, 120, 136,
and object of meditation, 135, and
shaktipat, 133–134, and *shaktopaya*,
259, mandala of the *malas* and
upayas, 119, meditation on, 138–139,
three *malas* and three *upayas*, 117–
127, *See also Upayas*
Anupaya, 274–284, and *samavesha*,
135–136, and Shiva Process, 241, as
experience of the Lord, 136–137, as
methodless method, 125–126, as
pathless path, 30–34, mandala of the
malas and *upayas*, 119, three *malas*
and three *upayas*, 117–127

About Swami Shankarananda

Swami Shankarananda (Swamiji) attained the state of Self-realisation at the feet of one of the 20th-century's greatest masters of yoga and meditation, Swami (Baba) Muktananda Paramahamsa. Baba Muktananda's teaching and inspiration was a key factor in the reinvigoration of the revered mystical tradition of Kashmir Shaivism in our time.

Swamiji grew up in Brooklyn, New York, and as a graduate of both Columbia and New York universities, began a promising career in English literature at Indiana University. However, in the late sixties, a dramatic turn of events profoundly altered the direction of his life.

In 1970, he travelled to India in search of a great teacher and a spiritual path. He practised Buddhist Vipassana meditation with Master Goenka, and hatha and raja yoga with Hari Dass Baba. He spent time with the mysterious Neem Karoli Baba; the great sage Nisargadatta Maharaj; and the holy mother, Anandamayi Ma. His search culminated in the meeting of the powerful and charismatic Baba Muktananda, under whom he studied for 12 years until Muktananda's death, and who initiated him into the Saraswati order of teaching swamis. Swamiji carries on the Siddha tradition of Muktananda and his teacher, Bhagawan Nityananda. In 2010, in recognition of the length and quality of his international work, Swamiji received the prestigious Hindu title, Mahamandaleshwar, meaning 'great teacher'.

Swamiji was instrumental in disseminating Baba Muktananda's Kashmir Shaivism in the West beginning in the 1970s. In 1974, he established the first Western ashram of this tradition, in Ann Arbor, Michigan. Later, he also directed centres in Los Angeles, New York, and Melbourne.

Motivated by the significance and value of the Shaivite teachings to Western spirituality, Swamiji edited *Siddha Meditation*, a collection of Baba's writings and one of the first commentaries on Kashmir Shaivism written specifically for Westerners. Swamiji also wrote *Muktananda Siddha Guru*, essays on the Guru-disciple relationship, and was the founding editor of the *Siddha Path* magazine.

Swamiji is the author of the Australian bestseller *Happy for No Good Reason*, also published in India by Motilal Banarsidass, *Carrot in My Ear*, a compilation of questions and answers about spiritual practice and philosophy, and *Self-Inquiry: Using Your Awareness to Unblock Your Life*. Other titles by Swamiji include a five-CD lecture series, *The Yoga of Gurdjieff*, and the audio and video series, *Great Beings*, including *Volume I: The Wisdom of Anandamayi Ma*.

Swamiji is Shivacharya (spiritual director) of the Shiva School of Meditation and Yoga, near Melbourne, Australia. His reputation as a Shaivite master is drawing national and international recognition as students from around the world gather, inspired by these profound teachings and his compassionate and wise guidance.

SHIVA

SCHOOL OF MEDITATION AND YOGA

The Shiva School of Meditation and Yoga is a non-profit organisation.
It offers a range of courses and training in meditation, hatha yoga,
Shiva Process Self-inquiry, and Kashmir Shaivism.

If you would like further information, you can contact:

Shiva Ashram
27 Tower Road
Mt. Eliza, Victoria 3930
Tel: +61 3 9775 2568
Fax: +61 3 9775 2591
Email: askus@shivayoga.org
Website: www.shivayoga.org

Lightning Source UK Ltd.
Milton Keynes UK
UKOW06f2013190616

276665UK00004B/195/P